Nigeria and the United States

Twists and Turns through Five Decades

Nigeria and the United States

Twists and Turns through Five Decades

**Edited by
Shola Omoregie and Abiodun Alao**

AMVPS

Published by

AMV Publishing Services
P.O. Box 661,
Princeton, NJ 08542-0661
Tel: 609-785-5135 Fax: 609-7164770
emails: publisher@amvpublishingservices.com &
customerservice@amvpublishingservices.com
worldwide web.www.amvpublishingservices.com

Nigeria and the United States
Twists and Turns through Five Decades
Copyright © Africa Peace Support, LLC, 2014

All rights reserved. No part of this publication may be reproduced, stored in a retrieval system, or transmitted in any form or by any means, electronic, mechanical, photocopying, recording or otherwise without the written permission of the publisher.

Book & Cover Design: AMV Origination & Design Division

Library of Congress Control Number: 2014900786

ISBN: 978-0-9894917-2-3

First meeting between Presidents Goodluck Jonathan and Barack Obama in the White House

Table of Contents

Organizations and their Acronyms ix
Foreword xi
Preface xiii

Introduction: Fifty Years of Twists and Turns
Shola Omoregie and Abiodun Alao 1

Chapter One: The Antecedents: America's Relationship With the Entity That Was to Become Nigeria
Adebayo Oyebade 11

Chapter Two: Independence and the Establishment of a New Relationship
Joseph Aihie 31

Chapter Three: The United States and the Nigerian Civil War
Olukunke Ojeleye 53

Chapter Four: Dealing with the Generals: Human Rights and Democracy as Issues in Nigerian US Relations
Funmi Olonisakin 79

Chapter Five: Convergence and Divergence in Nigerian/US Policy on the Issue of Majority Rule in Southern Africa
Shola Omoregie 101

Chapter Six: The Military Dimension in the Relationship Between the United States and Nigeria
Abiodun Alao 127

Chapter Seven:	Relationship under the New Democratic Dawn: The Nature and Dynamics of Nigeria/US Relations from 1999 to 2010
	Funso Adesola and Ronke Iyabo Akonai 151
Chapter Eight:	Trade and Economic Relations
	Bolaji Kehinde and Temilade Abimbola 179
Chapter Nine:	The Nigerian Diaspora in America
	Adebayo Oyebade 195
Chapter Ten:	The Nigeria-United States Bi-National Commission: Scope, Achievements, Limitations and Suggestions for Review
	Suleiman Baba Ali 217
Chapter Eleven:	Trends in Goodluck Jonathan's Foreign Policy
	Fumni Olonisakin and Penda Diallo 233
Chapter Twelve:	Looking at the Public Perception of Nigerians in the United States from Within: President Goodluck Jonathan and the Making of a New Image
	Laolu Akande 253
Conclusion:	Surveying the Past and Seeing the Future
	Shola Omoregie and Abiodun Alao 273
List on Contributors	285
Index	291

Organizations and their Acronyms

Abia State National Association of North America, USA (ASNANA)
Acquired Immunodeficiency Syndrome (AIDS)
Action Congress (AC)
African Academy of Arts and Research (AAAR)
African Crisis Response Initiative (ACRI)
African Growth and Opportunity Act (APGOA)
African Union (AU)
American Council on African Education (ACAE)
American Federation of Labor – Congress of Industrial Organizations (AFL-CIO)
Association for Better Nigeria, (ABN)
Association of Nigerian Physicians in America (ANPA)
Civil Liberty Organization (CLO)
Comprehensive Africa Agricultural Development Program (CAADP)
Cooperative for Assistance and Relief Everywhere (CARE)
Democratic Republic of The Congo (DRC)
Eastern Regional Government (ERG)
Economic and Financial Crime Commission (EFCC)
Economic Community of West African States (ECOWAS)
European Union (EU)
Federal Military Government (FMG)
Foreign direct investment (FDI)
Global Peace Operations Institute (GPOI)
Home Town Associations (HTA)
Human Immunodeficiency Virus (HIV)
Independent Corrupt Practice Commission (ICPC)
Independent National Electoral Commission (INEC)
Institute of International Education (IIE)
International Committee of the Red Cross (ICRC)
International Criminal Police Organization (INTERPOL)
Joint Development Zone (JDZ) between Nigeria and Sao Tome
Kwara State Association of Nigeria, North America (KSANG)
National Agriculture Investment Plan (NAIP)
National Council of Nigeria Muslim Organization in the USA (NCNMO)
National Drug Law Enforcement Agency (NDLEA)
National Rehabilitation Commission (NRC)
New Partnership for African Development (NEPAD)
Nigerian-American Public Professionals Association (NAPPA)
Nigeria Independence Day Family Fun Fair (NIDFFF)
Nigerian Bar Association (NBA)
Nigerian Information Technology Professionals in America (NITPA)

Nigerian Lawyers Association (NLA)
Nigerian National Petroleum Commission (NNPC)
Nigerian Nurses Association (NNA)
Nigerian Television Authority (NTA)
Nigerian Union of Journalist (NUJ)
Nigerian Women Association (NWA)
Nigerians in Diaspora Organization-Americas (NIDO)
Non-governmental organizations (NGOs)
Northern People's Congress (NPC)
Organization of African Unity (OAU)
Organization of Petroleum Exporting Countries (OPEC)
Oxford Committee for Famine Relief (OXFAM)
People's Democratic Party (PDP)
People's Movement for the Liberation of Angola (MPLA)
Redeemed Christian Church of God (RCCG)
South West African People's Organization (SWAPO)
Southern African Relief Fund (SARF)
Special Court for Sierra Leone (SCSL)
Supreme Military Council (SMC)
Trade and Investment Framework Agreement (TIFA)
Unilateral Declaration of Independence (UDI)
Union for the Total Independence of Angola (UNITA).
Union of Soviet Socialist Republics (USSR)
United Nations (UN)
United Nations Children's Fund (UNICEF)
United Nations Development Programme (UNDP)
United Nations Educational, Scientific and Cultural Organization (UNESCO)
United States Africa Command (AFRICOM)
United States Agency for International Development (USAID)
United States Government (USG)
United States Information Service (USIS)
Universal Negro Improvement Association (UNIA)
Visit board, search, and seizure (VBSS)
World Council of Churches (WCC)
World Food Programme (WFP)
World Trade Organization (WTO)
Young Men's Christian Association (YMCA)
Zimbabwe African National Liberation Army (ZANLA)
Zimbabwe African National Union (ZANU)
Zimbabwe African People's Union (ZAPU)
Zimbabwe People's Revolutionary Army (ZIPRA)

Foreword

It is with joy that I am writing this Foreword to this book written on the strategic partnership between Nigeria and the United States in the last 50 years. In all my years of working in diplomacy – both as an Ambassador and as the Minister of Foreign Affairs – I have always been fascinated by the relationship that exists between countries that are key actors in the affairs of their respective regions. In my view, the most compelling element for such a relationship has been how both countries in this arrangement have coped and have managed their respective ambitions in ways that have continued to ensure friendship and collaborations between them. I have also been interested in the politics that often underline economic relations between such countries and how their citizens have manifested the healthy rivalries that emerge out of national pride. While, of course, Nigeria and the United States have not always had the same geopolitical interests, both are crucial players in the politics of their respective regions.

The United States remains, without doubt, one of Nigeria's most important friends. The extent of this friendship transcends what often exists between the governments of both countries. Indeed, perhaps more important is the string of informal friendships between the citizens of both countries. While, as the various authors in the book have noted, the relationship has suffered minor hiccups, it still remains particularly strong. Indeed, the fact that it has survived many vicissitudes shows the extent of its resilience. Before Nigeria's independence, many Nigerians came to the United States to undertake studies in various fields and their contributions to the achievement of Nigeria's independence were legendary. Today, many Nigerians reside in the United States and they are making significant contributions to the development of the country. I am indeed, very proud of the involvement of Nigerians in almost all spheres of American life.

Against the foregoing background, the effort to document various aspects of the relationship between Nigeria and the United States is a welcome addition to the various studies looking at the relationship between Nigeria and some of its major partners. Indeed, this would be in line with the charge which President Goodluck Ebele Jonathan gave in his opening address to the Conference on the Review of Nigeria's Foreign Policy in August 2011.

The Chapters in the Book look at various aspects of the relationship between the two countries and the Editors have done a good job in weaving them together. I also want to commend the Ambassador of Nigeria to the United States, Ambassador Ade Adefuye, for embarking on this task. It is my hope that detailed studies of this nature will be undertaken on the relationship Nigeria has with its other key partners. With this, the efforts of having a coherent history of our diplomacy would have been enhanced.

It is therefore with joy that I warmly recommend this book to the wider public.

Ambassador Olugbenga Ashiru, MFR
Minister of Foreign Affairs
Federal Republic of Nigeria
Abuja
September 26, 2011

Preface

Nigeria's relationship with the United States is important for a number of reasons. First, it is the relationship between two countries that have sought to play important roles within different but deeply related geographical spheres: the United States in the world and Nigeria in Africa. The desire of each to harness its resources in the pursuit of its objectives has inevitably introduced twists and turns in the relationship, especially as each nation's goals are, in some ways, not mutually exclusive. Second, it is the relationship between the two of the countries with the largest populations of blacks in the world. Consequently, how both countries relate is of considerable interest to blacks all over the world. Indeed, until the independence of South Africa, the relationship between the United States and Nigeria was used by many people as the yardstick for American attitudes toward the entire African continent. Third, from the Nigerian perspective, the relationship with the United States is arguably the most important in terms of complexity and scope, especially as the United States is Nigeria's most important trading partner. Even Nigeria's relationship with Britain, though historically longer and with many other links and institutions to further entrench it, still comes after the relationship Nigeria has with the United States.

A detailed study of the relationship between the two countries not long after the celebration of Nigeria's fiftieth independence anniversary has additional importance. Both nations are at decisive phases of their history, with the United States having its first African-American President while Nigeria consolidates its democracy with its first civilian-to-civilian leadership transition. Numerous recent developments suggest that the relationship between the two countries will continue to assume greater importance for quite some time to come. For example, the United States indicated in 2000 that up to 25% of its oil supply would be coming from the Gulf of Guinea by the year 2015.[1] This is a region where Nigeria plays a particularly strategic role.

The relationship between Nigeria and the United States reaches far beyond economic concerns. As Nigeria celebrated its fiftieth anniversary in 2010, citizens of the country had contributed significantly to the socio-economic life of the United States, in enterprises ranging from business, sports and academics, to medicine, banking and entrepreneurship. Indeed, not even in Britain are there more Nigerians making significant contributions to their adopted country as in the United States.

Finally, shortly before Nigeria's fiftieth independence anniversary, the relationship between the two countries passed through perhaps a critical test with the December 2009 attempt by a Nigerian, Umar Mutallab,[2] to bomb an American Airline. This development, which was widely condemned by the government of Nigeria and its citizens, especially those in the United States, brought home to both countries the need to stem the flow of religious radicalisation in Nigeria. But while this and previous hiccups in the relationship created their own challenges, they have also led to a deepening and strengthening of ties between the two countries. This calls for a detailed analysis of the relationship between Nigeria and the United States between 1960 and 2010.

This book is a step in this direction. We hope to discuss the links between the two countries, focussing on how the relationship has been able to withstand political and diplomatic vicissitudes. The objectives of this book are three-fold: first to document some of the key ramifications of American-Nigerian relations over five decades, highlighting the ups and downs of the relationship and their consequences; second to assess the impact of the "past" on the "present" and the "future" of Nigerian-America relations. This is particularly important because a complex tapestry of dreams and desires seem to govern the political, economic and security relations between the two countries. Third, the book provides a detailed study that can assist the process of policy formulations in both Nigeria and the United States. In a broader sense, as Nigeria begins its second 50 years of independent existence, there is a need to begin the process of documenting, in a detailed manner, its relationship with key countries. Such a detailed study will assist the foreign policy formulation of the country.

The methodology adopted in this book is to identify all the key aspects of the relationship between the two countries and provide a detailed analysis of how these key issues have impacted the social, economic, political, diplomatic and military relations. Although the focus is mainly on Nigeria and the United States, the book also touches on situations in other countries that inevitably became intertwined with American/Nigerian relations, especially the situation in South Africa during the era of apartheid and minority rule as well as in Liberia, during the country's bitter civil conflict. On the whole, it is our conviction that while fifty years may be a short time in a relationship that has every prospect of perpetual survival, it is almost certainly enough for some form of stock-taking, even if preliminary.

We would like to acknowledge the assistance of those who have been instrumental in getting this book out. We want to thank Nigeria's Ambassador to the United States, Ambassador Adebowale Adefuye for commissioning this project. Apart from commissioning the work, Ambassador Adefuye also assisted by providing us with the materials from the embassy. We are also grateful to the staff of the Nigerian Ministry of Foreign Affairs for the assistance they offered. Finally, we thank all our contributors for heeding our call and for accommodating our invitation amidst their respective tight schedules.

Shola Omoregie and Abiodun Alao

Introduction
Fifty Years of Twists and Turns

Shola OMOREGIE and Abiodun ALAO

Nigeria's relationship with the United States has remained one of the most controversial of Nigeria's diplomatic relationships and scholars have variously described its different aspects. For example, George Obiozor described it as an "uneasy friendship", activated only when the US has needed Nigeria's resources or assistance to solve its problems. For him:

> Americans are not yet prepared to enter into active partnership with Nigeria or any other African country as they have done in Europe and with a few countries in Latin America and Asia.[3]

For Bassey Atte, Nigeria's relationship with the US, except for the brief periods of the Mohammed and Obasanjo regimes, has been characterized by an unusual level of dependency on economic patronage thereby making Nigeria almost totally subservient to the US. Atte argues that successful decolonization requires a change in relationships to assure the ability of the former dependent territory to act independently in the international arena.[4] Yet for Fred Agwu, the very idea of a US-Nigerian Policy, despite the orchestrated importance of Nigeria in Africa and the world, is itself a fallacy. US African policy, for him, had always

> treated Nigeria as a mere footnote, a complete adjunct, which is meaningful only in geo-strategic terms... As an adjunct of America's African policy, Nigeria is only embraced by the US when it is absolutely necessary to do so. Otherwise, it is simply disregarded.[5]

He cited an example of the speech former President Bill Clinton made when he visited Nigeria in August, 2000. According to Agwu, Clinton never spoke in terms of any conceivable US-Nigerian policy. Rather, he dwelt on the US-African partnership to combat disease (HIV/AIDS, tuberculosis, etc.) on the African continent. Clinton's own words were chosen entirely in terms of a "partnership with your continent", not with Nigeria, a country in which he said "so many of the great human dramas of our time are being played out." Equally, public opinion in the US is no more complimentary about Nigeria, an example being George Soros' description of Nigeria as a country where all conceivable policies have been tried, but where nothing works. As if to confirm Agwu's postulations, many Nigerians felt that President Barack Obama, the first African-American President of the United States, greatly "embarrassed" Nigeria when he clearly shunned the country in his first ever African visit and went to Ghana instead – a country he said was making great strides in building a virile democratic structure and enduring institutions. There are also those who consider what they see as the lack of American interest in Nigeria as part of the general lack of American interest in Africa.

But while all the above may give the impression that Nigeria is viewed as being only marginally important to the United States, there are also many who see Nigeria as vitally important to the US and one whose friendship the American government and people hold very seriously. Robert Shepard[6], Adebayo Oyebade and Toyin Falola have all looked at Nigerian/US relations from different vantage points and concluded that it is long and deep and also one that has every prospect of perpetual survival, even if there continue to be occasional hiccups.[7]

A number of things come out distinctly from the different positions on Nigerian-American relations expressed above. First, the debate shows clearly that in the fifty years since Nigeria's independence, the relationship between the two countries has gone through thick and thin, and with its own ups and downs. Second, it reflects that the relationship is important to both countries. Indeed in the last fifty years, Nigeria's relations with the United States have grown tremendously. For example, while there were less than twenty thousand Nigerians in the United

States at the time of independence in 1960, the figure had grown to more than a million by 2010, with the population of Americans in Nigeria also increasing significantly from the few hundred in 1960 to thousands in 2010. Again, while the volume of trade was in the region of few million dollars in the period immediately after independence, it had risen to several billions per annum by the time Nigeria turned fifty in 2010, surpassing even that of Britain with whom Nigeria has had a longer historical relationship. It was, indeed, beyond any shadow of a doubt that the United States was Nigeria's most important trading partner. Both countries have always been eager to advertise how close they are and how much they want to maintain that closeness in ways that will be mutually beneficial. Apart from consular and economic relations, many key global events have emerged over the last five decades that have brought the two countries together.

Two mutually reinforcing issues serve as the bedrock for the relationship: The geo-strategic importance of Nigeria as a key African nation and the continent's most populous sovereign state; and the central position of the United States as a Super Power and a principal actor in the global economy and world politics. As Bassey Atte has noted, Nigeria is important to the United States for a number of reasons: First, Nigeria is one of the most influential African countries; second, Nigeria is the largest black country in the world and up to about 15% of US population is made up of people of African descent; third, the establishment of a thriving democratic polity in Nigeria represents a successful export of American political value; and fourth, a modernized Nigerian economy constitutes the largest market place in Africa for American companies and citizens. At a stage, in fact, a social science survey showed the US as the foreign power most admired by Nigerian elites.[8] Despite a souring of relations after the civil war, the importance of Nigeria increased significantly after the 1973 Middle East war and the subsequent Arab oil embargo. During that critical period, Nigeria emerged as the second largest supplier of crude oil to the US. By 1977, the US had replaced Britain as Nigeria's principal trading partner. That year, the country purchased US$975 million worth of American goods, while it sold goods worth US$6.2 billion to the United States. The flow of trade was so important that the former United States Secretary of State, Cyrus Vance, noted in March 1978 that America's trade with Nigeria was "double the value of that with South Africa". Things have also moved significantly on the diplomatic front. Indeed, at a stage, Nigeria almost became a barometer with which 26 million black Americans measure America's policy in Africa. Consequently, the American leadership realised that for its policy in Africa to have credibility at home and abroad, it must have implicit Nigerian endorsement.

However, while there can be no doubt as to the closeness, it is also clear that the relationship has encountered a number of major hiccups, some of these quite profound. While the grounds for disappointments have varied, most of these have been woven around the dissatisfaction felt by one against the other over policies and actions that are considered inimical to the advertised friendship and boisterous camaraderie between both countries. It seems, over the last fifty years, the United States has felt disappointed that Nigeria had not maximised its potential and had persistently failed to take policies that can advance the lot of its population. Specifically, there have been concerns at the failure of Nigeria for several decades to establish a credible democracy. American governments have been so concerned about this that a former American President, Bill Clinton, described the era of military rule in Nigeria as that of "Plunder and Despair". The country has also been disturbed at the actions and activities of some Nigerians who are doing things or taking actions that are detrimental to American interest, even if conceding that a greater part of the population, especially those living in the United States have been law-abiding. On its part, Nigeria seems to have been unhappy with the United States for not showing sufficient support for causes that are supposed to advance the situation in Africa. Indeed, it is the belief of most Nigerians that, despite the much-advertised desire to assist Africa, the United States has contributed, directly or indirectly, to continued political instability on the continent. Nigerians are also uneasy about activities of key American politicians and business conglomerates which have a role in corruption and other activities inimical to Nigeria's economic and social interests. For example, the actions of American multinationals like Chevron in Nigeria have been a subject of concern while other companies like Halliburton conjure negative impression in the minds of many Nigerians.[9]

Disagreements of this nature are neither new nor unusual in international diplomacy. Within a period of fifty years, it is inevitable that paths will cross and disagreements will occur between nations. In the case of Nigeria and the United States, what is important is that both countries have realised the value of one another and the inevitability of sticking together. This explains why the relationship between the two countries, though sometimes battered and bruised, has remained strong for fifty years and will likely continue to be so for quite some time to come.

This book seeks to detail key aspects of Nigerian/US relations over the last fifty years. In the first chapter, Adebayo Oyebade takes a detailed look at the nature of the relationship between the United States and the entity that was to become Nigeria. Oyebade discusses the trans-Atlantic trade, the exportation of Yoruba captives from what later became Nigeria to the United States, the idea of black emigration back to Africa, the search for resettlement by American blacks in Lagos and Abeokuta, the impact of World War II, especially America's economic and military interests in West Africa (including Nigeria) and the economic need to have access to Nigeria's agricultural and mineral resources.

The second chapter takes a detailed look at the relationship between the two countries at the time of independence and how this was sustained by the two countries during the period of Nigeria's first republic. Here, Joseph Aihie focuses the discussion on crucial issues like the reaction of the United States to Nigeria's independence, the relationship between Kennedy and Balewa; initial technical assistance to Nigeria; the loan to assist in Nigeria's 5 year Development Plan; grants from the USAID, the assistance by American educational funding bodies like the Ford Foundation, the Carnegie Endowment and others to Nigeria's tertiary institutions, the activities of the Peace Corp and the Scandal of the Marjorie Michelmore Post Card,[10] the Syncom Communication Satellite launch and the assistance given by the United States for the construction of the Dam on River Niger.

In Chapter three, Olokunke Ojeleye discusses the role of the United States in the bitter Nigerian civil war. Here, the author first discusses the initial reaction to the military coup that overthrew Prime Minister Abubakar Tafawa Balewa. It then identifies the American position at the outbreak of the war. Other issues discussed in the chapter include the propaganda undertaken in the United States by the warring sides and the impact on American people and government, the balancing of the reaction to Biafra's allegation of starvation not the desire for Nigeria's continued unity, the reaction to Soviet support for the Federal cause during the period of the Cold War, American aid to the population affected by the war, diplomatic initiatives undertaken by the United States through the Organisation of African Unity (OAU), American humanitarian organisations and the Nigerian civil war, the end of the civil war, and American reactions to Nigeria's post-war reconciliation and reconstruction activities.

The relationship between Nigeria and the United States during the period of military rule occupies Funmi Olonisakin in Chapter Four. The chapter looks at some of the peculiarities in the US/Nigerian relationship during this time, considering the relationship that various military rulers were able to develop with American administrations. Among the crucial issues discussed is the initial reaction of the United States to the overthrow of democracy in Nigeria, and how the US dealt with the cases of human rights violation and suppression of democratic agitation by Nigeria's military leaders. The chapter also looks at America's support for the re-establishment of democracy in Nigeria, especially support given to civil society groups in Nigeria by America's human-right and democratic groups.

Chapter Five focuses on the ways both countries have reacted to developments in South Africa. Since South Africa was long one of the most important issues in the relationship between Nigeria and the US, Shola Omoregie focuses on areas of convergence and subjects of divergence between the two countries on the politics of the struggle for the end of apartheid and the establishment of majority rule. Omoregie discusses the positions of both countries on South Africa and the principles that guided their policies and positions over the decades; the entrance of South Africa into the position of importance in Nigeria's foreign policy; the Kissinger Connection; the entrance of US President Jimmy Carter and the new phase in American policy in South Africa; the Reagan policy reversal and the response from Nigeria, and the ultimate independence of Southern African countries.

Abiodun Alao in Chapter Six examines the military dimension in the US/Nigerian relationship. The discussion here includes the training of Nigerian officers in America's military institutions; support for the Nigerian Military in UN international peacekeeping; the U.S, Nigeria and conflict resolution in Africa, the support (logistical, troops training, financial) for African initiatives (e.g. ECOMOG) championed by Nigeria; the divergence of position on the African High Command; the sharing of views on Africa's security challenges (Darfur, Somalia, Sierra Leone, Zimbabwe, etc.) and the politics of weapons procurements and military exchanges. The chapter also discusses the nature and extent of America's support for Nigeria's post-military rule and security sector reform in the country. Finally, there is a discussion on the activities of Nigerians serving in the armed forces of the United States.

In Chapter Seven, Funso Adesola and Ronke Iyabo Akonai discuss the developments that have occurred since the dawn of the democratic era in Nigeria. They look at the reaction of the United States to Nigeria's democratic transition, especially the encouragement and support given to supporters of democracy. Specific activities of individuals like former Presidents Jimmy Carter and Bill Clinton as well as philanthropist Bill Gates in the promotion of democracy and the eradication of diseases are examined. The chapter also discusses the euphoria and expectations that came with the ascendancy of Barak Obama and the subtle disappointment from Nigeria about the non-inclusion of the country on his first African tour. Adesola and Akonai cover the whole debate surrounding the global war on terror and how this affects Nigerian/US relations. Among others, the chapter discuses the origin of the global war on terror and how the concept of "terror" manifests in both societies. As would be expected, the central focus of attention of the section is the December 2009 attempt by the Nigerian youth Umar Muttallab to bomb an American Aircraft and the subsequent placement of Nigeria on America's Terror Watch List. Other subjects discussed in the chapter include, Nigeria's reaction to the Bombing of United States Embassies in Kenya and Tanzania and to the World Trade Centre; America's reaction to incessant religious riots in Nigeria; America's discussions with Nigeria on other issues of terrorism in other African Countries like Somalia and the support by US agencies of understanding and religious harmony in Nigeria.

The focus of Kehinde Bolaji and Temilade Abimbola in Chapter Eight is on trade and economic relations between Nigeria and the United States. Here the chapter looks at key issues like the primary importance of oil in Nigerian/South African relations. Bolaji and Abimbola also examine other trading activities apart from oil, the establishment and development of the American-Nigerian Chamber of Commerce, the reaction of American leadership to the issue of corruption in Nigeria; the future of the Gulf of Guinea in view of America's determination to diversity the source of its oil supply from the Middle East; the various trade agreements signed between the United States and Nigeria, the African Growth and Opportunities Act (AGOA), the Trade and Investment Framework Agreement, and the Nigerian-American Bi-National Commission.

Attention in Chapter Nine moves to the activities of the Nigerian Diaspora population in the United States. Here, Adebayo Oyebade again traces the origin of the migration of Nigerians to the United States and the influence of Nigerian academics, medical professionals, entrepreneurs and others on American society. The chapter also looks at the cultural dimension of the activities of the Diaspora population, including the establishment of American Yoruba communities (e.g., Oyotunji village in South Carolina). Other issues discussed include the establishment of indigenous Nigerian churches, the establishment of local and state groups by Nigerians and the contribution to socio-economic development at home, the activities of American nationals in Nigeria, and the contributions of the Diaspora to the development of the relationship between the two countries. The chapter does not limit itself to the positive

INTRODUCTION

side of the Diaspora population. Oyebade also discusses the activities of criminal Nigerian networks operating in the United States.

The last three chapters deal with facets of the US/Nigerian relationship that are serving as platforms for the next phase in the countries relations as the 21st century advances. Suleiman Baba Ali examines the Nigeria-United States Bi-National Commission in detail in Chapter Ten. Chapter Eleven sees Fumni Olonisakin and Penda Diallo looking at the trends in President Goodluck Jonathan's foreign policy, charting how a relatively young administration has gained confidence and its own policy identity. Fittingly, the last chapter by Laolu Akande looks at the perceptions of Nigeria held by Americans and documents the most recent twists and turns in these perceptions.

In the Conclusion, Shola Omoregie and Abiodun Alao review fifty years of Nigerian-American relations and take a look at the future of the relationship.

End Notes

[1] See, Abiodun Alao: *Natural Resources and Conflict in Africa: The Tragedy of Endowment*, Rochester: University of Rochester Press, 2007.

[2] Indictment in *USA v Abdulmutallab*, Case: 2: 10-cr-20005, retrieved from http://www.cbsnews.com/htdocs/pdf/Abdulmutallab Indictment.pdf on 09/04/2011

[3] George Obiozor, *Uneasy Friendships: Nigeria-United States Relations* (1992), Fourth Dimension, Enugu, 1992: p. 211.

[4] Bassey Atte, *Decolinization and Dependence: the Development of Nigerian-US Relations 1960 -1984* Boulder Colorado: Westview Press, 1987.

[5] Fred Agwu, "Beyond the Clenched Fist: A Contemplation of the United States' Nigerian Policy Under barack Obama" *Igbinedion Journal of Diplomacy and Strategy*, Vol.1 No. 1 2009, p. 35

[6] Robert B. Shepard, *Nigeria, Africa and the United States*, Bloomington and Indianapolis: Indiana University Press 1984.

[7] Adebayo Oyebade and Toyin Falola, 2008

[8] Bolaji Akinyemi and John Stremlau Report on Nigerian-American Dialogue October 9-12 1978

[9] Chevron has been accused of environmental degradation of the oil producing regions while Halliburton has come to the fore of controversy over alleged bribery scandals.

[10] This was the story of a Post-Card sent by a Corp member to her boyfriend depicting Nigerians as backward.

Chapter One

The Antecedents: America's Relationship with the Entitiy that Would Become Nigeria

Adebayo OYEBADE

The relationship between the United States and Nigeria predates the independence of both nations, stretching as far back at the sixteenth century, when Europeans, in the guise of trading, carted away millions of Africans from the west coast of their home continent to work as slaves on farm plantations or as indentured servants in the colonial Americas. Many Nigerian towns were prominent during this period.[11] Indeed, the slave trade marked the very first relations between the Americas and Africa south of the Sahara.

Before the emergence of Nigeria as a colonial state, the region had been peopled for hundreds of years by disparate ethno linguistic groups; some large, and others of medium or small size. The advent of Europeans on the west coast of Africa and the subsequent institution of the trans-Atlantic slave trade brought some of the peoples of the region that would become Nigeria into contact with New World societies. By the early nineteenth century, a large number of ethnic Nigerians—the Yoruba, Igbo, Edo, Nupe, Hausa, and others—had been transported to and enslaved in the New World.[12] This chapter examines the sporadic contacts between the developing United States and the geographical area that would become Nigeria before its attainment of statehood on October 1, 1960.

Contacts in the Age of the Slave Trade

The European slave trade in Africa across the Atlantic to the New World which began in earnest in the sixteenth century and lasted until the nineteenth century was one of the most epochal events in human history. Perhaps its most significant repercussion was the making of African identities in the Americas. By the peak of the infamous trade during the eighteenth and early nineteenth century, the Bight of Benin (the so-called Slave Coast) and the Bight of Biafra, a broad region bordering the modern state of Nigeria to the south, were noted as principal catchment areas for New World-bound slaves. Major European slave trading ports such as Badagry, Lagos, Bonny, Calabar, and Elem Kalabari flourished on this coastal stretch along the Atlantic.[13] Thousands of captured people of various ethnic groups in the interior of Nigeria were exported to the Americas through these ports.

The Yoruba of present-day south-western Nigeria constituted a significant number of Nigerians transported to the Americas as slaves. Trafficking in Yoruba slaves across the Atlantic seemed to have commenced in earnest by the middle of the eighteenth century. The disintegration of the great Oyo Empire in the early nineteenth century and the series of inter-group wars throughout Yoruba land that followed its collapse after the 1840s affected the export of slaves from the region. War captives became destined for the Atlantic slavery market, shipped from ports such as Lagos and Badagry. The volume of exported Yoruba slaves increased considerably from the early eighteenth century, reaching a peak by the middle of the century. Slaves from Yoruba land were predominantly headed for Brazil, Cuba, Haiti, Barbados, Trinidad and Tobago, and other countries of South and Central American as well as the islands of the Caribbean and West Indies. Yet, a good proportion of Yoruba slaves landed in the United States, particularly in the southern colonies, from Virginia to Florida.[14]

The Igbo-speaking people of modern eastern part of Nigeria also supplied large numbers of slaves to colonial America. It is true that the interior of the Bight of Biafra lacked powerful, centralized slave trading states in the caliber of the Oyo Empire in Yoruba land. Yet the region was a major slave exporting area from the mid-eighteenth century to mid nineteenth century. Here, the slave trade with the Europeans was dominated by the prominent Aro merchants of Igbo and Ibibio extraction who, through brigandage, and particularly the use of their powerful oracle, the Arochukwu, procured slaves for the Atlantic market. From ports on the Niger Delta to the Cross River valley, slaves of Igbo origin and allied groups in the region were herded away to the United States, many of them landing on plantations in the American south.[15]

The presence of millions of enslaved ethnic Nigerians in the United States played an important role in the development of black cultural identities in America. The attempt of slave owners to divest Africans of their culture never wholly succeeded. Aspects of African culture survived one way or another throughout the period of slavery. This is particularly true of the Yoruba, a people of rich and resilient culture. Indeed, in antebellum America, even though the Yoruba never constituted the majority of the enslaved Africans, the tenacity of their culture generated interest in their home land in the American black community. This interest was promoted in the late-nineteenth century when a few proponents of black emigration to Africa within the antislavery movement called for the resettlement of willing free blacks in Yoruba land. Noted black emigrationists, Martin Robinson Delany and Robert Campbell, visited the Yoruba town of Abeokuta in late 1859 to purchase land for colonization by returning blacks from America. Although this venture failed, in part, because of the outbreak of the American Civil War, Yorubaland remained important in the antislavery emigration and colonization project.

Aside from the unsuccessful Abeokuta project, Lagos, the heart of budding British colonial power in Nigeria, saw the immigration of a few American blacks as part of the influx of emigrants of African descent from the New World, principally Brazil. Robert Campbell was one of the American returnees who later became a prominent Lagosian. From 1863 to 1867 he published the first newspaper in Lagos, the *Anglo-African*, modelled after the influential African American newspaper, *Anglo-American Magazine*, which saw circulation between 1859 and the end of the American Civil War in 1865. Although, the emigration and colonization project did not find wide support among African Americans, the interest it generated helped to promote American-Nigerian ties. The existence of elements of Yoruba culture, particularly traditional religions, in contemporary America could be partly traced to the transplantation of Yoruba slaves in the United States.¹⁶ Despite the fact that historians estimate the deaths of between 1.5 and 2 million slaves during the journey to the New World, various accounts put the number of African slaves that successfully landed in the United States to "at least 3.36 million"[17] to as many as 4 million.[18]

The abolition of the slave trade and slavery altogether saw many of the ex-slaves settling and integrating themselves into American society. However, the years 1859-1860 represented a crucial and significant period of emigrationist activities among black Americans. While some of these ex-slaves were in favour of emigrating and searching for a "black nationality" whether in Africa or in Haiti and the islands and countries bordering the Caribbean, other black leaders opposed the idea and termed it a deceptive designs of the American Colonisation Society, which they saw as the vehicle for the final expatriation of the free black population and the continued enslavement of their brothers in the South. The increasing restrictions imposed on the free black population by the Fugitive Slave Act of 1850, the Kansas-Nebraska Act of 1854 and the Dred Scott Decision in 1857 strengthened the emigrationists' resolve to leave America. In this, however, they were in the minority. Dr. Martin Delany and Robert Campbell were both prominent leaders of the emigrationism school. After toying with the idea of immigrating to the Caribbean, perhapsHaiti where a sizeable population of blacks had already established political communities, it was to Lagos and Abeokuta that they headed in search of an African colony of selected and skilled individuals.[19]

This colony would be composed of agriculturalists, mechanics, competent businessmen, teachers, qualified clergy, a photographer and artist, a surveyor and civil engineer, a geologist and chemist and persons to fill every vocation necessary to an intelligent and progressive community.[20] This African or black nationality was to be sustained by the production of cotton and other tropical crops, which could find an easy market in industrial Europe. This was based on reports on the extensive growth of cotton, the fertility, the untapped resources, and the potential for huge profits in Yorubaland, which they believed, could accommodate more than 100, 000 black American returnees.[21] The emigrationists were greatly encouraged and inspired by the great successes being recorded by ex-American slaves who had settled and were managing their affairs in an admirable way. They hoped their proposed colony would operate under the auspices of the Liberian government.

Delaney and Campbell settled down to work – mobilizing, raising funds and going on expedition to the entire Yorubaland. Eventually, on December 27, 1860, a treaty was signed with the Alake of Egbaland and the Chiefs of Abeokuta allowing for the settlement of emigrants from America in the area around Abeokuta. The Alake and his Chiefs were optimistic that the black American settlers would bring their skills and resources to educate and develop the whole area and would also provide additional security from the ravaging inter-tribal wars ravaging Yorubaland at that time.

As Delany and Campbell went back to America to mobilize willing black Americans to relocate, English missionaries already working in Abeokuta Henry Townsend especially who had long held the view that "the negro was naturally not suited for leadership and could be of no good to his fellow negro" mounted a sustained attack on the entire scheme and caused the Alake to repudiate the treaty. As Towsend argued "… the negro feels a great respect for a white man that God kindly gives a great talent to the white man in trust to be used for the negro's good. Shall we shift the responsibility? Can we do it without sin?"[22]

Still undeterred, Delany and Campbell succeeded in getting a large number of young black Americans willing to settle in Yorubaland. But just as they were about to set forth, the Civil War broke out in America and the blacks turned their attention to participation in the war in the hope of winning their freedom and rights as citizens. The Reverend King described the situation:

> In the spring of 1861 I had several young men prepared to go out as pioneers of the colonies. While I was corresponding with the Society (A.A.S) …about sending the young men out, the Southern States seceded and war was declared. I then wrote to the Society….that the sword had been drawn from the scabbard and would not be retuned, until liberty was proclaimed to the captives. The market for slaves as far as the United States

was concerned would come to an end with the war. The young men interested to go out to Africa to colonise the West Coast were prepared to go south to fight for liberty as soon as the opportunity would be given them to enter the Northern Army".[23]

Surprisingly, even Delany was commissioned to raise black troops for the Northern Army and later given the rank of Major. Campbell, on the other hand, was not to be distracted by the war from returning to Africa. He later came down to Lagos, became a prominent citizen and founded the *Anglo-African Weekly* newspaper and served as its editor.[24] In all, the efforts to establish a "black or African nationality" in Lagos and/or Abeokuta ultimately collapsed due to the hostile opposition of the English missionaries, English imperialist expansion (which had by then seen Lagos annexed) and the outbreak of the Civil War in America.

The United States and Colonial Nigeria

By the second half of the nineteenth century, the British had annexed and established a consulate in Lagos, and set to expand their colonial dominion into the interior.[25] In the years before World War I, British attempts at colonization stepped up. However, it was not until 1914 that a full-fledged colonial state emerged when the British amalgamated the hitherto separately ruled Northern and Southern Protectorates of Nigeria. British colonial rule in Nigeria was to last till October 1, 1960 (1914 – 1960), when the state achieved political independence.

As might be expected, British interest largely defined Nigeria's relations with other powers including the United States. Despite Britain's predominance, the United States maintained some links, principally commercial, with Nigeria. America's trading relations were in the areas of agriculture, mining, transportation, and shipping. The principal Nigerian exports to America during this period were cocoa and palm produce, while Nigeria imported few manufactured products from the United States including automobiles. However, America's commercial intercourse with colonial Nigeria before World War II was rather modest; Britain and other European powers were the big players in Nigeria's international economic relations.

Although commercial ties between the United States and Nigeria increased modestly in the interwar years, Britain's restrictive economic policies severely curtailed a continued growth of trade between the two countries. In any case, the Great Depression of the 1930s that followed the New York stock market crash in October 1929 had a significant impact on the Nigerian economy just as it affected many other parts of the world. The slump in the global economy deeply affected the export-driven Nigerian economy. The prices of major Nigerian export crops such as cocoa and palm produce fell drastically as American demand weakened.

The occupation of Southeast Asia by the Axis during World War II helped to focus America's attention more on Nigeria. Officials in Washington learned during the war how much the sub Saharan region could serve America's war efforts.[26] The fall of the Far East (Malaysia and Singapore) to Japan was crucial in changing American attitudes towards West Africa. Both Malaysia and Singapore were the world's major sources of rubber supply. The seizure of these products by Japan created a sharp spike in demand for rubber, and consequently its price rose astronomically. This created a national crisis for the Allied powers particularly the United States because natural rubber was a strategic commodity in the war effort. It was vital to the production of tires for war planes and military vehicles. It was also required for aircraft guns and sensitive radar equipment, portable bridges, gliders, oxygen masks and many other war supplies. Civilian and military demand for rubber was so monumental, and supply was so tight relative to demand, that a law was enacted in the United States, reducing the speed limit to 35 miles per hour, and limiting the mileage of individual cars to 5, 000 miles per year, to preserve the life of tyres. Attempts to develop synthetic rubber substitutes were still in their infancy and could offer little hope of resolving the shortage. Naturally, the Allied powers turned to West Africa (particularly Liberia and Nigeria) for their supplies of the scarce commodity. The entire region's economy was directed to the servicing of the Allies' war needs, to the detriment of food production.

The interests of the United States in West Africa grew rapidly as the provision of war supplies to the North African war zone became difficult, expensive, and time consuming. US military supplies were taken from Florida, transported through South America to Brazil, then flown from the Parnamirim air base in Natal, Brazil to the military depot at Roberts Field, Liberia, where 5,000 American troops stored and maintained inventory. From Roberts Field, war supplies were flown to Morocco, Tunisia and Algeria. The use of the West African corridor to transport American soldiers and war supplies to North Africa was necessary, since German U-boat activity had made shipping in the North Atlantic Ocean hazardous to American war and merchant vessels. The situation became even more problematic for the Allies after the fall of France in 1940. Hundreds of Allied ships were sunk by German submarines in the North Atlantic. To make matters worse, not even the best military planes could make the direct flight from the United States to North Africa. In General Eisenhower's "Crusade in Europe," he admitted that he seriously considered using Liberian territory as the initial staging ground for the invasion of North Africa and Europe. The ports of Dakar, Gambia, Sierra Leone, Liberia and Nigeria became strategically important to American war planning, especially after it assumed responsibility for the running of the Trans-African Air Ferry Service. Through this service, military supplies including combat aircraft were flown from the United States along points in West Africa to the Allied troops in North Africa and the Middle East. The Nigerian cities of Lagos, Kano, Maiduguri, and Oshogbo, were transit points along this ferry route, putting Nigeria on the map of America's military strategy in the Southern Atlantic.

West Africa, and particularly Nigeria, played an invaluable role militarily and economically in the defence of the Western Hemisphere during the Second World War. During the war the volume of United States trade (imports and exports) with Nigeria rose appreciably.[27] Prior to this period, the government of the United States had never shown any special consideration for the people of Africa and their aspirations. After the war, however, the US government demonstrated feeble and half-hearted support for the European colonial powers and supported speedy decolonization of the African continent.

Pioneers of American Education in Nigeria

Tertiary education was not always readily available to willing Nigerians during the colonial period, particularly in the early part of the era. It was thus commonplace for those seeking post-secondary education and professional training to go abroad to obtain it. Given that Britain was Nigeria's colonial master, Nigerians who had the privilege of studying abroad headed to the United Kingdom.

Though the first generation of educated Nigerians and professionals was a product of British education, in the years immediately after World War I, a handful of young Nigerian students were already attending American colleges and universities. One of the most prominent among these students was Nnamdi Azikiwe, a future leading figure in the Nigerian nationalist movement and later a political leader in post-colonial Nigeria. Popularly called "Zik," this young Nigerian came to the United States in 1925, and his sojourn in the country would last nine year during which he studied at some of America's finest institutions, both historically black and white-dominated. Azikiwe began his American college education at Storer College in Harpers Ferry, West Virginia, and consequently attended Lincoln University in Pennsylvania, and Howard University in Washington D.C., both predominantly black institutions. His educational pursuit also saw him attend leading white-dominated institutions such as the University of Pennsylvania in Philadelphia, and Columbia University in New York. By the time Azikiwe returned to Nigeria in 1934, he had acquired a chain of American degrees including an MA in Political Science and an MS in Anthropology. Azikiwe also served as an instructor at Lincoln.[28]

Encouraged by Azikiwe, a few more Nigerians went to the United States to study in the late 1930s. Twelve left in 1938, among who were Azikiwe's fellow Igbo, Mbonu Ojike, Nwafor Orizu, and Kingsley Ozumba Mbadiwe. Both Ojike and Orizu attended Lincoln University, Azikiwe's alma mater. Also, like their mentor, both of them went on to attend predominantly white institutions after leaving Lincoln. Ojike studied at the Ohio State University and thereafter attended the University of Chicago where he bagged an M.A degree. Orizu also attended Ohio State University and later obtained an M.A. from Columbia University. On his part, Mbadiwe studied at Columbia and New York Universities where he earned the B.Sc. and M.A degrees respectively.[29]

This generation of Nigerian students in the United States extolled the American educational system. Orizu described American education as "horizontal," by which he meant it was broad-based, providing opportunities for more people to obtain higher education. He contrasted this to the British system which he termed "vertical," in the sense that it was more restrictive. Orizu and others not only adored the American educational system, they played an important role in promoting it in Nigeria upon their return. Orizu and Mbadiwe travelled the length and breadth of the country giving lectures on American education to audiences, and encouraging more Nigerians to pursue their studies in the United States. Orizu was perhaps the most vocal of these ambassadors of American education. He promoted relentlessly an elaborate scholarship scheme under the sponsorship of an organization he had founded in New York in 1943, the American Council on African Education (ACAE), to aid Nigerians willing to study in the United States.[30] His public lecture tours on behalf of American education took him to major Nigerian cities and all the regions of the country including Lagos in the West; Onitsha, Oguta, Calabar, Enugu, Port Harcourt, in the East; and Jos, Kano, Sokoto, and Zaria, in the North.[31] The colonial authorities frowned at the promotion of American-style education by Orizu and other American-trained Nigerians, and tried to discourage Nigerians from studying in the United States. Nevertheless, partly because of their campaign, the post-World War II period saw an influx of Nigerians into the United States in search of post-secondary education. A Nigerian newspaper reported in 1949 that 248 Nigerians were studying in American institutions.[32] Between 1947 and 1953, the number of Nigerians who had received ACAE scholarships was 121.[33]

Nigeria long remained grateful to American institutions for the assistance they offered to Nigerians who came to the United

States to study in the period before independence. For example, when General Obasanjo visited the United States in 1977, he had this to say about Howard University:

> From the 1930s Howard University has provided succor to hundreds of Nigerians, quenched their thirst for knowledge, and provided jobs at all levels ... To the greater glory of this institution, it can name among its alumni, a past president of Nigeria, a former ambassador of Nigeria to the United States of America and innumerable highly placed person in all walks of life in my country.[34]

Howard continues to attract Nigerian scholars long after independence. For example, in 1985, 18 of the 73 Ph.Ds. and 15 of the Masters degrees awarded by Howard went to Nigerians.[35]

American universities had a profound impact on these leaders at a key moment in their lives. For example, Dr Nnamdi Azikiwe was to note much later:

> Deep in my heart I can honestly confess the United States of America impressed me as the haven of refuge for oppressed sections of humanity in Europe, Africa, Asia and the rest of the world. My life is a testimonial that Americans shared life's pleasures and walked the honest road with me.[36]

This, undoubtedly, was to be a major factor in the nationalist agitation of Dr Azikiwe and his co-nationalists.

Nigerian Nationalism and American Influence

Anti-colonial sentiment in Nigeria before World War II was not overtly radical. Nationalist leaders of the period stopped short of expressly demanding independence, instead pushing for reform of the colonial system. Rather than self-determination, nationalist agitation focused more on narrow demands such as the inclusion of educated Nigerians in the colonial administrative apparatus. Except for Azikiwe and a few other Nigerians such as Eyo Ita, a Columbia University alumnus who had spent eight years in America, most Nigerians who studied in the United States before World War II did not become actively involved in the educated class-led anti-colonial protest once they returned. As noted above Azikiwe's experiences during his nine-year stay in the United States greatly influenced his political outlook and nationalist thoughts in subsequent years. His first-hand experience of Jim Crow segregation and black subordination in America predisposed him to an anti-colonial mind-set. He was inspired by the radical black consciousness thought of activists such as the New York-based Jamaican nationalist and pan-Africanist, Marcus Garvey. Azikiwe claimed that he was influenced, in particular, by Garvey's call for Africa's liberation from colonialism.[37] Garvey's influence on Azikiwe was so great that when he (Azikiwe) became Nigeria's first governor-general in November 1960; one of the dignitaries who graced his inauguration was Garvey's widow, Amy Jacques Garvey. Azikiwe had personally invited her to the august occasion.[38]

Like Azikiwe, many of the Nigerian students in America during the Second World War were politically conscious. At Lincoln, Ojike was actively involved in African students' politics, at one time serving as president of the African Students Union. His activism compelled him to travel extensively in America, attending conferences and giving lectures on Nigerian and African affairs to American audiences. In 1940 he attended the convention of the Universal Negro Improvement Association (UNIA), Garvey's grassroots radical organization.

In 1943 Mbadiwe and his compatriots, Ojike and Orizu, founded the African Academy of Arts and Research (AAAR), dedicated to educating the American public about Africa, promoting African culture, and supporting the course of African independence. Both Mbadiwe and Ojike were executive officers of the organization which, by 1946, boasted over a thousand members. Its board members included prominent Americans including Eleanor Roosevelt, the former First Lady. In his capacity as executive director of the academy, Ojike attended the United Nations Conference on International Organization held on April 25, 1945, in San Francisco, as an observer. During the time of the academy's existence from 1943 to 1957, it worked relentlessly through cultural awareness programs to foster Nigerian-American relations. It also tried to support African students in the United States through fundraising. In 1947 the academy established Africa House in New York City, which became a rendezvous for African students. On his return from the United States, Mbadiwe continued the course of the AAAR by establishing branch offices in many parts of West Africa including Nigeria. Mbadiwe travelled extensively in Nigeria in an effort to raise money for the organization to foster its scholarship scheme.[39]

Orizu's organization, the ACAE, was also dedicated to the fostering of African and American cultural relationships, and promoting the prevailing anti-colonial sentiment in wartime America. The organization impressed prominent African Americans and White liberals who served on its advisory board. These Americans included Harlem Renaissance writer Alain Locke, Civil Rights advocate Mary McLeod Bethune, radical activist and singer Paul Robeson, scholar and anthropologist Melville Jean Herskovits, Vice President Henry Wallace, and Eleanor Roosevelt. After his return to Nigeria, Orizu established ACAE branches in Port Harcourt, Calabar, Aba, Enugu, Jos, Onitsha, Lagos, and Ijebu Ode,[40] principally to serve the organization's course of propagating American education in the country.

A major influence on the Nigerian students in wartime America which helped to sharpen their nationalist inclination was the United States' anti-colonial foreign policy which particularly opposed the continued existence of the British Empire after the war. In 1941, American president Franklin D. Roosevelt and British Prime Minister Winston Churchill signed the Atlantic Charter, a document that expressed the right of self-determination belonging to the colonised peoples of the world. While Churchill interpreted this document to exclude Britain's African colonies, Roosevelt gave it a broader interpretation, meaning that it was applicable to all peoples still under colonial rule. America's anti-colonial pronouncements became a source of encouragement to Nigerian nationalists. They relished Roosevelt's interpretation of the Atlantic Charter and considered it an expression of support for self-determination in Nigeria.

A number of the American trained Nigerians were destined to play a prominent role in the nationalist struggle in Nigeria, and subsequently in its post-colonial politics. The most recognizable of them was Azikiwe, who, from the time he returned from the United States in 1934, entered the centre stage of Nigerian nationalism. Azikiwe eventually became Nigeria's first governor-general and later president.[41] Orizu, Mbadiwe, and Ojike, also emerged as leading figures in Nigerian nationalism and in the politics of the First Republic. Orizu was the first president of the Nigerian Senate, and he also served as acting president of the republic in 1966 shortly before the military take-over of the government. Mbadiwe served in various political capacities, in the First Republic as minister in various departments including Trade and Communications, Aviation, and Lands and Natural Resources, and as a presidential adviser in the Second Republic. Ojike's political portfolios included Deputy Mayor of Lagos, member of Eastern Region's House of Assembly, Minister of Works, and of Finance, in the region.

Nigerian nationalism in turn provided inspiration for the black community in America in its struggle for racial equality and justice. The demand for civil rights in the late 1950s brought the issue of racial discrimination against America's blacks to the attention of many Nigerians. The politically conscious Nigerian populace was very critical of racial inequality in American society, and often expressed support for black civil rights leaders and their struggles. The success of the nationalist struggle in Nigeria and other African states was reassuring to African Americans in their own fight against racial oppression. The Rev. Dr Martin Luther King, Jr., the charismatic leader of the Civil Rights Movement in the early 1960s, once noted that African leaders like Azikiwe were popular in black institutions in America because of their role in the African liberation movement.[42] Dr King himself was in attendance at Azikiwe's inauguration as governor-general in November 1960.

The Early Cold War and Nationalism

The post-war period saw the emergence of the United States and the Soviet Union as global superpowers. Their engagement in an ideological confrontation, the Cold War, became the new dynamic in international relations. From the 1950s to the 1960s, the age of decolonization in Africa, the overriding interest of the superpowers was to keep the emerging independent

African states within their respective ideological blocs. As Nigeria moved towards self-determination in the late 1950s, the United States, driven by Cold War considerations, cooperated with the colonial power, Britain, to ensure the emergence of an independent Nigerian state firmly in the Western capitalist bloc, endowed with Western-style democracy and free trade.

To some extent, post-1945 radical nationalism in Nigeria drew on leftist ideology and fed on Soviet-bloc support and inspiration.[43] Left-leaning Nigerian nationalists, though small in number, were impressed and encouraged by the Soviet Union's anti-colonial credentials. These militant nationalists operated within mainstream nationalism or through their own organizations such as the Nigerian National Socialist Party formed in 1945, and the militant Zikist Movement established in February 1946.[44] Marxist nationalists also constituted a small but vocal sector of the Nigerian labour movement. Apart from receiving inspiration and non-tangible support from communist organization in Britain and other parts of Western Europe, some of the leaders of the radical left wing of the Nigerian nationalist movement also received funds from Soviet-bloc states.

Leftist and militant brands of nationalism in colonial Nigeria were necessarily viewed in London and Washington threats to Anglo-American interest in the colony and in the rest of the sub-Saharan region of West Africa. Nigeria was clearly of strategic and economic importance to the West, and thus a sovereign Nigeria planted in the Soviet bloc and hostile to Western interests could not be allowed to materialize. This trajectory underlined the colonial power's determination to contain communist infiltration into Nigeria, a policy that was wholly supported by the United States. During World War II, the United States had largely pushed an anti-colonial policy, even opposing post-war survival of the British Empire. Now Cold War considerations compelled the reshaping of US policy toward European colonialism. Britain was not to be rushed into granting independence to its African colonies. Also, African nationalism must be shaped and guided to eschew any communist subversive influence.

In Nigeria in the 1950s, the American consulate in Lagos was an important source of support for the Britain's anti-leftist campaign. In addition to the consulate, a government agency, the United States Information Service (USIS) which had offices in Lagos, Enugu and Kaduna, acted as an instrument, not only for countering communist propaganda, but also for propagating American values. As parts of the agency's strategy to undermine communist influence and appeal to young Nigerian minds, it produced and disseminated pro-Western propaganda literature and organized scholarships for Nigerians to study in the United States.[45] Generally, in the decade before Nigeria's independence, the USIS collaborated with Nigerian colonial officials, departments, and colonial agencies, in the task of containing the activities of militant nationalists and leftist organizations.

The United States government instituted other initiatives in Nigeria aimed at propagating Western ideals and thereby stifling any communist agenda. For example, Nigeria was one of the beneficiaries of the Truman administration's technical assistance initiative for developing countries christened the Point Four Program, instituted in 1950. Under this program, in 1957, the Department of State sponsored the training in American institutions of the first generation of Nigerian diplomats to serve in the Nigerian Foreign Service.[46]

The United States and Nigeria: Formal Diplomatic Relations

On October 1, 1960, Nigeria was formally granted independence by its colonial master, Britain, and the United States immediately recognized the new state. At the independence ceremonies, the United States was officially represented by New York governor, Nelson Rockefeller. Meanwhile, American President Dwight Eisenhower sent a congratulatory message to Nigeria's Prime Minister, Sir Abubukar Tafawa Balewa.[47] The Secretary of State, Christian Herter, also sent a goodwill message to the Nigerian people. Both countries went on to immediately establish formal diplomatic relations as they opened embassies in each other's capital. The Nigerian Embassy in Washington, D.C., was headed, in the interim, by M. J. Garba as Charge d'Affaires, while at the helm of affairs in the American Embassy in Lagos was Joseph Palmer II, who formally presented his letter of credence to the Nigerian government on October 4, becoming America's first ambassador in Nigeria.

THE ANTECEDENTS

At the time of Nigeria's independence in 1960, the United States hoped to build a strong and cordial relationship with the new state which boasted an enormous size and population, vast natural and human resources and, therefore, great potentials for economic and political development. In the prevailing Cold War era of superpower ideological competition, the United States' foreign policy toward Nigeria was shaped by the prospect of the country becoming a model of a successful western-type democracy and free enterprise economy in Africa and the rest of the developing world. With the prospect of the emergence of a viable democratic African state which was expected to become a regional power and assume a leadership role on the continent, the administrations of Presidents John F. Kennedy and Lyndon B. Johnson hoped to maintain an influence in the new state. Although, it appeared at first that Nigeria would fulfil America's hope of a democratic, capitalist state whose example other emerging African states would follow, in the final analysis, this expectation was not realized. By the mid-1960s, after groping from one crisis to another, Nigeria's First Republic collapsed, courtesy of a military coup d'état.

End Notes

[11] Olufemi Vaughan, "Traditional Chief and Rulers in Nigeria", *West Africa,* London 1989.

[12] For more on this, See, Ade Ajayi and Okon Uya, *Slavery and the Slave Trade in Nigeria,* Ibadan: Safari books, 2010

[13] See Ibid

[14] For more on this subject, see S. Adebanji Akintoye, *A History of the Yoruba People,* (Dakar: Amalion Publishing, 2010).

[15] See Ade Ajayi and Okom Uya, *op-cit*

[16] This subject is discussed in details in Adebayo Oyebade, "Yoruba Culture in Contemporary America," in Toyin Falola and Adebayo Oyebade, (eds.), *Yoruba Fiction, Orature, and Culture: Oyekan Owomoyela and African Literature and the Yoruba Experience,* (Trenton: Africa World Press, 2010), 321-340.

[17] *(Joseph Inikori,* 1992).

[18] *(Eltis et al,* 1999).

[19] Blackett, R., "Martin R. Delany & Robert Campbell: Black Americans in Search of an African Colony", *The Journal of Negro History,* Vol. 62, No. 1, January. 1977.

[20] Ibid, p. 5.

[21] ibid.

[22] (*Eugene Stock, 1899, J.F.A. Ajayi, 1959*).

[23] (Cited in Blackett, 1977; 5) *The Autobiography of the Rev. William King,* (unpublished) — William King Papers.

[24] Fred Omu, *Press and Politics in Nigeria 1880 – 1937,* Ibadan: Longman 1966)

[25] For a more detailed discussion on this, see, Tekena Tamunu, *The Evolution of the Nigerian State,* Ibadan Longman.

[26] *(Oyebade,* 1995).

[27] This subject is further developed in Adebayo Oyebade, "Feeding America's War Machine: The United States Economic Expansion in West Africa during World War II," in *African Economic History,* 26, (1), 1998.

28. For a discussion of the impact of Lincoln College on the thinking of Azikiwe.See Pearl T. Robinson, "Area Studies in Search of Africa", in David Szanton (ed) *The Politics of Knowledge: Area Studies and the Disciplines*, Berkeley and Los Angelis, University of California Press, 2004.

29. Lynch, Hollis. "K.O. Mbadiwe, 1939–1947: The American Years of a Nigerian Political Leader," *Journal of African Studies*, 7 (4), Winter 1980–1981, 184–203.

30. More discourse on this subject is provided in Michael M. Ogbeidi, "Non-Governmental Organization and the Promotion of American Education in Nigeria, 1941–1953," *Nebula*, 6 (4), Dec., 2009.

31. See ibid., 7-8. See also Kalu Ogbaa, *The Nigerian Americans*, (Westport, Conn.: Greenwood Press, 2003)

32. *African Echo*, 11 Feb., 1949, 5, cited in Ogbeidi, "Non-Governmental Organization, 16

33. The figure is obtained from ibid.

34. Steven Monblatt, "Nigeria and the United States: 25 Years of Cooperation", Lecture delivered at the Nigerian Institute of International Relations, October 24 1985.

35. Ibid

36. ibid

37. See James G. Spady, "Garvey's Influence on Owelle Nnamdi Azikiwe and West African Nationalism," *Garvey's Voice*, Nov. – Dec. 1981.

38. See Ula Y. Taylor, *The Veiled Garvey: The Life and Times of Amy Jacques Garvey*, (University of North Carolina Press, 2002), 214.

39. For more details on the AAAR, see LaRay Denzer, "Black Cultural Nationalist Network in the United States and Nigeria after World War II: The Example of the African Academy of Arts and Research," *Nigerian Journal of American Studies*, 3, July 1993; and K. O. Mbadiwe, "African Academy of Arts and Research," *Africa: Today and Tomorrow*, (New York: African academy of arts and research, 1945).

40. Ogbeidi, "Non-Governmental Organisation," 6.

41. The literature on Azikiwe's political career is quite extensive. See the following, for example: L.B. Ekpebu, *Zik of Africa: God's Special Gift to Nigeria, Africa, and the World*, (Ibadan: Sam Bookman, 1998); Rhoda Osemene, (ed.), *Zik: the African Legend*, (Lagos, Nigeria: Times Books, 1996); Michael J. Echeruo, "Nnamdi Azikiwe and 19th Century Nigerian Thought," *Journal of Modern African Studies*, 12 (2), 1974, 245-263; Nnamdi Azikiwe, *My odyssey: An Autobiography*, (London, C.

Hurst, 1970); and Nnamdi Azikiwe, *Renascent Africa,* (London, Cass, 1968).

[42.] James Melvin Washington, (ed.), *A Testament of Hope: The Essential Writings and Speeches of Martin Luther King, Jr.,* (San Francisco: HarperCollins Publishers, 1991), 162.

[43.] Important sources on this subject are Hakeem Ibikunle Tijani, *Britain, Leftist Nationalists and Transfer of Power in Nigeria,* 1945-1965, (New York: Routledge, 2006); and Hakeem Tijani, "Communist and the Nationalist Movement," in Toyin Falola, *Nigeria in the Twentieth Century,* (Durham, NC: Carolina Academic Press, 2002), 293-313.

[44.] The Zikist Movement is discussed in the following works: Ehiedu E.G Iweriebor, *Radical Politics in Nigeria, 1945-1950: The Significance of the Zikist Movement,* (Zaria, Nigeria: Ahmadu Bello University Press, 1996); and G.O. Olusanya, "The Zikist Movement: A Study in Political Radicalism," *Journal of Modern African Studies,* 4 (3), 1996, 323-333.

[45.] Tijani, *Britain, Leftist Nationalists,* 78

[46.] Ibid., 76

[47.] See U.S. Dept. of State, Office of the Historian, "A Guide to the United States' History of Recognition, Diplomatic, and Consular Relations, by Country, since 1776: Nigeria," retrieved on Feb. 28, 2011, from http://history.state.gov/countries/nigeria.

Chapter Two

Independence and the Establishment of a New Relationship

Joseph AIHIE

As noted in the last chapter, although United States – Nigerian relations formally started in 1960 with the attainment of political independence by Nigeria, there had been quite some level of interaction between the two countries prior to that time. Nigeria, in fact, did maintain some form of external relations, but under British tutelage rather than as a mark of sovereignty.[48] The United States, for its part, had repeatedly demonstrated interest in Nigeria's economic development by giving assistance through Britain. In 1958, for example, the US approved 10 mostly agricultural projects whose value was estimated at $700,000.[49] There were considerable expectations of a relationship with the US at the time Nigeria became independent. President Dwight David Eisenhower specifically noted that he was "confident that, in the years to come, our two countries will stand as one in safeguarding the greatest of all bonds between us, our common belief in a free and democratic way of life".[50]

This chapter discusses the relationship between Nigeria and the United States from the time of independence up to the time of the military intervention in Nigerian politics in January, 1966. The chapter specifically focuses on all the ramifications of the Nigerian/US relationship and the interpretations both sides gave to the connection between them. The main argument advanced in the chapter is that the foundation laid at the time of Nigeria's independence and during the First Republic was to play a major part in what subsequently occurred in the relationship between the two countries in subsequent years.

Diplomatic Relations

At the independence of Nigeria, the American President, Dwight Eisenhower, extended his best wishes and congratulations to the country and assured Nigeria that the United States stood "ready to work with the people of Nigeria to reach the goals we shared of health, enlightenment and material well-being".[51] Shortly before independence on September 23 1960, President Eisenhower had appointed Joseph Palmer II as his first Ambassador to Nigeria. When Nigeria became a Republic in October 1963 Palmer was again re-accredited as Ambassador to the country. At the same time, Dr. Matthew Mbu was designated as Nigeria's first Ambassador to the United States. Diplomatic visits started almost immediately afterwards, with Nigeria's foreign Minister, Jaja Wachukwu, meeting President Eisenhower in the United States while attending the third Annual Conference of the American Society of African Culture in Philadelphia.

Quite early in 1961, the Prime Minister, Sir Abubakar Tafawa Balewa, had, on the invitation of President John F. Kennedy, paid an 8 day official visit to the United States where discussions for loans and grants were initiated. But why did newly-independent Nigeria command such attention from the United States, which had consistently maintained a policy of non engagement with Africa, regarding its nations as being within the spheres of imperial Europe? Several reasons have been advanced to explain the interests and attention of the United States on Nigeria in the years before and after its independence. Firstly, it is argued that both countries shared similar colonial experiences – each experienced Britain as a colonial master. The only difference was that while Nigeria gained independence through a largely peaceful and a negotiated constitutional process, the United States had to fight its way to sovereignty through force of arms. Secondly, both countries are characterized by ethnic heterogeneity. The United States boasts of being a plural society with ethnic groups from almost all parts of the world. Though Nigeria's inhabitants are of the same racial stock, the country harbors some 250 culturally, historically, politically, and socioeconomically disparate groups. The only difference again remains that while all the diverse racial groups in the United States have largely succeeded in subordinating their differences under an American identity, Nigeria has been struggling with synthesizing the different cultural and political ethnics into what could represent a Nigerian character or consciousness.[52] Thirdly, Nigeria, with its vast size (923, 853 square kilometers) and huge population, remains the largest black nation in the world and since independence has been poised to play a strong leadership role not only in Africa, but in the world at large. As L.A. Nwachuku argues, the United States, psychologically impressed with size, feels that its own large size has contributed to its material success. Therefore, it feels that Nigeria, with all its promise at independence, has the potential to develop an economy on a scale that would accelerate its own material progress. The prospect that Nigeria would assume a leadership role in the African continent and become a key player in the international community made it desirable for the big powers to gain Nigeria's friendship.

Nigeria, on the other hand, having grown up in the best traditions of British capitalism, was ideologically oriented to the West and the United States in particular and earnestly sought its friendship. Prime Minister Balewa, in an address in the Nigerian House of Representative in 1961 declared emphatically: "we admire the American way of life, and we respect the people of the United States for their love of freedom".[53] He repeated similar declarations on various occasions, including his official visit to the United States.[54] Similarly, David Apter, in his testimony before the Senate subcommittee on Africa, affirmed that "Nigeria was much more of a western country than we [Americans] tend to think it is".[55] But that was as far as United States—Nigerian relations went, and despite America's obvious interest in Nigeria's economic development and the prospects of a flourishing diplomatic and political relation, US/Nigerian relations during the First Republic started and ended on a low note.

During the First Republic, the attitude of the United States towards Nigeria was somewhat complex, as it was a mixture of political indifference and economic involvement. This was not unconnected to its traditional attitude towards African countries at the time. Despite supporting independence after the Second World War, the United States continued to view Africa as within the orbit of European political influence, noting that the new African nations were former European colonies. The US was therefore reluctant to deal directly with African states in political matters. The clear exception was Liberia, which for historical reasons had closer political ties with the US, and Congo, whose leaders had shown signs of intercourse with communism. Again, since Nigeria was ideologically a democracy, had indicated its continuing tutelage to Britain and the capitalist word by signing a Nigerian-Anglo Defence Pact, and had endlessly courted American friendship despite proclaiming itself to be "non-aligned", the United States felt comfortable restricting its relations with Nigeria to economic interactions, informed by its belief that such economic and moral vigour could be used to erect a better world. Nigeria, or more particularly its northern dominated leadership, delighted the US by rapidly exhibiting an anti-communist posture. Nigeria's relations with the USSR and other communist states during this period bordered on hostility. This was partly informed by Balewa's personal fears of the dangers of communism – which he saw as an evil from which Nigeria must be shielded.[56] According to Billy Dudley, this posture was due to the inability of Nigeria's leaders to get over the image of the Soviet Union created by the colonial administration.[57] Nigeria maintained a ban on literature originating from the Eastern Bloc (even though such a ban was not in place in Britain and the United States), rejected Soviet aid and trade and discouraged contact with the East.[58] This was despite the willingness of the Eastern Bloc countries to contribute to the development of Nigeria and the inability of the West to provide substantial aid to the country. The Balewa administration also provided generous incentives to Western foreign investors even where such investments were likely to weaken local entrepreneurs.[59]

The Nigerian government rejected all scholarship awards from Eastern Europe, and it also denied employment to Nigerians who secretly went to acquire education there. Particularly interesting is the fact that Balewa's government denied the

USSR the facility to open an embassy in Lagos, even though the Soviets had expressed a desire to open diplomatic relations with Nigeria. The Nigerian authorities stated that the country did not have the resources at that stage to reciprocate with a Nigerian embassy in the Soviet Union. But the same government during that period gave a £40.000.00 grant to the British government to assist it in building its diplomatic mission in Lagos.[60] Even when the government eventually permitted the Soviet Union to establish an embassy in Nigeria, the number of its personnel was restricted. This was on the

> understanding that the number of embassy staff would be restricted; it was claimed that that was the advice of the British government, the understanding being that since Nigeria did not have the personnel to keep Soviet representatives under effective surveillance, the numbers to be allowed had to be such that the British High Commission could keep a check on them.[61]

With such a posture, the United States had no reason to engage Nigeria politically, even when Nigeria desperately courted that friendship.

It should be noted however, that Nigeria's pro-American stance was mostly limited to the North and that the Northern People's Party controlled the Balewa government. The mainly southern opposition and nationalists had always maintained an anti-American and anti-capitalist stance long before and after independence. This seems like a paradox especially if juxtaposed against the current anti-American sentiments in the north of Nigeria and the pro-American attitude in the south. In the days before and after independence, religious affiliations did not play any role in shaping relations between the United States and Nigeria. Rather, they were strongly influenced by the British colonial legacy of giving priority to the Muslim north.[62] The early exposure of the predominantly Christian south to western influences and processes of social change led to their early radicalization and politicization. They subsequently played a dominant role in the creation and leading of the Nigerian nationalist movements demanding independence and the emancipation of the black race. Beginning with the period of decolonization in the 1950s, politicization of the masses was much more noticeable in the south than in the north and Christian graduates of the mission institutions in the south and of educational institutions abroad, such as Nnamdi Azikwe, became the ideological avant-garde of the anti-colonial movement.[63] The intellectual wing of the southern nationalist movement, on the other hand, grew very critical of capitalism and what they termed "American imperialism," becoming great advocates of socialism. This position was carried right into independence and as Back contends, "in the first decades after independence, the tradition of anti-establishment (and thus anti-U.S.) criticism seems to have been a salient feature of the Christian elites –both political and intellectual."

Muslims in the north, on the other hand, were exposed to reduced levels of both social change and political participation, which were led mainly by Muslim leaders. The tradition of collaboration between these elites and the British authorities, shaped during the colonial era, strengthened as independence approached. The southern element in Nigerian nationalism was perceived as subversive, and the British preferred to strengthen the dominance of the North. This spirit of collaboration continued after independence and, despite Nigeria officially proclaiming itself to be 'non-aligned' and 'neutral', its actions betrayed it as pro-western. For instance, records of Nigerian voting pattern at the United Nations showed that for the period 1960 – 1965, Nigeria voted on the side of the Western powers on most issues of any significance.[64] That was also the major reasons behind the Anglo-Nigerian Defence Pact which gave Britain military facilities and included the training of British personnel in Nigeria. This was interpreted as a subtle handing over of the defence of the NPC controlled government to Britain and to prevent its overthrow by the loquacious and rebellious southerners, who by then controlled the top officer cadre of the Nigerian army until such a time when the north could restore parity with the south or even take over control of the army. It is still being debated how the first military coup could have succeeded if the defence pact had not been abrogated.

So, while this spirit of admiration and a desire for strong cooperation continued to shape Nigerian attitudes toward the

United States in the First Republic, the same did not hold true for American attitudes toward Nigeria. America simply did not have any strategic interest in Nigeria or sub-Saharan Africa and so did not need to establish any special relationship with Nigeria. Even if there was a need to keep Nigeria and other African countries pro-western to avoid the incursion of the Soviets, the US trusted Britain and the other European imperial powers to ensure that African countries remained within the western sphere of influence. That was the same attitude that guided the America response to the Nigerian civil war – it stayed aloof and refused to sell weapons to Nigeria until the Soviets came to Nigeria's aid. It was not until the post civil war oil boom that the United States warmed up to Nigeria, and even that was more in the area of trade as Nigeria being one of its main suppliers of crude oil.

In the prevailing Cold War era of superpower ideological competition during the early 1960s, the United States' foreign policy toward Nigeria was shaped by the prospect of the country becoming a model of a successful western-type democracy and free enterprise economy in Africa and the rest of the developing world. With the prospect of the emergence of a viable democratic African state which was expected to become a regional power and assume a leadership role on the continent, the administrations of Presidents John F. Kennedy and Lyndon B. Johnson hoped to maintain an influence in the new state.

At first, it appeared as if Nigeria would fulfil America's hope of a democratic, capitalist state in Africa, whose example other emerging African states would follow. The United States policy in Nigeria, consequently, aimed at assisting the state in the task of nation building. Nigeria became the principal beneficiary of United States' foreign assistance program. Particularly during the Kennedy presidency, American dollar aid fuelled a number of developmental projects in Nigeria. In the early 1960s, bilateral trade between the two countries expanded as Nigeria opened more of its market to America. American imports from Nigeria and investments in the country increased, although the greater volume of Nigeria's external trade still resided with its erstwhile colonial power, Britain.

Economic links during the First Republic

Independence brought an increase in economic assistance from the American government. Barely eight months after the country's independence, President John F. Kennedy, sent a special economic mission to study Nigeria's 6-year development plan. Following the recommendations of the mission, the US government provided economic and military assistance with loans and grants that ranged from US$25 million in 1962, US$30.2 million in 1963, US$51.6 million in 1964, US$36.4 million in 1965, to US$30.5 million in 1966.[65] While President Kennedy was in office, Nigerian-American cooperation further increased, with the US respecting Nigeria's non-aligned stance. In 1961, Kennedy openly praised Nigeria for detailing police and army units to the United Nations Command in the Congo during the country's intense struggle to maintain peace soon after its independence. In 1962, the US gave a US$225 million in loans and grants to Nigeria. At this time, this was the largest single US aid commitment to any sub-Saharan country. Indeed, in a special message to the Congress in April 1963, President Kennedy singled out Nigeria for:

> meeting those high standards of self-help and fiscal and economic progress which permit our aid to be directed towards ultimate full self-support.

In December, 1961, Gulf Oil, Texaco, Mobil and Philips Petroleum were granted off-shore prospecting licenses. In December 1963, after 2 years of intensive exploration, Gulf drilled Nigeria's first successful offshore well in Escravos Bay and in April 1965, Gulf shipped the first cargo of offshore oil in Nigeria.

Apart from Washington's aid program, the United States also exerted a major presence in Nigeria in the early 1960s through Kennedy's Peace Corps, a program designed to assist the course of nation-building in the developing world. Under this program, about three hundred American Peace Corps volunteers, the largest number sent to any country, served in Nigeria, mostly in educational institutions such as schools, colleges, and universities. This was, however, to lead to another development which almost marred the relationship, when, in October 1961, the infamous Postcard incident occurred. The story centred round a postcard sent by a Peace Corps volunteer, Marjorie Michelmore, to her boyfriend in Cambridge, Massachusetts, depicting Nigeria and Nigerians in very negative light. The actual content of the postcard is presented below:

> Dear Bobbo:
>
> Don't be furious at getting a postcard. I promise a letter next time. I wanted you to see the incredible and fascinating city we were in. With the training we had, we really were not prepared for the squalor and absolute primitive living conditions rampant both in the city and in the bush. We had no idea what "underdevelopment" meant. It really is a revelation and after we got over the initial horrified shock, a very rewarding experience. Everyone except us lives in the streets, cooks in the street, sells in the street, and even goes to the bathroom in the street. Please write.
>
> Marge.
>
> P.S. We are excessively cut off from the rest of the world.[66]

Fortunately, this unfortunate incident did not derail the Peace Corps effort and between 1962 and 1967, Nigeria had more Peace Corps Volunteers than any other African country and ranked the second in the world after India.

Political and economic ties between the United States and Nigeria in the early years of Nigeria's independence remained cordial despite some divisive issues. The struggle for civil rights by African Americans in the 1960s brought the issue of racial discrimination against America's black population to the attention of many Nigerians. The politically conscious Nigerian populace was very critical of the racial inequality in the American society, and often expressed support for black civil rights leaders and their struggles. The militant civil rights leader Malcolm X was well received on his visit to Nigeria in April 1964 and was even given a Nigerian name. On this occasion, he said, Nigerians are interested in every aspect of the plights of blacks in America and that they study black Americans struggle for freedom. Nigerian criticism of America's racial problem was related to the condemnation of Washington's support for apartheid South Africa with its virulent racist policies towards its black population. The United States had always maintained very strong presence in South Africa, where its investment was enormous, far outweighing its total investment in the rest of Africa combined. The condemnation of US support for South Africa came from both the Nigerian people and the government. Though important, these issues did not destabilize the broader US/Nigerian relationship.

For the United States, the overriding determining factor in its relations with Nigeria remained one of support for a budding democracy on the way to being firmly planted within the capitalist bloc. The Nigerian government was a functioning parliamentary democracy agreeable to the US and its leader, Prime Minister Abubakar Tafawa-Balewa was a moderate, pro-Western politician. Although the Balewa government formally professed nonalignment, its foreign policy behaviour and pronouncements suggested that it was favourably disposed toward the United States.

However, by the mid-1960s, the fundamental basis of American relations with Nigeria had floundered. Bitter and often violent political and ethnic divisions as well as lack of real economic development as envisaged at independence had seriously hampered Nigeria's ability to emerge as a viable democratic state. Indeed, by early 1966, the First Republic had collapsed, ignominiously terminated by the first coup d'état in the country, a bloody putsch executed on January 15, which claimed the lives of the Prime Minister, a number of prominent politicians, and senior military officers. From then on, Nigeria groped from one crisis to another until a civil war began in 1967, which threatened to destroy the federation.

As the expectation that Nigeria would serve as a shining example of a democratic state evaporated, the United States was less enthusiastic in fomenting a special relationship with the country. In any case, the war in Vietnam was consuming a great deal of America's energy by this time and the Johnson administration shifted most of its attention away from Nigeria until the onset of the Nigerian Civil War.

The low-keyed relation between the United States and Nigeria or perhaps the refusal of the United States to engage

Nigeria fully continued throughout the First Republic up until the government of Sir Tafawa Balewa was toppled in the 1966 bloody military coup championed, in the main, by middle rank officers of predominantly eastern Nigerian origin. The ease with which the coup was carried out and its success exposed the fact that optimistic American views of the strength of Nigerian democracy and unity were premature and that the hope for a united and strong Nigeria to represent Africa was not practical in the near future. This may have further convinced the United States of the need to keep relations with Nigeria very low-keyed so as not to be drawn into a conflict it had no interest in.

As will be shown later in this book, the same kind of attitude guided the United States' response to Nigeria throughout the period of the Nigerian civil war where it stayed aloof and refused to sell weapons to Nigeria until the Soviet Union came to Nigeria's aid. That period also saw a more positive approach towards the Soviet Union and the Eastern Bloc. The civil war lasted between July 1967 and January 1970. On May 30, 1967, the former Eastern region of Nigeria seceded and declared itself the Republic of Biafra. This secession followed the large scale massacre of people from eastern Nigeria in other parts of the country from October 1966, triggered by a counter coup staged by officers from Northern Nigeria against their fellow officers from the east who were accused of eliminating politicians and senior military officers from the north and west in the January 1966 coup d'état. The easterners therefore felt their safety could no longer be guaranteed in a united Nigeria and wanted out of the federation. This led to the civil war.

Both sides in the dispute (the Nigerian government under General Yakubu Gowon and the Biafran government under Colonel Odumegwu Ojukwu) sought military and diplomatic assistance from the United States. Under the circumstance, the United States found itself caught in a diplomatic crossfire and responded in a very ambiguous manner. The US announced at the beginning of the war that it intended to stay aloof from the whole affair since the conflict fell "within Britain's sphere of influence", making it a British rather than an American problem.[67] The American government followed this statement up four days after the beginning of hostilities by declaring that it would neither sell nor otherwise supply arms to either side in order not to deepen the conflict. However, many see the United States as intervening in favor of Nigeria when in a statement, the first United States' Ambassador to Nigeria, Joseph Palmer assured General Gowon that it was "the wish of the American government that this Federal Republic of Twelve States remains a united and indivisible country".[68]

On the other hand, due to the efficient Biafran propaganda machine, the US was compelled by public opinion to offer humanitarian assistance to Biafra. The sight of children dying of starvation was enough to push the US to get itself heavily involved in aid provision, while still refusing to sell arms to the Nigerian government. President Johnson explained this position thus: "while we have no intention of interfering in Nigerian affairs, we do not believe innocent persons should be made victims of political manoeuvring". It was estimated that the US contributed more than $9 million for airlift support and transportation costs to the voluntary agencies operating relief efforts in Biafra.[69] In fact, on assumption of office, US President Richard M. Nixon wanted to increase the scope of the relief efforts, but was unable to do so given the strong pro-Federal bias in the US embassy at Lagos, the Department of State in Washington, and the apparently anti-Biafran stance of Dr Henry Kissinger in the White House.[70]

Although the US easily explained its humanitarian involvement as a natural call to assist in times of disaster, it did not escape suspicion from the Nigerian government which saw US assistance as crucial to the sustenance of the secession. This was because the US relief efforts involved direct dealings with the secessionist authorities, which indirectly strengthened the status of Biafra in striving for international recognition. Besides, it led to an increase of the pressure by the ever-active Biafra lobby in the US for some kind of diplomatic relationship, and this, in turn, led to false hopes within Biafra.

There were, of course, many reasons why the United States adopted this ambivalent posture. Washington was naturally wary about any deep involvement in another civil war, with the Vietnam War still on, the international difficulties which it had created, and the memory of the American involvement in the

Congo. It also could not ignore public opinion from home and across many European cities that had come to believe that the war was an ethnic one – the Hausas trying to eliminate the Igbos. So, even though the Nigerian government was greatly angered by America's ambivalence and were turning to the ever willing Soviet Union, Washington did not find it necessary to review its stance in favour of Nigeria. This was because it felt that Britain's commitment to the Federal cause would check, if not neutralize, Moscow's efforts, and partly because it had worked out the Nigerian equation and came to the conclusion that as General Gowon was hardly a Bolshevik, there were obvious limitations to the degree to which he would flirt with the Russians.[71]

Nigeria also was wary of any confrontation with the US as it tried to downplay the refusal of the US to sell arms to it as much as possible on the official level. For one thing, with the Soviets on its side, Lagos was anxious to avoid a cold-war confrontation. It issued a statement that Britain, and, to a lesser extent, the US, were the traditional arms suppliers to the Federal Armed Forces, and "both countries still remain Nigeria's first choice for the purchases of arms for many reasons".[72] While the statement regretted the US refusal to issue permits for Federal arms purchases, it pointed out that:

> The recent purchases from Soviet sources have been strictly for cash on commercial basis. The Nigerian government maintains its traditional friendship and foreign policy of non-alignment. The Federal Military Government expects its friends, particularly in the West, not to do anything to hamper its current efforts to defend the territorial integrity of the Federation of Nigeria and to guarantee justice to all communities.[73]

The Russians, on the other hand, were most willing in supplying Nigeria all the arms it needed to prosecute the war, including fighter jets. The assistance even extended to training Nigerian pilots to man the jets. The war obviously opened a new vista in Nigerian-Soviet relations. The Russians soon flooded the country and even won the contract for the construction of Nigeria's first iron and steel mill. After the war, Gowon became the first Nigerian leader to pay a state visit to the Soviet Union.

However, the Russians greatly misjudged Nigeria's deep attachment to capitalism or were downright over-optimistic. Not long after the war, relations between Nigeria and the USSR became sour because of Nigeria's continued romance with the West. The USSR had thought that the goodwill and friendship resulting from its supply of heavy guns and aircraft that enabled Nigeria to successfully prosecute the war, from the loan of N120 million it gave Nigeria (which was quite huge in 1968), and from the Soviet-built iron and steel complex, would establish it as the dominant foreign power in the politics, diplomacy and economy of Nigeria. That Nigeria drifted back to Britain and the US after the war was extremely frustrating for the Soviet Union.[74]

Meanwhile, America, through the State Department, became even more pro-Federal as the war drew to a close in 1969. Many Americans had been quite incensed with Ojukwu's apparently cavalier attitude towards the sufferings and starvation of his own people. Biafra never got the recognition it badly sought from the US, and when the war ended in January of 1970, President Nixon dispatched his Secretary of State William Rogers with a personal letter to Gowon, congratulating Nigeria and expressing his admiration for Gowon's leadership in the reconciliation and reunification of the country.

Rogers also used the opportunity of his physical presence in Nigeria to patch-up, at least in official quarters, the hidden rift in US-Nigerian relations caused by the US policy of formal neutrality during the war. While the Nixon administration fully recognized that the arms embargo and the US relief efforts seriously strained American – Nigerian relations, it was convinced that the policy was the right one given the circumstances surrounding the Nigerian conflict. Even the Federal government later realized how difficult it was for the US, in terms of the domestic political constraints under which it was operating, to offer formal support for the Federal cause. In retrospect, it was clear that the ban on sales of arms to Lagos was beneficial to Nigeria. Sympathy for the Biafrans became so strong and vocal that if the American government had permitted the sale of arms to the Federal government at the outbreak of hostilities, it might ultimately have been obliged to apply a ban.

In all, the events of January and July 1966 and the consequent civil war made the United States quite cautious in relating to Nigeria since it appeared America's initial hopes and expectations about the country were exaggerated. George Obiozor described relations between the two countries during the period as "uneasy friendship".[75] But it must be emphasized that the factor of uneasiness can mainly be ascribed to the attitudes of the United States toward Nigeria and not the other way around. Nigerian leaders, for the most part, tended to maintain consistently pro-American attitudes no matter what the Americans did. This can be seen in the way the Nigerian government tried to downplay the refusal of the United States to sell arms to it and American provision of generous humanitarian aid to Biafran civilians, even when it was clear that such efforts were greatly beneficial to the continued resistance of Biafra. It can also be seen in the subsequent trade dependence on the United States by Nigeria.

Assistance and activities of US AID

America's first Ambassador to Nigeria, Joseph Palmer, noted that "The United States looks forward to continuing co-operation with Nigeria's programmes of economic and social development. We admire Nigeria's determination to achieve rapid progress, and recognise our common interest in furthering the emergence of a world of prosperous and free people".[76] Assistance from the US took several forms, which are reviewed below.

(a)   **Assistance in the Field of Agriculture**

During the First Republic, the efforts to develop Nigeria's agriculture were central to the country's development plans. Indeed, over four-fifths of the population of the country depended on, and more than half of the Gross National Product was derived from agriculture, livestock and fisheries. The expansion and modernisation of agriculture and related production was thus of crucial importance to the development of the Nigerian economy, and here, the United States offered tremendous assistance. The United States became involved in livestock development in Nigeria during the First Republic and one of the areas where emphasis was placed was in the animal fattening exercise that was undertaken by the Northern and Western regional governments. Specifically, the United States government was helpful in the construction of modern abattoirs in Enugu and Fashola (Eastern and Western regions respectively) and in the establishment of cattle breeding ranch in the Bornu Province. There was also assistance rendered in the tsetse fly eradication project in Hedejia in Northern Nigeria. In the area of poultry, American poultry specialists worked in the three regions.

Since lack of water was a major challenge facing cattle raising, American specialists came to Nigeria to assist in water development experiments with Nigerians. For example, in 1962, the USAID assisted the Nigerian Ministry of Mines and Power to undertake water development projects in the Chad and Sokoto basins of Northern Nigeria. Also in the Katsina and Sokoto provinces, a joint programme was carried out in range management.

Another area where the United States made considerable investment was in the area of agricultural cooperative programmes. In 1957, before independence, Nigeria and the United States began a crop research project in Moor Plantation, not far from Ibadan in the Western region. Here extensive research activities were devoted to crop improvement. The United States also constructed a new classroom and a library worth £36, 000 and also provided £8,000 for soil survey laboratory.

This also extended to the field of educational institutions, where the United States contributed significant assistance to the development of agriculture in educational institutions across the country. For example, the United States provided £120,000 to help construct and equip a new institution for general agricultural training in Kabba. This was in addition to a Veterinary Assistant School in Kaduna. This also extended to Agricultural Faculties in Universities across the country. For example, the United States provided £72,000 to assist in increasing the number of Junior Officer graduates at the Samaru School of Agriculture from forty-five to ninety. This was in addition to more than £30,000 that was given for laboratory equipment and books. With the School of Agriculture in Eastern Nigeria, the United States government, through the USAID gave equipment worth £250,000. The Faculties of Agriculture at the former University of

Ife, the University of Nigeria and the Ahmadu Bello Universities all received significant financial assistance from the United States government for the expansion of their programmes.

(b) Contribution to Education

During the years immediately after independence, educational links between Nigeria and the United States increased significantly. On the eve of independence in 1959, 258 Nigerians were studying in American institutions and the United States had committed £6,000,000 in grant assistance towards Nigeria's educational development. This was apart from the £2 million specifically given for agricultural education. The assistance in the area of education was to supplement the educational goal in the First National Development Plan, which was to "increase as rapidly and as economically as possible the high manpower which is indispensable to accelerated development".[77] As with most assistance to Nigeria during this period, assistance in the field of education was carried out through the USAID and it specifically focused on the areas of teacher training, technical education and assistance to Universities. A number of American Foundations like Ford, Rockefeller and Carnegie were among those that assisted in promoting exchange, seminars and conferences. Some of the key assistance provided in this area is recorded below:

(i) Federal Advanced Teachers College Lagos

In its origin, this college was a joint initiative between the Federal Government of Nigeria, UNESCO, Ford Foundation and USAID. The main objectives were to increase the number of teachers qualified to teach in Nigerian secondary schools, to develop a nation-wide approach to education, and to increase the number of teachers qualified to train primary school teachers in Nigeria. During the First Republic, this College received considerable assistance from the United States. A contract was established with the University of California, Los Angeles through which senior faculty members came to the College. The United States also gave approximately £180,000 for the construction of the College.

(ii) University of Nigeria, Nsukka

Of all the first group of universities in Nigeria, the University of Nigeria, Nsukka benefitted most from the American government during the years immediately after independence. In fact, the United States offered significant assistance in the planning of the University. This is possibly because Nigeria's first President and a person whose ancestral home was in the Eastern region (where the University was located), Dr. Nnmadi Azikiwie received his university education in the United States. Not long after the establishment of the University of Nigeria, Michigan State University provided assistance. With the sum of £357,140, the United States also constructed a Continuing Education Center. Americans were also involved in supervising and developing research and training programmes for the University.

(iii) Establishment of Comprehensive Secondary Schools

Through the assistance of the United States, a number of Comprehensive Secondary Schools were established during the First Republic. The Aiyetoro Comprehensive High School was established in Abeokuta, which was then part of the Western region making it the region's first genuinely comprehensive secondary. Apart from contributing £228,570 towards construction costs, the United States government also established a contract with Harvard University to offer assistance to the school. A similar school was established in Port Harcourt and here again, the United States government worked out arrangements with University of California Los Angeles to assist the school in its initial development. A Day Training College was also established in Kano through the assistance of the United States government and American educators from Ohio University assisted in teaching at the school. A Technical College established at Ibadan also benefited from this assistance. A two-year contract established by the United States government in October 1962 with the Western Michigan University assisted this school. The US government also offered 60 two-year scholarships to students who could not get industry or government sponsorship. Also, in collaboration with the Western Region Ministry of Education, USAID trained more than 3,000 teachers and, like most other initiatives of this nature, an agreement was reached with an American Institution, in this case Ohio University, to assist in the training.

(iv)   Seminars and Workshops

A number of publishing workshops and seminars were organised to advance education in Nigeria by the United States government during the First Republic. For example, in 1961, a Workshop on the Education of African Women and Girls was held at the University of Ibadan with the support of the United States government. Also in 1961, another seminar sponsored by the American government brought together educational leaders to the University of Nigerian Nsukka to examine University's role in Nigerian educational development

(v)   Radio and Television Education

As is well known, Nigeria was significantly advanced in the area of Radio and Television in Africa and indeed, Africa's first television station was established in Ibadan even before independence by the administration of the late Chief Obafemi Awolowo. The United States assisted in radio and television education and after independence, showing considerable interest when Nigeria decided to expand its activities in this area. In the effort to extend radio and television to schools, a contract team of specialists from the Board of Education of Washington County, Maryland assisted the Nigerian government. Other aspects of Radio and TV education where the United States assisted during the period included: T.V. education, film bank and radio vision.

(c)   Industries

The United States tried to assist the Nigerian government in its first national Development Plans. The Nigerian government's major aims in the National Development Plans were: (i) to stimulate the establishment and growth of industries which contribute both directly and materially to economic growth; and (ii) to enable Nigerians to participate to an ever increasing extent in the ownership, direction and the management of Nigerian industry and trade. Specialists from the US firm of Arthur D. Little Inc. were brought in to assist the Nigerian government. Industry specialists came from the United States to assist

Nigeria and new equipment was brought in to assist Nigerian institutions like the Industrial Development Centre in Owerri, eastern Nigeria.

(d) Public Administration

To meet the immediate post-Independence need in the field of public administration, the Nigerian government sought the assistance of the United States and the latter offered a number of seminars aimed at developing skill of Nigerians. Specifically the US offered training in areas like government budget and fiscal operations, personnel system and management, principles and practice of effective leadership and Federal and State governmental organisation and relationships. Under the programme about 150 senior civil servants from all over the country were sent to the United States for training. But apart from external training, the United States also supported the Institute of Administration that had been established in Zaria, northern Nigeria.[78] The University of Pittsburgh, under a contract with the United States government cooperated in the development of curriculum and course materials for the institute and a sum of £32,140 was arranged for the construction of a library. Also, the Ford Foundation helped to finance a field programme conducted by the Ministry of Local government for the training of local councillors in all the thirteen states of northern Nigeria.

In the area of economic and finance, an American financial adviser was seconded to the Nigerian Central Bank to assist in the development of a research facility and another adviser was sent to help in developing a Nigerian unit at the Central Bank that could compile and analyse data concerning Nigeria's international financial position. In the area of Housing, four Americans were sent to assist the Eastern Nigerian Housing Corporation shortly after it was established in 1961. In the field of urban water supply, the United States assisted in supplementing the inadequate water system of towns like Gusau, Ilorin and Maiduguri in Northern Nigeria. In the area of road construction, a team of American engineers undertook a technical and economic feasibility study on the Calabar, Ugep and Ikom road in what was then eastern Nigeria. The American government also extended three development loans to Nigeria – for a warehouse in Apapa, for railway track replacement, and an expansion of the Ibadan water system for a total of £5,607,000. Also, the United States Export-Import Bank gave loans for the establishment of two manufacturing enterprises - £471,000 for Flour Mills and £714,000 for Aba Textile Mills Ltd. The railway tracks that were replaced were those between Enugu and Markurdi and between Minna and Kaduna. A development loan of £1,070,000 was used to finance rail for 176 miles.

But as we have seen above, the 1966 coup that overthrew the First Republic and the civil war that followed placed severe strain on the relationship between Nigeria and the US. It is a testament to the resiliency of the relationship that involvement continued during these years and resumed more fully later.

End Notes

[48] Dudley, B. (1982), *An Introduction to Nigerian Government and Politics.* London & Basingstoke: Macmillan Press Ltd. P. 278).

[49] *Briefing on Africa,* 1960.

[50] Steven Monblatt: "Nigeria and the United States: 25 Years of Cooperation".

[51] Official Letter from the White House, October 1 1960.

[52] Nwachuku, L.A., "The United States and Nigeria – 1960 to 1987: Anatomy of a Pragmatic Relationship," *Journal of Black Studies,* Vol. 28, No. 5, 1998, p 576)

[53] Balewa, A.T. (1964), *Nigeria Speaks,* Lagos, Nigeria: Longman, p. 104).

[54] Back, I, (2004), "Muslims and Christians in Nigeria: Attitudes towards the United States from a Post-September 11th Perspective" in *Comparative Studies of South Asia, Africa and the Middle East,* 24:1 p. 212.

[55] Briefing on Africa: Hearing before a subcommittee on Africa of the Committee on Foreign affairs, House of Representatives, 86th Cong., 2d Sess, (1960) p.104.

[56] Osaghae E.E. (1998), *The Crippled Giant: Nigeria Since Independence,* London: C. Hurst & Co. Publishers Ltd, p. 50.

[57.] Billy Dudley, *An Introduction to Nigerian Government and Politics.* London & Basingstoke: Macmillan Press Ltd, 1982 p. 27).

[58.] (*The Post Express,* 2001: 39),

[59.] Akintola, B.S. (2007), "Nigeria and the World: A Review of Nigeria's Foreign Policy (1960-2007)," *The Nigerian Army Quarterly Journal* vol 3, No. 4, December. 2007: 444

[60.] Dudley, 1982 p 279; and *The Post Express,* 2001, 39.

[61.] Billy Dudley: p.279.

[62.] Back, I, (2004), "Muslims and Christians in Nigeria: Attitudes towards the United States from a Post-September 11th Perspective" in *Comparative Studies of South Asia, Africa and the Middle East,* 24:1 p. 212.

[63.] (Back, 2004: 213).

[64.] (Dudley, 1982: 280).

[65.] US Agency for International Development, 1972.

[66.] *To Preserve and to Learn: Original Essays About the history of the Peace Corps* at http://www.peacecorpswriters.org/pages/2000/0001/001pchist.html retrieved 10/04/2011.

[67.] Oye Ogunbadej0, Nigeria and the Great Powers: The Impact of the Civil War on Nigerian Foreign Relations", *African Affairs,* Vol. 75, No. 298, January 1976, p. 18

[68.] Ngoh, 1982: 176

[69.] (US Assistance to Refugees, 1969)

[70.] Ibid

[71.] Ogunbadejo, 1976: 18.

[72.] Ibid

[73.] Cited in Ogunbadejo, ibid

[74.] Ofoegbu, R. (1979), "Foreign Policy and Military Rule," in Oyeleye Oyediran (ed.) *Nigerian Government and Politics Under Military Rule 1966 – 1979.* London and Basingstoke: The Macmillan Press Ltd, p, 138 – 9

[75.] George Obiozor, 1992: 211

[76.] From Programme for Progress: US AID Document

[77.] National Development Plan, (1962 – 1968)

[78.] This institute was established in 1954 and was later integrated into the Ahmadu Bello University when (1992: 211) the University was established.

Chapter Three

The United States and the Nigerian Civil War

Olukunke OJELEYE

It is axiomatic to state that Nigeria occupies a place of importance in the geo-political and strategic calculations of the foreign policy of the United States of America. The special relationship existing between the United States and Nigeria has been fostered not only because of a shared experience of having the same colonial master, but also because both nations are ethnically heterogeneous in nature. As such, it is not surprising that even before Nigeria became independent in 1960, the United States government through the British government had started to demonstrate the special regards it had for the country by committing about $700,000 to Nigeria's economic development through support for various agricultural projects. Once Nigeria gained independence from Britain, US-Nigeria relations were deepened further by the United States' support for Nigeria's developmental plan and extensive economic and military assistance through loans and grants.[79]

The historical legacy of being a British colony dictated a Nigerian foreign policy posture that was pro-Western in a significantly bi-polar system characterised by the cold war between the capitalist and communist blocs. In this same period, the United States, Africa and consequentially Nigeria as part of the European orbit of political influence, in view of the strong link with Britain and the allied powers. Independence for Nigeria on 1 October, 1960 was immediately followed by a congratulatory message to the Nigerian people from the US Secretary of State Christian Herter, the consolidation of formal diplomatic relations through the simultaneous establishment of the Nigerian Embassy in Washington and the American Embassy in Lagos on that day, and the United States Government (USG)'s recognition of Nigeria as a sovereign state via a congratulatory letter on 2 October, 1960 from President Dwight D. Eisenhower to Prime Minister Sir Abubukar Tafawa Balewa. On 12 December, 1961, the USG of President John F. Kennedy pledged the sum of $225 million as long-term development aid to Nigeria, and fifty (50) per cent of the external loan and grant needed to finance public expenditure of $949.2 million under the Nigerian National Development Plan 1962–68 was met by the USG.[80] This depth of friendship between Nigeria and the United States led to Sir Abubakar Tafawa Balewa's declaration in the Nigerian House of Representatives in 1961 that "we admire the American way of life, and we respect the people of the United States for their love of freedom".[81] As a result, the first six years of relations were marked by conviviality.

The outbreak of civil war in Nigeria in 1967 marked a turning point in a seemingly amicable Nigerian-US relationship. Indeed, for the USG, the civil war period was one of the most trying eras of political and diplomatic relations with Nigeria. The USG's policy and attitude towards the Nigerian civil war has been categorised as one of "non-involvement". However, this is a contradiction because the various attempts to induce both sides to find a negotiated settlement to their difference, the recognition of the Federal Military Government (FMG) of Gen. Yakubu Gowon as the de facto and de jure Nigerian administration, as well as the refusal to sell arms to either side in the conflict amounted to some form of US involvement.

As such, it is necessary to point out from the onset that the US policy of non-involvement in the Nigerian civil war meant a policy of no military intervention in the war and/or no military support for either party in the imbroglio. In casting a reflection on fifty years of US-Nigerian relations, this chapter re-examines the course of relations between the two countries from 1967–1970 with the purpose of determining if the US policy of non-involvement in the Nigerian Civil War was misplaced or justified.

Diplomatic Efforts by the United States' to Prevent the Nigerian Civil War

For discerning observers including the USG, the Nigeria civil war which was Africa's first modern and brutal civil conflict was an event waiting to happen. The crisis that befell the country which had begun to take shape shortly after independence had its origin in the artificial creation of a British dependency consisting of over 250 diverse and often antagonistic ethnic groups at varying degrees of socio-economic and political development. Various dates and occurrences have been indicated as being the "turning-point" in the commencement of the war. While some traced it to the "amalgamation" of the north and south protectorates in 1914, others have traced it to the politics of the independence struggle, while others still have sought explanation in the complications of the elite politics that characterised affairs in the country shortly after independence.[82] The internal strains within the artificial state were initially concealed by the federal parliamentary political system bequeathed to the nation at independence but by 1965, the USG had begun to wonder if the Nigerian nation could survive as a single entity 'in the face of the many internal strains and tensions'.[83]

The strains and tensions in the Nigerian polity culminated in the first military coup on 15 January, 1966 in which the Nigerian Government was overthrown and many senior politicians and military officers lost their lives. In the immediate aftermath of the military counter coup of 29 July, 1966 by officers of northern origin to correct the perceived injustice of January 1966 and the anarchy that set in, the military governor of the Eastern Region Col. Emeka Ojukwu expressed the doubt that the people of Nigeria could continue to live together as members of the same nation, and requested that Nigeria be split into component parts with Northerners and Southerners repatriated to their regions of origin. Given Ojukwu's statement, the US became concerned that Nigeria was 'moving at an accelerating rate along a downward slope with a consequent diminution of its prospects for unity and stability. Unless present army leaders and contending tribal elements soon reach agreement on a new basis for association and take some effective measures to halt a seriously deteriorating security situation, there will be increasing internal turmoil, possibly including civil war'.[84]

The position of the Eastern Region was already clear to the USG by 4 November, 1966. By this time, Col. Ojukwu had started sounding out American diplomats as to the possibility of military aid from the USG if the East was attacked by Northern troops, and whether the USG 'would recognize Eastern sovereignty if the East declared independence'.[85] It became apparent that the Eastern region had taken the position that continued association with the rest of Nigeria was not the best and was already reconciled to secession. As a result, in a diplomatic dispatch on 11 November, 1966, US diplomats urged Col. Ojukwu to give careful consideration to the consequences a unilateral secession would have not just on the Eastern region but the rest of Nigeria and Africa as a whole, and reiterated the American conviction that a dissolution of the Nigerian union would exacerbate rather than resolve the problems and animosities in the country. In response to such a development which the US considered as setback to independent Africa and a major political and economic disaster for Nigeria as a nation, it began to make frantic diplomatic efforts to oppose the secession of any component part of Nigeria through formal and informal representations to both the Federal Military Government (FMG) of Gen. Yakubu Gowon and the Eastern Regional Government (ERG) of Col. Emeka Ojukwu.[86]

As far as the US was concerned, Nigerian unity was incontrovertible and to give credence to its position, the USG gave its unalloyed support to the reconciliatory meeting of the Supreme Military Council (SMC) held at Aburi in Ghana from 4 to 5 January 1967, which resulted in four important agreements. First was the renunciation of force in resolving the conflict on the ground. Second, were the re-organisation of the army and the functioning of the SMC to allay fears of domination of one ethnic group by the other. Third was the repeal of all the decrees that encouraged over-centralisation of the political and administrative system, which had fuelled mistrust and hostilities. Fourth was the agreement by the SMC for the federal government to rehabilitate all displaced persons following the riots and the Igbo massacre in the north.

From the outset, the Aburi agreement had a fundamental problem of interpretation. Whilst Gowon saw the agreement as reinforcing a political system based on a strong federal government with regions subordinate to the centre, Ojukwu interpreted the same agreement as promoting a confederation that allowed each of the regions to run its own affairs as it deemed fit. The steps subsequently taken by Gowon to implement parts of the Aburi agreement were therefore seen by Ojukwu as a breach of trust, and a repudiation of the mutually agreed terms. In spite of the deteriorating relationship between the FMG and the ERG, the USG continued in its diplomatic effort by reaffirming its support for the Ghanaian initiative of General Joseph Arthur Ankrah and encouraging him to take the lead in a mediatory role to resolve the Nigerian crisis. In view of his earlier intervention which resulted in the Aburi Agreement, Ankrah was regarded to have special knowledge of the Nigerian situation and the USG wanted to remain in the background to avoid being seen as the overseer of Nigerian unity in a conviction that if Ojukwu and Gowon could not be persuaded to resolve their differences, and threats or sanctions needs to be applied as a means of inducement, 'the British and their fellow Commonwealth members should be way out in front.'

Secession of the Eastern Region and the Onset of the Nigerian Civil War

Before hostilities began, intelligence reports had indicated the preparation of both sides in the conflict for a forceful resolution of the crisis. First, the federal military authorities decided to allow armed forces personnel of other regions leaving the eastern part of the country to do so with their weapons, whilst personnel of eastern origin were not allowed to return to the region with their weapons. This tactically depleted the eastern region of any weaponry that could effectively aid rebellion and secession. Second, an aircraft en-route the eastern region filled with arms for the Eastern regional government had crashed and there were un-refuted allegations of Italian arms purchase by the Nigerian government.[87] The assertion that there was a secret build up of arms and ammunitions by both sides before the first military clash is further given credence by Atofarati's assertion that 'on the Biafran side, preparation for war was put into high gear as soon as the troops of non-Eastern origin withdrew from Enugu in August of 1966'.[88] Alexander Madiebo also recollects that recruitment into the Army had begun throughout Nigeria except in the Eastern Region where the federal government had placed a hold on such an exercise. However, following reports that a Major Appolo had travelled to Europe to procure arms for the federal government, the East felt under threat and a conference of senior army officers in the region was convened in Enugu in January 1967 to explore the possibility of setting up an Eastern Nigeria Command. The result of that conference was the establishment of a training depot inside the Enugu Prisons to prevent the federal government from suspecting that soldiers were being recruited and trained, as well as the setting up of an officer cadet school outside Enugu to be run in absolute secrecy.[89]

On 30 March, 1967, Ojukwu in his role as the military administrator of the Eastern Region sought to carry out a unilateral implementation of the Aburi Agreement based on his own interpretation of a decentralisation of power, by enacting three edicts. The Revenue Collection Edict ordered that all revenues originating from the east be paid to the eastern regional treasury rather than the federal government. The Legal Education Edict broke ties in education between the eastern region and the rest of the federation, and the Court of Appeal Edict ended the right of judicial appeal to the Federal Supreme Court. As a further step, Ojukwu decided to sequester all federal institutions and properties that were situated in the eastern region. In taking those steps, Ojukwu virtually declared the eastern region a separate political and administrative entity, but fell short of an official declaration of independence and statehood.

On 26 May, 1967, a joint conference of the eastern region consultative assembly and leaders at Enugu 'unanimously passed a resolution mandating Ojukwu to declare the sovereign Republic of Biafra at an early practicable date'.[90] In reaction to Ojukwu's actions, the resolution of the eastern region consultative assembly, and to anticipate any attempt by the eastern region to secede, Gowon proclaimed a state of emergency over the whole country on 27 May, 1967, assumed full powers over the armed forces and the government, banned all political associations and gatherings, divided the country into twelve states,[91] and announced measures to safeguard federal interests in the eastern region. On 30 May, 1967, Col. Ojukwu as military governor of the Eastern Region of Nigeria, addressed a gathering of civilian authorities, military leaders, journalists and diplomats at the State House in Enugu and declared the birth of an independent sovereign state called 'The Republic of Biafra'.[92] On 6 July, 1967, the first military clash between Federal and Biafran troops occurred. The advancement of the federal forces into the Eastern Region was beaten back by the Biafrans and what the federal forces thought was a "police action" to deal with an errant brother turned out to be a full scale civil war – Africa's first modern and internationalised conflict.

US Policy of Non-Involvement in the Nigerian Civil War of 1967–1970

Once the Aburi agreement failed and war commenced, there was little prospect that there would be a quick resolution. Indeed, the failure of the Aburi meeting extinguished any flicker of hope that a local settlement to the dispute could be found and focus became centred on international mediators. Up until May of 1967, the US continued to make efforts to persuade the Eastern Region to seek a peaceful solution to the differences with the rest of country within the framework of one Nigeria. The various American attempts to persuade both sides to negotiate their differences and reach a mutually beneficial position were predicated on the view that unless the Federal and Eastern governments reconciled, Nigeria had little or no prospect for peace, stability and economic growth. Hence, the USG made it clear to the Eastern region that no government, including by extension the US, could afford to recognise or support the region's secession at the expense of relations with the rest of Africa who would likely give political support to the Federal Military Government.[93]

As soon as secession was declared by the Eastern Region and civil war began, both the Nigerian military government under Yakubu Gowon and the Biafran government under Emeka Ojukwu sought the military and diplomatic assistance of the

United States. Right from the onset of the civil war, the USG clearly pointed out that it intended to stay aloof from the whole affair, and that the war was a British problem since the conflict fell within British "sphere of influence". For the United States, the war was an additional irritation in view of the outbreak of the Six-Day War in the Middle East between Israel and its Arab neighbours Egypt, Jordan and Syria. The US regarded the Nigerian civil war as an internal affair that at best must be resolved by Nigeria or by the Organisation of African Unity (OAU).[94] It was against this background that President Lyndon Johnson, in a message to the Fifth Annual Conference of the OAU meeting in Algiers on 13 September, 1968, said "it is to the Assembly of the OAU as the highest voice and conscience of Africa that the world now looks to break that Nigerian deadlock".[95]

Various factors contributed to the American attitude towards the Nigerian-Biafran war. First, because the United States did not have colonies in Africa, its concerns with Africa were minimal compared to that of Great Britain and it felt less obligated to formulate an independent policy toward the continent. As far as the USG could see, the Biafran secession did not threaten any of its vital interests, and military involvement on the side of the federal forces would have been seen as foreign interference in Africa since there was neither a request from the Nigerian government for assistance to a friendly government threatened by an internal minority or terrorist group, nor a request to help repel external aggression or internal revolt encouraged by external assistance. Secondly, the experiences of the Vietnam War and the quagmire in which the USG was trapped dictated the attitude that the US must not be seen as the policeman of the world. As much as possible, given its limited military and economic resources vis-à-vis commitments elsewhere, the USG wanted to avoid being drawn into an increasing military and political role in Nigeria and gave preference to the military and economic burden of Nigeria being carried by Britain as the former colonial master. Furthermore, by getting involved in the Nigerian civil war, it was felt that a precedent would be set for other African nations to enlist the USG's intervention when faced with similar circumstances in the future. Thirdly, the US involvement in the Congo in 1964 aroused considerable controversy in Africa with many African states accusing the USG of supporting Belgian imperialism following its' involvement in rescuing white hostages.[96] The United States thereafter became apprehensive of the implications of future involvement in African crises.

Finally, the possibility of Nigeria disintegrating into three or four independent countries was real. By May 1967, there were indications that the Western region under the influence of the Yoruba Leader Chief Obafemi Awolowo was leaning towards secession if the Eastern region was to pull out of the federation. Even though this danger of fragmentation of the country did not materialise, the USG considered it of utmost importance to protect American interests in the face of uncertainties by maintaining the best of all relationship with whatever political entities may emerge from a "disintegrated" Nigeria. The American attitude to the war is best summed up by Legum's report of the US Secretary of State's statement on 6 April, 1969 that 'in the civil war in Nigeria, we are not militarily, politically, or economically involved, and we have resisted pressures to become so ... We will continue our humanitarian involvement and do all we can to prevent disease and starvation'.[97]

Towards an official policy of direct non-involvement – politically and militarily – in the conflict, the USG on 10 July, 1967 placed an arms embargo on both sides, four days after the outbreak of full-scale war. This policy was not farfetched. As early as February, 1967, the USG had already indicated to the FMG its resolve not to be seen as militarily involved in the Nigerian crisis. Considering the hardening positions of the FMG and the ERG and the likelihood of a resort to force by both parties to resolve their disagreement, the USG had politely turned down an FMG request for the supply of 106 mm ammunition in the view that an approval of a sale to Nigeria would harm its relation with both parties as well as with the Congress in Washington.[98] A further request for the supply of 12 fighter-bombers, 6 PT-boats, and 24 anti-aircraft guns by the FMG of Gen. Gowon in July 1967 was also turned down. The FMG had requested delivery of the weapons within 48 hours by the US and the British governments with the underlying threat that a failure to honour the request would force the Nigerian government to procure the arms from any other source – a reference to the Union of Soviet Socialist Republics (USSR). Even though the USG knew that the Gowon government had started negotiation with the USSR and Czechoslovakia for the purchase of weaponry, the USG stuck to its position that it would not interfere in Nigeria's internal problem and that the supply of any weaponry to the FMG or the ERG would be tantamount to such, fuelling the looming civil war in the country.[99] From a geo-political perspective, it is remarkable that in spite of the Cold War climate and subsequent Soviet involvement through open supply of arms and ammunitions to the federal forces, the US saw no political or economic gain in the crisis and Washington refused to sell arms to either side in the conflict.

Nevertheless, the USG's dispatch of three C-130 military aircrafts and the sending of arms and paratroopers to the aid of Mobutu Sese Seko on 14 July, 1967 was seen by the FMG and ERG as a negation of its policy of non-interference in the internal affairs of another state under which it refused to sell arms to them.[100] In spite of the USG's explanation that its' involvement in Congo was due to an external threat and in line with a standing United Nations' (UN) resolution, the American aloofness from giving any firm commitment to either side not only soured relationship with both sides in the imbroglio, the refusal to allow the FMG to buy arms and ammunitions from American suppliers became the most significant sticky point in US-Nigeria relations throughout the course of the war and in the immediate aftermath.

The United States and Humanitarian Involvement in the Nigerian Civil War

The hawks in Gowon's government were of the view that the quickest and most effective way to end Biafran secession was to take advantage of it being a landlocked enclave by cutting off the food supply. The use of starvation as a legitimate weapon of war led to the death of many Biafrans, especially children and by June 1968, journalists who visited Biafra had managed to uncover instances of this starvation, particularly among the young. By the summer of 1968, the International Committee of the Red Cross (ICRC) reported that three million children were near death. A combination of the vast numbers of displaced persons throughout Nigeria and the federal blockade on food was driving more than 2,500 people into the hospital every week.[101]

The harrowing descriptions and pitiful pictures which soon flooded the media awakened a number of relief organizations to the vast needs that existed in Nigeria. This resulted in the involvement of international non-governmental organizations (NGOs) in the distribution of relief materials in the Biafran enclave. These NGOs included the ICRC which is credited for leading humanitarian operations during the war, the United Nations Children's Fund (UNICEF), OXFAM, CARE, Caritas, the World Food Programme (WFP), the United Nations Development Programme (UNDP), the World Council of Churches (WCC) and the Young Men's Christian Association (YMCA). With assurances from both sides of the conflict that the Geneva Conventions would be respected, the relief agencies set out to ameliorate the effects of the war on civilians. The federal government created two corridors for the supply of relief material, and the ICRC was allowed to engage in its relief operations without restrictions in those areas that were under federal control[102] visiting prisoners of war, facilitating the exchange of personal messages across both sides of the imbroglio via its Central Training Agency, providing and distributing food to the needy, and giving medical care to the wounded. ICRC's coordination of relief activities in federal areas began in July, 1968 and the Nordchurch aid airlift to Biafra began in August, 1968.

In the face of severe attack from a strong pro-Biafran lobby following press reports of starvation and suffering among the Biafran civilian population, Washington had to change its policy of non-involvement to one that aimed to provide relief for the secessionists. The United States there and then became the largest contributor to relief efforts in the Biafran enclave during the war.[103] The American approach to relief and humanitarian assistance in the war was in five main directions. First, was to effectively use the Red Cross as the main tool for international involvement in relief operation; second, was to influence both parties in the conflict towards agreeing a settlement or at best, an agreement that allows relief operations to take place; third, was to persuade the FMG to prove that it was not deliberately keeping food out of Biafra in line with an alleged policy of starvation; fourth, was to offer all help that would make relief operations possible and effective; and fifth, was to work out the logistics of the relief operation once a formal agreement for its operation was in place.

As of 30 June, 1969, estimated world-wide donations to Nigerian (and Biafran) relief and rehabilitation during the conflict was put at US$160 million, of which US$66 million originated from the American government and another US$11 million from American voluntary agencies. By June, 1970, total contributions were put at nearly US$170 million. US$76.5 million out of this came from within the United States and US$61.2 million specifically from the USG. The USG also donated 94 million francs, almost 60% of the total cash donation made to the ICRC for its operation in Biafra.[104] In a telegram to the American Embassy in Nigeria on 11 January, 1969, Department of State officials re-emphasised that since the outbreak of civil war in Nigeria, American policy of non-involvement had been complimented by the parallel policy of providing assistance to civilian victims of warfare, a commonly accepted obligation of all nations which is deeply rooted in American tradition. 'USG has accordingly since early 1968 provided assistance in various forms to Nigerian National Rehabilitation Commission, Nigerian Red Cross, ICRC and private voluntary relief agencies for relief of civilian victims of Nigerian civil war wherever located.'[105]

In spite of the good intention of the United States, its relief and humanitarian policy did not go down well with either the Federal government or the Biafrans. On one hand, humanitarian involvement entailed direct dealings with Biafran authorities and this had the political implications of giving a false hope of diplomatic recognition by the United States to the Biafrans whilst on the other hand, the federal government viewed American direct dealings with the Biafrans as strengthening the latter's bid for international recognition given the increased momentum from pro-Biafran lobbyists asking the US for some level of diplomatic relation.

More importantly, the futile attempts by the USG to effect an agreement on relief operation between the FMG, the ERG and the NGOs especially the ICRC resulted in bitter dispute between all the parties involved. The situation was not helped by the level of mistrust between the two warring parties. Once civil war began, and Biafra became landlocked with the blockade of all access to the sea by the federal forces, the only way arms and ammunitions could get into the enclave was through illegal airlifts using international arms dealers. The open air corridor through which the NGOs were flying relief into Biafra became exploited by gunrunners and the FMG was convinced that some of the humanitarian airlifts were simultaneously stocked with arms and ammunitions for Biafra.[106] On 5 June, 1969, a clearly marked ICRC DC-7 aircraft on a relief mission into Biafra was shot down by the Nigerian Air Force over Eket in South Eastern Nigeria killing the four aid workers on board. This led to the suspension of all ICRC relief activities on 10 June, 1969 and failure to reach mutually acceptable agreement between the warring parties and the ICRC led to the termination of ICRC operation in federal controlled territories (and effectively Nigeria) on 2 October, 1969.

US involvement in relief efforts in the Nigerian civil war thus became the second source of contention between the USG and the FMG during the war. While recognising the problem created by the fact that arms and relief flights into Biafra were using the same flight corridor and airfield, the USG was unequivocal in its condemnation of the downing of the ICRC relief plane by the federal forces. The USG was particularly piqued that if its efforts to get an agreement from the warring sides for daylight flights and surface corridors for relief arrangements had met with acceptance, such a needless destruction of life saving cargo and human lives would have been avoided.[107] The US was of the strong viewpoint that the humanitarian aspects of the civil war was completely distinct from the political and military aspects, and with cooperation from both sides of the conflict, there was no reason why the former could not be attended to subject to adherence to three fundamental concepts namely: the participation of the international community in providing assistance to both sides in the war to ensure relief efforts were administered for the benefit of the civilian victims of the war; the transportation and distribution of relief materials was done in such a manner that gave no military advantage or impose any military liability on any of the parties; and the restrain by both parties from turning matters of relief and humanitarian assistance into issues of politics and propaganda.[108] The US National Archives reveal these attitudes held by the Nixon administration:

> The FMG opposition to night flights, in which it has acquiesced in the past, is hardening because of arms flights tailgating relief planes into Biafra for protection. It has endorsed the principle of both daylight flights and a land corridor into Biafra with outside supervision to avoid military violation by either party. But it insists that: (a) the relief airlift should be inspected for arms and (b) the land corridor not interferes with military operations. FMG suspicions of all foreign relief agencies are growing. It prefers that all international relief to Biafra be channelled through Nigerian territory. Biafra refuses daytime flights into its one working airstrip for fear FMG aircraft will tailgate to the airfield. Biafra also values the protection given nighttime arms flights by the intermix with relief flights which the FMG is either reluctant or unable to interdict. It has thus far opposed (or countered with proposals unacceptable to the FMG) every land corridor proposed by the FMG on the grounds that it would be militarily exploited by the FMG and that the food might be poisoned. Both sides have obstructed relief, but on balance, the FMG has indicated more flexibility in its willingness to consider alternate relief routes and possibilities than have the Biafrans. The beleaguered Biafrans give priority to arms shipments over relief and they also know the suffering is a political asset.[109]

The scathing criticism of the FMG given its curtailment of the role of the International Committee of the Red Cross and of the ERG in view of its frequent unsubstantiated allegations against the ICRC did not go down well with both parties. On the one hand, from the standpoint of the FMG, the USG was becoming less neutral but more politically vocal on behalf of the Biafrans, whilst from the ERG perspective, the American posture was becoming antagonistic and anti-secession. In justifying its humanitarian intervention, the USG insisted that it had no intention of interfering in Nigerian affairs, but at the same time did not believe innocent persons should be made victims of political manoeuvring. In a passionate appeal to Gen. Gowon, President Johnson stated that he had been kept fully informed of the efforts of the International Committee of the Red Cross to make arrangements for the supply of urgently needed food and other relief supplies to the civilian victims of the Nigerian war:

> We have supported those efforts in the past and continue to do so now. Knowing that you share my own deep concern over the suffering of those innocent persons, I feel justified in addressing this personal appeal to you to give your urgent agreement to the ICRC proposals for an air mercy corridor. Hopefully, this can be followed by rapid agreement on a land corridor...the conscience of the world has been deeply moved by reports of starvation in Nigeria, and tons of food are already in position near the most needy areas. The world will not easily understand any failure on the part of those most concerned to agree to effective, international, humanitarian arrangements to alleviate this suffering. I therefore most earnestly urge you to make it possible for relief supplies to move rapidly into the hands of the needy by facilitating the establishment of this relief corridor on an urgent basis. I trust that I need hardly add...that in sending you this message I am motivated solely by compelling humanitarian concerns.[110]

Realising these consequences, the state department sought clarification of its intention to deliver eight C97 cargo planes to Biafra relief purposes by declaring that American relief efforts did not either directly or indirectly reflect support by the USG for Biafra secession, or portend such a support. However, all United States government donations whether monetary, food, medical supplies, or vehicles were primarily channelled through American voluntary agencies or the ICRC. Such donations assisted the NGOs in their programs which they had already largely shaped with their own venture capital, and did not compromise their integrity.

US-Nigeria Relations in the Immediate Aftermath of the Nigerian Civil War

With the collapse of Biafra, President Nixon sought to regain Nigeria's friendship. In a telephone conversation on 15 January, 1970, Nixon expressed his desire to make sure that the US took 'leadership on humanitarian problems'[111] in the former Biafra, and sent a congratulatory letter to General Yakubu Gowon praising him for not showing vindictiveness to the defeated Biafrans. In spite of the consistent pro-united Nigeria position of the US during the civil war, the humanitarian efforts of the American government and people to aid the Biafrans made the Nigerian government ungrateful of American diplomatic support and friendly gestures in the immediate post war environment.

An American embassy official noted the discomfort of the Nigerian government in a memo to the Department of State on 15 February, 1970 stating that the relationship with the Nigerian government had been brought close to a breaking point by the American pressure during the war on the relief front. He was of the view that in the immediate aftermath of the war, the US needed to maintain a low profile 'until the irritations recently created have subsided' since any vigorous action by the American embassy in Lagos would worsen relations rather than improving them. Visits by American diplomatic personnel had been barred at this point, and there was the likelihood of Americans being excluded from the war-affected areas at the slightest provocation. He therefore insisted that 'the kind of concerted country team approach envisaged in ... your message – no matter how adroitly it was carried out – would be promptly identified as renewed U.S. pressure campaign. The result could be disastrous, for the immediate relief program and for our longer-term position here. I must repeat that we are very close to the edge here'.[112] As a result, Nixon's Secretary of State, William Rogers visited Nigeria to demonstrate to the federal government American satisfaction over the outcome of the war, and to reiterate that the United States understood Nigeria's discomfort at its policies during the civil war.

Following an express request to the US by the Nigerian government, the US changed its support from relief activities to reconstruction in Nigeria offering assistance in housing and road reconstruction in the belief that it would be the only real long-term solution to the restoration of normalcy in the country. This change in attitude was also predicated on the view that such a shift would in the long-term augur well for the relationship between the US and Nigerian governments, which had suffered considerably. In his memorandum to President Nixon on 1 June, 1970, the President's Assistant for National Security Affairs Henry Kissinger felt that the US needed to show its readiness to discuss with the federal government how the Americans could assist in 'the immediate and urgent task of reconstruction and in longer range development. By participating in reconstruction, which holds more promise than relief, we will be contributing to a return to normal'.[113] The US initiated several emergency rehabilitation projects in war-affected areas, and supported the SNDP by granting about $8 million aid for reconstruction and development in 1970. The US also gave capital assistance through program and sector lending, collaborated with UNICEF in school restoration and feeding projects, and assisted the federal government in the construction of a new Police College. In agriculture, the US provided technicians and specialists to work in the field, supported yam and maize planting programs and supplied agricultural tools.[114]

In Retrospect

In any conflict, the weaker party (the opposition and/or secessionist minority) in the imbroglio is bound to seek external support towards redressing the perceived existing imbalance, whilst the stronger party (the incumbent government) reinforces efforts to solidify its position of authority and control. In such a situation – which describes effectively the Nigerian Civil War – international involvement is unavoidable. Consequently, the response of states to civil conflicts can be one of non-involvement, or passive neutrality; involvement as an intermediary or mediator; partisan involvement in support of the incumbent government; or partisan involvement in support of the opposition movement. The two main modalities of international involvement in civil wars are tangible, and political-diplomatic or moral involvement. The tangible involvements include material aid through the supply of arms, ammunition, aircraft, other military equipment and means of transportation, funds, foodstuffs, medicine, and fuel; access to communications media and transportation and other networks; and provision of services and assistance rendered within or outside the conflict zone such as sanctuary, asylum, a base for operations, military training, personnel as advisers on various issues, military personnel, and, in rare instances, direct military assistance by combat units, artillery cover in border skirmishes, and armed intervention. The political-diplomatic or moral involvement include verbal statements of concern by governments, support in International Governmental Organisations, diplomatic pressure, campaigns in support of protagonists in the civil war, and diplomatic recognition.[115]

Throughout the ten years of relations with Nigeria from independence in 1960 till the end of the war in 1970, the United States of America was consistent in its support for Nigerian unity. For the USG, the Nigerian civil war was primarily a Nigerian and African problem. This position accounted for all the diplomatic efforts it made especially in April and May of 1967 to find a mutually beneficial and acceptable solution to the crisis between the Federal Military Government under Gen. Yakubu Gowon and the Eastern Regional Government under Col. Emeka Ojukwu. When the ERG decided to secede and the Republic of Biafra was proclaimed, the USG not only deplored it but refused to give any form of support to either side that could be expressly construed as having preference for one against the other. In that context, the US continued throughout the sad period of conflict to seek for a peaceful settlement of the conflict.

American refusal to get involved in the Nigerian civil war beyond humanitarian and mediatory efforts was informed by: the need to promote peaceful resolution of the crisis; a desire not to be seen as interfering in the internal affairs of Nigeria; the necessity to avoid further international commitments given its political and military involvement in other global hotspots; and the possibility of being on good terms with any number of state(s) that might have risen from the ashes of the Nigerian civil war. Hence, the imposition of an arms embargo on both warring factions, the continued recognition of the Gowon government as the de jure Nigerian administration, the deference to the British, the OAU and the Commonwealth to undertake peacemaking roles, and the massive material, diplomatic and moral support given to relief agencies and relief efforts especially in the Biafran enclave.

However, while the USG in pursuit of the policy of neutrality and non-involvement participated in international relief efforts to provide food, medical supplies and other emergency aids to the civilian victims of the war, its insistence to provide relief directly to those inside the Biafran enclave did not go down well with the FMG. The Nigerian government could not see any clear distinction between humanitarian and political aspects of the civil war as the US wished, especially given that the humanitarian factor was susceptible to manipulation by the Biafrans culminating in recognition being accorded to the "Biafran State and Government" by some countries.[116] Although the USG continued to recognise the federal government as the legal authority, its policy of non-involvement, the decision not to sell arms and weaponry to either side in the Nigerian civil war, as well as the politics of relief operations in Biafra led not only to a resentment of the USG by the federal government and the Biafran government, but to a deeply strained US–Nigeria relations.

Looking at the politics of the Nigerian Civil War, the experience of the United States has raised a number of questions, two of which are particularly important: first, to what extent can a foreign state be even handed in its relationship with both sides enmeshed in a civil conflict?; and second, what is the limit of resistance that a foreign government can muster in the face of local public opinion to take a side in an imbroglio? Addressing these two questions will enable one to assess whether the USG policy of non-involvement in the Nigerian civil war was justified or not.

While the USG tried to be even handed and neutral in the Biafran war, its policy was more of benevolent neutrality. On the one hand, its humanitarian impulse dictated economic assistance for Biafra, whilst on the other it was firmly in support of the idea of one Nigeria.[117] The support for one country made the Biafrans to be suspicious and wary of its humanitarian assistance, whilst its refusal to sell arms to the federal forces when a request was made angered the Nigerian government whose suspicion of U.S. policy grew even more when the latter contributed more than US$9 million for airlift support and transportation costs to the voluntary agencies operating relief efforts in Biafra.[118] As noted by an American diplomat, 'equal treatment of an internationally accepted national government and a dissident and subsequently rebellious regional government could only [be] to the advantage of the latter'[119] As a result, the United States could not successfully balance the equation created by its humanitarian desire to assist the Biafrans economically in terms of relief, and its willingness to satisfy Nigeria's political demands. Apart from this, American pilots are recorded to have piloted the Biafran aircraft that bombed Lagos in February, 1969[120] and the inability of the USG to prevent American citizens from openly selling arms and ammunitions to Biafra did a lot of damage to US position in the eyes of the federal forces.

In regards to the second question, it is evident that public opinion in the US added pressure on the USG to change its posture in regards to the Nigerian civil war. Students of Eastern Region origin living in the US played significant roles in raising awareness of the civil war in the international arena, generating sympathy for Biafra and sending home money as well as relief items to support the cause. Biafran Friendship Associations were established in the United States, and the group lobbied US officials and leveraged public opinion through various publicity activities including public protests and demonstrations.[121] The interest in Congress which increased significantly following trips to Lagos and Biafra by members ranged widely from calls to the USG 'to increase significantly the amount of surplus food stocks, relief monies, non-combat aircraft, and such other vehicles of transportation as may be necessary for relief purposes' to those who wanted the USG to 'lend its good offices and utilize all of its diplomatic resources for the purpose of bringing about an immediate cease-fire between the Nigerian and Biafran forces and thereafter to promote the conclusion of a just and durable settlement of the Biafran conflict' as well as those who asked for the USG to become politically involved by exercising its role as a Great Power to bring an end to the civil war.[122]

By July 1969, the USG was almost buckling under the strain of pressures to adopt a radical position in regards to the Nigerian crisis. In an instruction from the Under Secretary of State Richardson to the US Ambassador in Nigeria Mathews, the latter was asked to inform Gen. Gowon as the head of the FMG that 'if the relief impasse continued much longer, the question of possible new U.S. approaches to the problem would undoubtedly arise.'[123] The question is whether the USG position would have swung from humanitarian involvement to a political and military involvement assuming the Nigerian civil war had continued beyond January, 1970. Notwithstanding all the various pressures and the influence exercised by the Biafra Lobby[124] not just on Congress but the sentiment of ordinary American citizens, the USG refused to alter its foreign policy course of non-interference and non-involvement as regards the war on the argument that it could neither determine a settlement of the war nor impose a cease-fire.

Regardless of the inability to please either side in the Nigerian civil war, it is to the credit of the USG that its basic policy of non-involvement beyond encouraging the two warring sides to negotiate a peaceful settlement of the conflict did not change even when it became apparent that the FMG was militarily stronger than the Biafrans and that federal victory was inevitable. Furthermore, the saying that the piper dictates the tune was not true in regards to the American relief efforts in Biafra. Even though the bulk of donations to the Biafran relief operation came from the USG and American sources, frontline operations and distributions were carried out by NGOs who had their own individual operational modalities and were not influenced in any way by the USG.

Conclusively, the USG made a wise judgement by towing the line of non-involvement and non-interference in the Nigerian civil war. By distancing itself from a political and military involvement on the side of any of the warring parties in the Nigerian civil war and refusing to play the role of a big power by intervening in the conflict, the USG not only prevented the triggering of an arms race with the communist bloc in Nigeria (the consequences of which no one would have known), but also significantly positioned itself in a place of favour with Nigeria regardless of what the outcome of the war could have been. In the immediate aftermath of the Nigerian civil war, the US emerged as Nigeria's dominant trading partner and by 1976, forty (40) per cent of the total US imports from Africa was from Nigeria alone and from 1973 to 1979, Nigeria sold almost fifty-six (56) per cent of its oil export to the United States.[125]

Fifty years after the formal establishment of political and diplomatic relations between the US and Nigeria, forty years after the end of the Nigerian civil war and regardless of what many regard as a snubbing of the country by the USG of President Barrack Obama following his first Presidential visit to Africa which did not include the country, Nigeria remains a very valued ally of the United States. Indeed, the failure of President Obama to visit the country as part of his first Presidential African tour is more of a protest that Nigeria has not lived up to the expectation of one of its most important partners, rather than the demotion of the country from its status as *primus inter pares* in the centre of American Foreign Policy in Africa, the West African sub-region and especially the Gulf of Guinea.

End Notes

[79.] Levi A. Nwachukwu, "The United States and Nigeria – 1960 to 1987: Anatomy of a Pragmatic Relationship", *Journal of Black Studies*, Vol. 28, No. 5 (May, 1998), 575-593.

[80.] National Development Plan, Progress Report (Lagos: Federal Ministry of Economic Development, 1962), p. 31.

[81.] A. T. Balewa. *Nigeria Speaks*. (Lagos: Longmans, 1964), p. 104.

[82.] For a detailed history of Nigeria, please see Michael Crowder, *The Story of Nigeria* (London: Hutchinson, 1971); Michael Crowder, *West Africa Under Colonial Rule* (London: Hutchinson, 1968); Okoi Arikpo, *The Development of Modern Nigeria* (Harmondsworth: Penguin, 1967); Elizabeth Isichei, *A History of Nigeria* (Harlow: Longman, 1983); and T. Falola et al *History of Nigeria: Nigeria in the Nineteenth Century* Vol. II (Lagos: Longman, 1991), pp. 17-38.

[83.] National Intelligence Estimate/1/NIE 64.2-65 Washington, August 26, 1965. /1/Source: Central Intelligence Agency: Job 79-R01012A, ODDI Registry of NIE and SNIE Files.

[84.] Intelligence Memorandum Prepared in the Central Intelligence Agency/1/ Washington, October 1, 1966. /1/Source: Johnson Library, National Security File, Country File, Nigeria, Vol. I, Memos & Miscellaneous, 6/64-8/67.

[85.] Telegram From the Embassy in Nigeria to the Department of State/1/Lagos, November 11, 1966, 1510Z. /1/Source: Department of State, Central Files, POL 23-9 NIGERIA.

[86.] Circular Telegram From the Department of State to All African Posts/1/ Washington, August 2, 1966, 5:45 p.m. /1/Source: Department of State, Central Files, POL 23-9 NIGERIA.

[87.] Michael J. Draper, *Shadows: Airlift and Airwar in Biafra and Nigeria 1967 – 1970* (Aldershot: Hikoki Publications Limited, 1999), pp. 10-14.

[88.] Abubakar Atofarati, "The Nigerian Civil War: Causes, Strategies and Lessons Learnt", (US Marine Command and Staff College, 1991/92).

[89.] Alexander Madiebo, *The Nigerian Revolution and the Biafran War* (Enugu: Fourth Dimensions Publishers, 1980), p. 98.

[90.] C. Legum (ed.), *African Contemporary Records*, 1968-1969 (New York: Africana Publishing Company, 1969), p. 649.

[91.] The twelve states were made up of six in the north, three in the east, one in the west, one in the mid-west and Lagos as a state on its own.

[92.] C. O. Ojukwu, *Biafra: Selected Speeches with Journals of Events* (New York: Harper & Row, 1969), pp. 146-147.

[93.] Telegram From the Embassy in Nigeria to the Department of State/1/Lagos, November 11, 1966, 1510Z. /1/Source: Department of State, Central Files, POL 23-9 NIGERIA.

[94.] Now known as the African Union (AU).

[95.] L. B. Johnson, *Public Papers of the President of the United States,* (Washington, DC: Government Printing Office, 1970), p. 960.

[96.] The airborne rescue mission on 24 and 25 November 1964 was a joint venture between the United States and Belgium, the colonial power.

[97.] C. Legum, "America's Year in Africa" in *Africa Contemporary Record 1969-70* (New York: Africana Publishing Company, 1970), p. A44.

[98.] Department of State Bulletin, September 11, 1967, p. 320.

[99.] Washington, July 3, 1967. /1/Source: Johnson Library, National Security File, Country File, Nigeria, Vol. I, Memos & Miscellaneous, 6/64-8/67.

[100.] Cervenka, Z. *The Nigerian Civil War 1967-1970: History of the War, Selected Bibliography and Documents* (Frankfurt am Main: Bernard & Graefe, 1971), p. 109

[101.] Caroline Moorehead, ibid. pp 615 -616

[102.] See Laurie Wiseberg, *The International Politics of Relief: A Case Study of the Relief Operations Mounted During the Nigerian Civil War (1967-1970)* (Los Angeles: PhD Thesis, University of California, 1973), and Caroline Moorehead, *Dunant's Dream,* (New York: Harper Collins Publishers, 1988).

[103.] R. Sheppard *Nigeria, Africa and the United States: From Kennedy to Reagan* (Indianapolis: Indiana University Press, 1991), pp. 34 – 49; and W. Rostow *The Diffusion of Power: An Essay in Recent History* (New York: Macmillan, 1972), p. 472.

[104.] Morris Davis, "Audits of International Relief in the Nigerian Civil War: Some Political Perspectives", *International Organization,* Vol. 29, No. 2 (Spring, 1975), pp. 501-512.

[105.] Telegram 5133 from the Department of State to the Embassy in Nigeria, January 11, 1969, 2050Z, National Archives, RG 59, Central Files 1967-69, POL 27-9 Biafra-Nigeria.

[106.] The FMG specifically accused Caritas and the World Council of

Churches of prolonging the war not just by "feeding" Biafran soldiers, but by airlifting arms and ammunitions into Biafra under the guise of relief materials.

[107.] National Archives, RG 59, Records of the Special Coordinator on Relief to Civilian Victims of the Nigerian Civil war, February 1969-June 1970, Lot 70 D 336, Box 517, ICRC, Records.

[108.] National Archives, RG 59, Central Files 1967-69, POL 27-9 Biafra-Nigeria.

[109.] National Archives, Nixon Presidential Materials, NSC Files, NSC Institutional Files (H-Files), Box H-20, NSC Meeting, Biafra, Strategic Policy Issues 2/14/69.

[110.] Telegram From the Department of State to the Embassy in Nigeria/1/ Washington, August 15, 1968, 1553Z. /1/Source: Johnson Library, National Security File, Special Head of State Correspondence File, Nigeria-Presidential Correspondence. Confidential; Flash.

[111.] Transcript of telephone conversation, Washington, January 15, 1970, 6:10 p.m., Library of Congress, Manuscript Division, Kissinger Papers, Box 361, Telephone Conversations.

[112.] Telegram 1699 from the Embassy in Nigeria to the Department of State, February 15, 1970, 0955Z, National Archives, RG 59, Central Files 1970-73, POL 1 Nigeria-US.

[113.] Memorandum from the President's Assistant for National Security Affairs (Kissinger) to President Nixon, Washington, June 1, 1970, National Archives, Nixon Presidential Materials, NSC Files, Box 742, Country Files, Africa, Nigeria, Vol. I.

[114.] Airgram A-22 from the Department of State to the Embassy in Nigeria, Washington, June 21, 1971, National Archives, RG 59, Central Files 1970-73, POL 1 Nigeria.

[115.] Alexis Heraclides, "Secessionist Minorities and External Involvement", *International Organization,* Vol. 44, No. 3 (Summer, 1990), p. 345; and Pierre Hassner, "Civil Violence and the Patterns of International Power," *Adelphi Papers,* No. 83, December 1971, p. 19.

[116.] Bassey Ate, *Decolonization and Dependence: The Development of Nigerian-U.S. Relations, 1960-1984* (Boulder, Colorado: Westview Press, 1987), p. 159.

[117.] This is reflected in the statement made by Joseph Palmer II, the first U.S. ambassador to Nigeria and later assistant secretary of state for African Affairs that it was the wish of the American government that this Federal Republic of Twelve States remains a united and indivisible country.

118. Nwachukwu, supra n. 1.

119. Airgram From the Embassy in Nigeria to the Department of State/1/ A-469 Lagos, March 7, 1968. /1/Source: Department of State, Central Files, POL 1 NIGERIA-US.

120. FCO 65/362, f. 23.

121. A. Nwankwo. *Nigeria: The Challenge of Biafra* 3rd edn. (Enugu: Fourth Dimension Publishers, 1972), pp. 76-77; G. A. Onyegbula. *Memoirs of the Nigerian-Biafran Bureaucrat: An Account of Life in Biafra and Within Nigeria* (Ibadan: Spectrum Books, 2005), pp. 163-178.

122. Paper Prepared by the NSC Interdepartmental Group for Africa, Washington, February 10, 1969 National Archives, Nixon Presidential Materials, NSC Files, NSC Institutional Files (H-Files), Box H-20, NSC Meeting, Biafra, Strategic Policy Issues 2/14/69.

123. Telegram 116458 From the Department of State to the Embassy in Nigeria, July 15, 1969, 0317Z1. National Archives, RG 59, Central Files 1967-69, POL 27-9 Biafra-Nigeria.

124. The lobby consisted of student groups, Peace Corps volunteers as well as US religious and charitable groups.

125. B. Ate, Supra n. 38.

Chapter Four

Dealing with the Generals: Human Rights and Democracy as issues in United States-Nigerian Relations

Funmi OLONISAKIN

A major issue of concern to successive administrations in the United States during most of the period Nigeria was under military rule was how to deal with its military rulers. As it is well known Nigeria's first fifty years of independence witnessed more than thirty years of rule by different military leaders. On the whole, during the period, the United States had to deal with eight different military rulers under seven different military administrations.[126] Even though the global antipathy that currently exists against military rule was not a phenomenon during most of the period that Nigeria was under military rule, relating with Nigeria's military rulers was not particularly easy for the United States for a number of reasons, two of which are particularly profound. First, the United States regards itself as the global bastion of democracy. Washington was not warmly disposed to be seen fraternizing very warmly with a country almost perpetually under military rule. Second, the activities of some Nigerian military rulers brought their human rights policies to the tribunal of international attention, such that the United States had to come up with positions that greatly affected the relationship between the two countries.

Although the relationships between the United States and Nigeria during the administrations of these military officers are discussed in different chapters in this book, this chapter specifically discusses how the American government related with each of the military rulers that managed the affairs of Nigeria. It also identifies and discuses the key diplomatic issues that underlined the relationship between the two countries. The chapter argues that the United States was left with no choice than to tolerate Nigeria's military rulers largely because of the depth of economic relations between the two countries. But even in doing this, encouragements were also given to the leaders to embark on the path of democracy. The extent to which this encouragement was received by Nigeria's rulers, however, depended on how willing they were to accept democracy. In discussing how the United States had managed relationships with Nigeria's military rulers, this chapter takes individual military rulers and discuss the relations each had with the United States. Consequently, this chapter is divided into seven substantive sections to cover each of the military administrations that governed Nigeria during the period of military rule.

The Aguyi Ironsi Administration and the United States

The assumption of power of General Aguyi Ironsi in early 1966 was like a bolt out of the blues for the United States. Before the coup, the United States was getting accustomed to Prime Minister Balewa and his administration and there were clear indications that both countries were about to consolidate a strong relationship. The close connection the Balewa regime had with the Britain also assured the Americans that Nigeria was firmly in the corner of the West on key diplomatic issues. To now see a violent overthrow was a major cause of concern for the Americans.

The initial concern of the United States was to be cautious, especially as the situation in Nigeria was fluid. Immediately after assuming power, General Ironsi promised a quick return to democratic rule. He attempted to restore discipline to the army which at this time had become unruly. It was also to his credit that he passed laws allowing for greater press freedoms and in May 1966, announced plans for a centralized Nigerian constitution after suspending regional constitutions and dissolving all legislative bodies.

It would appear that the prevailing circumstances and the relatively brief period of the administration meant that the United States did not have any time to really engage the Aguyi Ironsi regime. Also the general uncertainty that was looming and which was to ultimately result into a civil war was also such that the US was more concerned about the imminent danger to the unity of the country than the human rights and democratic credentials of the new military ruler. Also, since military intervention in civilian politics was not a common feature of the African nations at this time, the US had no clear template with which to engage the new military leaders in Nigeria. It was thus not surprising that it was not long before the regime was overthrown in another military coup.

The Yakubu Gowon Years

On issues surrounding human rights and democracy in the area of Nigeria controlled by the federal government, there were relatively few bones of contention between the United States and Nigeria during the Yakubu Gowon years. There are a number of reasons for this. First, the whole issue of democracy was not a major global issue during the Gowon era. Indeed, military rule was a common thing across the continent and the Cold War gave subtle endorsement of dictatorship. Consequently, the United States gave some form of endorsement, if not encouragement, to dictatorial regimes and human rights abuses, provided of course that the regime followed policies which were in America's interest. The main thing that attracted global attention during the Gowon era was the civil war (discussed above in Chapter 3) and it was the human rights issues surrounding this that was the main issue in American Nigerian relations. Although the United States insisted on not recognising Biafra, it also tried to ensure that the war was not used as an opportunity to abuse human rights in Nigeria. Against this background, the United States refused to sell arms to Nigeria. While the Nigerian government was willing to respect this position, the government was upset when the United States refused to give Nigeria export permits allowing the purchase of arms on commercial basis from US arms manufacturers ostensibly because the US argued that it would not want to interfere in the internal affairs of Nigeria.[127] Furthermore, the US Secretary of State, Dean Rusk, argued that the United States considered Nigeria a "British Responsibility".

Nigeria became upset by the American position for three reasons. First, Nigeria argued that it never, at any time, applied for military aid from the United States as the US had publicised and that it was dishonest of the US government to portray the impression that Nigeria needed aid from US to prosecute the war. Second, the government found Rusk's assertion that Nigeria was British responsibility condescending and insulting, and the Federal Government was forced to remind the American government that Nigeria was no longer a British colony.[128] Finally, the Federal Government of Nigeria argued that America's claim of not wanting to intervene in the internal affairs of another country contradictory as the US had a history of interfering in the internal affairs of other countries if it suited American national interest. Nigeria's position here seems valid. A few days after denying Nigeria export permit, the United States allowed three C130 Hercules transport planes with 150 personnel and 45 paratroopers to go into Zaire and assist President Mobutu in fighting his enemies. This was to be a low point in American-Nigerian relations. However, compared to what was to happen in future years, this was a mild disagreement on the issue of human-rights and their violations in Nigeria.

A key human right issue that the US contended with during the Gowon era was how relief assistance was offered during the civil war. The Gowon administration argued that two distinct sets of problems emerged with the distribution of relief assistance during the war. The first were the problems associated with the organisation of relief supplies to displaced persons in areas under lawful authority, while the second was those problems associated with foreign relief operations in the territory held by Biafran forces. The government thus saw the need to organise relief assistance for displaced persons and other needy in war affected parts of Biafra. In doing this, however, the Federal Government was concerned that appropriate distribution mechanisms be put in place, especially as it was suspected that many foreign relief agencies were getting arms to the Biafrans under the guise of supplying relief materials. Initially the government invited the International Committee of the Red Cross (ICRC) as the main organisation to coordinate international relief assistance. This was acceptable to the United States and quite a number of US relief assistance to Biafra was passed through the agency. However, it got to the stage where the government was no longer impressed with the activities of the ICRC and decided to terminate the relationship. To take over from the ICRC, the Nigerian government established the National Rehabilitation Commission (NRC) and it subsequently instructed all foreign assistance to war affected regions to be passed through the Commission. The United States did not feel very comfortable with this arrangement and it expressed subtle protest, even though it had to comply.

Nigeria also felt that the United States could have been a victim of misinformation about the goings on in Nigeria during the civil war and that this might be colouring the perception of events in Nigeria. Consequently, every effort was made by the Gowon administration during the early days of the civil war to impress upon the US that the situation was not as bad as it was often portrayed by the media.[129] The Gowon administration also felt that the reduction in the level of interest with which US projects in Nigeria that had earlier received American enthusiasm, could also be because of the perceived inaccuracy about reports on Nigeria.

Reports on Nigeria's behavior during the civil war continued to generate controversy even after the end of the conflict and this affected the relationship between Nigeria and the United States. The situation got a bit worse in February, 1970, when Nigeria expelled an American Military officer, Lt. Col. Eugene Dewey, from the country. Although the Nigerian government claimed that his expulsion was a "police matter", the suspicion was that he was expelled because he had earlier written an uncomplimentary report about the food situation in the war-affected region. Specifically, he noted that the war was far worse that it was often portrayed. The US was sufficiently annoyed by the expulsion to summon the Nigeria Charge d'Affairs to Washington, Mr Peter Udoh, to the State Department to express protest.[130]

The relative tension continued even after the end of the civil war. For example, in 1973, when the Nigerian Head of State, General Yakubu Gowon visited the United States, the White House arranged and then postponed so many appointments with President Nixon that Gowon was left seething in exasperation. In 1975, the Nigerian government gave the United States

Information Service two weeks to vacate its premises in Lagos. When the agency failed to move, Nigerian troops moved in and occupied the building.

Even after the end of the Civil war, there were those who believed that the United States' role during the war should not be forgotten and that friendship towards the country should be regulated. For example, an association, the Nigeria Afro-Asian Solidarity Organisation (NAASO) made it clear in February, 1970 that the visit that was proposed by the former United States Secretary of State, William Rogers, should not be allowed on the grounds that the country had played an unfriendly role during the Nigerian civil war.[131] It should, however, be pointed out that the organisation was known for its extreme views.[132]

Also, it seemed that the US was not willing to press Gowon on the issue of return to civil rule as it was appreciated that special post-war circumstances required some sympathy.

The second reason why there were few areas of contention between the US and the Gowon administration was that there were no serious cases of human rights violations during this period. While overzealous governors might sometimes go overboard,[133] the general impression, both at home and abroad, was that Gowon was a military leader who, compared to those who were to come after him, was relatively compassionate.

Third, the Gowon administration, at least at the beginning, had a clear idea of when it was going to hand over power to civilians. Following the end of the Civil war, Gowon announced that Nigeria would remain under military rule for six more years, promising to return the country to civilian rule in 1976. With this date, it was possible that the United States felt no urgent need to put the regime under any form of pressure. However, when the administration retracted its promise, another military administration took over. Gowon's statement after four years that it was not feasible to return to civilian rule sparked protests and instability throughout the country. On 29 July, 1975, Gowon was ousted in a bloodless coup led by Brig. Gen. Murtala Muhammed.

The Murtala Mohammed/Olusegun Obasanjo Years

It is ironic that to a very large extent, the Murtala and Obasanjo administration got on relatively well with the United States on issues surrounding democracy and human rights, despite the fundamental diplomatic disagreement on the issue of Angola. Against the background of the mistake made by the Gowon administration, the Murtala and Obasanjo administration made it clear from the outset that they had a definite agenda to hand over power in 1979. Even after Murtala was killed in an abortive military coup in February 1976, Obasanjo remained loyal and handed over power at the stipulated time. Against this background, there was no major disagreement between Nigeria and the United States on the issue of democracy under the Murtala and Obasanjo administration. Furthermore, it was during this period that Nigeria adopted the American system of government with an executive President. This, no doubt, would have increased the amount of admiration America had for the unfolding democracy in Nigeria under General Obasanjo. Also, to ensure free and fair elections, the Obasanjo administration established a Federal Electoral Commission in order to take the potentially rancorous election out of partisan hands. This is apart from a new constitution that was written. In short, along the lines of democracy, the American government rated the Murtala and Obasanjo administration quite high indeed.

The only major issue of human rights concern that occurred during the Murtala and Obasanjo administration was the execution of those convicted of the coup plot that killed General Murtala Mohammed. However, there seemed to be no formal criticism of the Obasanajo administration for taking this step, which was also the first time that coup plotters would be publicly executed in Nigeria.

The Mohammadu Buhari Phase

The Buhari administration made clear from its inception at the end of 1983 that democracy and human rights were not key issues of consideration. For one thing, the administration felt that the short period of civilian administration of President Shehu Shagari had brought about some of the worst levels of corruption and indiscipline that Nigeria had ever witnessed and that it was the responsibility of the military to clean up the mess of the politicians. Among the first steps taken was the arrest of all key politicians who had participated in the ousted regime and to institute military tribunals to try them. Those who were found guilty of corruption were give long jail terms, sometimes up to 100 years. The zero-tolerance the regime showed to corruption was also extended to general indiscipline, with a major "war" officially declared against it. Decrees were also made to address issues like press freedom, currency trafficking, drug peddling, etc. In short, right from the time of its inception up to the time it was overthrown, the Buhari administration did not leave Nigerians and the international community in doubt that strict adherence to human rights was not an option. Also on democracy, the Buhari administration did not make any promise about any imminent return to civilian rule. Indeed, the administration showed clear contempt for civilians and gave all indications that the mess the civilians had created would take a long time to clean up. Consequently, the possibility of a return to civilian rule was not on the table. The administration also went further to externalise the pursuit of accountability over human rights with the attempt the administration allegedly made to ensure the forceful return to Nigeria of a prominent member of the Shagari administration who had escaped to the United Kingdom, Umaru Dikko. This attempt, which failed after the heavily drugged Dikko was found in a container at Stanstead Airport in London, was to affect the relationship between Nigeria and the United Kingdom. Indeed, the general belief of most Nigerians was that the Buhari administration was, up to that time, the worst in terms of human rights violations, especially because laws were backdated so people could be executed for offences that did not carry death sentences at the time they were committed.[134] Even the regime that replaced him was to confirm that "He was too rigid and uncompromising in his attitude to issues of national significance".

    Despite the extent of human rights violation in Nigeria during the Buhari administration, the United States did not take any official position on the state of human right abuses and violations in Nigeria. Even after the abortive attempt to smuggle Umaru Dikko into Nigeria and the subsequent diplomatic problems between Nigeria and the United Kingdom, there was no formal involvement of the United States. All these, however, were to change after Buhari was overthrown in what was widely considered a palace coup and was replaced by another military leader, Ibrahim Babangida.

Dealing with Ibrahim Babangida

From the start of his regime in 1985, Ibrahim Babangida made it clear that he was of a different stock from Buhari and he immediately countered some of the negative impressions that Buhari had left on the Nigerian people. Specifically, he noted that his government "does not intend to lead a country where individuals are under the fear of expressing themselves." To show his desire to entrench human rights, Babangida released many political detainees, including former state governors and journalists, some of whom were detained without trial and he allowed public scrutiny of detention centres. This gave the impression that human rights and democracy would be respected by the new administration. The United States also showed interest to encourage the new leader. Indeed, the former United States President, Ronald Reagan, sent Mr. Justice Arlin Adams, a member of the United States Court of Appeal to Babangida to express his best wishes for Babangida's efforts to bring about democracy and human rights. The American President on the occasion also presented volumes of books on human rights as evidence of America's best wishes to Nigeria.

While the previous administration was somewhat short, the Babangida years lasted quite a long time and as such recorded a number of developments in the American-Nigerian relations. By the time Babangida assumed office, the United States seemed to have realized that military dictatorship would be around in Nigeria for quite some time, and for the first few years of his administration there was nothing beyond platitudinous call for the country to ensure a speedy return to democracy. The assistance Babangida gave in addressing conflicts in Liberia and Sierra Leone also added to the relative interest the American government gave his administration. What could also have been of initial interest to the United States was the impression of respect for human-rights that the administration portrayed at its inception. The abrogation of some of the oppressive decrees of the previous administration could have also given the United

States the impression that the Babangida administration could be a military rule with human face.

While there were no serious human right violations during the early Babangida years that the United States felt obliged to react to, things soon became difficult when a prominent journalist, Dele Giwa, was killed by a parcel bomb. Although the facts of the case were never clearly established, it was the belief of many Nigerians that the Government had a hand in his death. This was given credence by the vehemence with which the late human rights lawyer, Gani Fawehinmi, pursued the fight to get to the roots of the assassination. It is important to point out that there was no reaction from the United States to the new level of uncertainties descending on Nigeria. Even after Gani Fawehinmi and other human rights activists were arrested there were no comments from the United States Embassy in Nigeria. A more profound human rights issue came with the execution of those convicted for coup plots during the Babangida administration. On the whole there were two coup plots during the regime — one alleged and one attempted. All those found guilty of these plots were killed. On the whole about 70 people were executed for alleged involvements in coup plots against Babangida. It is also noteworthy to point out that there was no open criticism of the execution of these people by the United States government.

The United States appeared to have shown considerable interest in Babangida's agenda for democratic reform and all encouragements were given to the administration in its efforts to return Nigeria to democracy. Even though it was becoming clear to the Nigerian population that the occurrence of such a transition was questionable, the United States did not show any indication that it was concerned that any discussion of transition was not leading anywhere.

A major diplomatic face-off occurred between Nigeria and the United States over the issue of the election in June 1993. The circumstances leading to this event are worth recording. A few days before the presidential election, an organisation believed to have dubious credentials, the Association for Better Nigeria, (ABN) went to court to request that the election be postponed. This request was granted by a judge of the Abuja High Court, the late Justice Bassey Ikpeme. The impression most Nigerians had was that the request by the ABN and the judgement by Justice Ikpeme were all devices by the Babangida administration to delay a hand-over to a civilian government, especially because of the leader of the ABN, Arthur Nzeribe, was widely known to have advocated the interest of the military. Immediately after the judgement was made, the Director of the United States Information Service (USIS) in Nigeria issued a terse warning that the United States would not accept any postponement of the election. This drew an angry response from the Nigerian government which saw it as interference in Nigeria's internal affairs and the Director of USIS was issued with a 72 hours order to leave Nigeria. As a further reaction, the Chairman of the Centre for Democratic Studies, Professor Omo Omoruyi, withdrew the accreditation of 8 American who had earlier been accredited to observe the election. Omoruyi argued that the court ruling came out of the judicial process in Nigeria and that it was within the domestic jurisdiction of the courts.[135] He thus concluded that the Americans hitherto accredited to observe the election were not likely to show respect to Nigerians as contained in the manual for international observers.

When eventually Nigeria went to the polls after several prevarications, the American government was supportive and expected, at last, an end to military dictatorship. In the election held in June 2003, Moshood Abiola won the majority of votes, but Babangida's government nullified the results, citing an electoral process rife with fraud. This was marred with massive protests as thousands took to the streets protesting the move and accusing the government of trying to thwart the will of the people. At least 100 people were killed during the fighting. The military arrested human rights activists and shut down newspapers. When however the Babangida administration annulled the election result, the United States realized the somewhat peculiar problem Nigeria had on its road to democracy.

After the nullification of the election result, America's first reaction was to impose sanctions on the Nigerian Military. The Clinton administration invoked Section 212 (f) of the Immigration and Nationality Act to deny entry into the United States by senior Nigerian government officials and others who formulated, implemented or benefitted from policies impeding Nigeria's transition to democracy. The United States also suspended all military assistance and banned the sale and repair of military goods and refinery services to Nigeria. Other steps taken included the immediate cancellation of the $11 million assistance that had been intended as budgetary support to Nigeria's Ministry of Health; the termination of all government-to-government military assistance and training except for counter-narcotics and military training; the withdrawal of the Nigerian military attaché in Washington and the simultaneous withdrawal of his opposite number from Lagos and the termination of other development assistance, except for humanitarian aid channeled through non-governmental organizations.[136] This thus placed the United States above other Western European countries like Britain and Germany who continued arms sales to Nigeria. Furthermore, President Clinton sent Jesse Jackson as his special envoy to Nigeria to encourage concessions from the military. The failure of his visit made Jackson conclude that an assertive and aggressive diplomacy was needed to prevent an imminent civil war in Nigeria. But this was as far as the Clinton government went.

The U.S. ambassador to Nigeria during the period was not forceful in protesting detentions of political prisoners and neither did the Clinton administration put active pressure on its traditional European allies to take additional measures against the Babangida administration. Nigerian democracy activists would have also preferred stringent issues like a firm international arms embargo, freezing the foreign assets of regime members, and finding some way to block the military's access to oil revenues. Greater sympathy however came from some members of the U.S. Congress. For example, a concurrent resolution urging support for democracy in Nigeria, introduced by Rep. Donald Payne (D-N.J.) with 56 co-sponsors, passed the House of Representatives. The bill did not mandate specific action, but many of the sponsors maintained a continuing concern with the situation in Nigeria. Also many nongovernmental groups became very active, including human rights groups such as Amnesty International and Human Rights Watch, as well as the AFL-CIO's African-American Labor Center. Facing massive domestic and international opposition, Babangida resigned on

27 August, 1993. However, by the time he left office, there had also emerged a very strong Nigerian population in the United States clamouring for democracy in their home country. The role of this group, which was to continue to become even stronger during the administration of General Sani Abacha, is discussed in a separate chapter in this book on the activities of the Diaspora population.

Contending with Sani Abacha

When the late General Sani Abacha assumed office after the short interim administration of Ernest Shonekan, the general impression was that he had come to "right" the "wrong" that was done through the annulment of the June 12 election. There had in fact been rumours that he had been invited to come in and prevent the nation from descending into total chaos. However, not long after he assumed power, it became clear that he had a separate agenda and it was then that the United States and the entire international community realized that Nigeria was about to begin another long haul of military dictatorship.

The first step taken that marked the dawn of a new but dangerous era was the arrest and imprisonment of Moshood Abiola, the man who had won the annulled election. After Abacha had signified his intention to hold onto power, Abiola had gone around the world to canvass for support to reclaim his mandate. On his arrival in Nigeria, he declared himself as President. He was immediately declared wanted, accused of treason, and was arrested by the Abacha regime. While it is likely that the American government did not encourage Abiola to declare himself President, a decision that was most likely given endorsement by the Nigerian population, especially those in exile, the US was disturbed at the arrest and detention of the person that won an election that was adjudged the best the country has undertaken. However, from the time Abiola was arrested and detained, Abacha had signalled to the international community that he was ready to take them on.

After arresting Abiola, Abacha began efforts to metamorphose himself into a civilian president. It was at this stage that the American government fully realized that Nigeria was on the threshold of another long period of modified dictatorship. Initial assistance from America, albeit not often recognised, came from American Foundations, especially the Ford Foundation, to assist civil societies in Nigeria. Apart from the American foundations, government establishments like USAID also gave grants to civil society organisations fighting for democracy and human rights in Nigeria. One of the organisations that benefitted from this was the Centre for Democracy and Development.

Cases of human rights violations that existed during the Abacha administration also did not go unnoticed by the American government, although there was often no serious criticism or condemnation of them. For example, there were two cases of alleged coup plots against the Abacha regime. The first, which was reported to the nation in 1995, implicated the former military Head of State, Olusegun Obasanjo, his deputy, the late Shehu Musa Yar'Adua and a number of other military officers. At the end of a trial that many considered suspicious, 38 people were condemned to death, including Obasanjo and his former Deputy, Shehu Yar'Adua.

The United States had to intervene after the condemnation of Obasanjo and others. At the insistence of the US Ambassador to the UN Andrew Young and former American President Jimmy Carter who were close personal friends of the Obasanjos, President Clinton on 18th July wrote a letter to General Abacha urging him to grant clemency to the 40 people convicted in secret trials of being coup plotters, including several who are believed to have been sentenced to death. In the letter, President Clinton urged the Nigerian Government to allow fair and open appeals and said relations between the United States and Nigeria would be hurt if executions went forward. Although the United States government praised Nigeria's recent cooperation in fighting drug trafficking, it warned that if the executions were carried out the United States might impose economic sanctions or tighten visa restrictions. In October, Abacha announced that the death sentences were commuted and Obasanjo's sentence was reduced to 15 years.

Although there were difficulties in the relationship between the Abacha administration and the United States, there were attempts at a point by the Nigerian government to go on a charm offensive and to see whether it could sell its position to the United States. For example, in August 1995, the regime's Foreign Affairs Minister, Tom Ikimi, went on a visit to the United States where he attempted to defend the situation in Nigeria. While he was in the United States, the Minister met prominent individuals and media institutions like the *Wall Street Journal, The New York Times, Business Week, Time Magazine, Journal of Commerce; The MacNeil Lehrer News Hour,* the Carnegie Endowment for International Peace, the Business Council for International Understanding; Salomon Brothers; James Bourdley Business Development; business representatives of US Companies in Nigeria; and Dr. Coretta Scott King, the wife of the late Dr. Martin Luther King. During the trip, Chief Ikimi touched on a number of issues including the progress being made in the country's democratisation process and the human-rights situation. Specifically, he noted that the democratisation process in the country was making progress and that the government was determined to continue with the democratisation agenda promised by the President. He, however, requested that Nigeria should be allowed to develop at its own pace and also to evolve the type of democracy that took into consideration the country's peculiar socio-political, cultural and economic situation. Moving on to the fate of those convicted of coup plots, Ikime told his American audience that Abacha was personally distressed about the calibre of those indicted in the coup plot, especially General Obasanjo, but that the government would take into consideration the plea from President Clinton and other leaders from across the world. On the continued detention of Chief Abiola and Ken Saro-Wiwa, Ikime made it clear to the Americans he met during his trip that the detention of the two of them was not because of their political views but for the civil offences of treason and murder which they allegedly committed and for which the courts in the country were then looking into.[137]

The relatively soft gloves with which the American government had been fighting the Abacha administration was completely thrown overboard when, in November 1995, the government executed Ken Saro-Wiwa and other 8 other Ogoni activists who had been fighting the environmental degradation of the oil-producing Ogoni region of the Niger Delta. Despite global appeals for clemency, the Abacha administration carried out the hanging of these activists after a deeply flawed judicial procedure. The hanging received global condemnation and the United States immediately recalled its Ambassador to Nigeria, Walter Carrington, who had himself long shown deep interest in democracy and human rights in Nigeria. This was the lowest point in US-Nigerian relations and it continued until June 1998, when General Abacha died and was replaced by General Abdulsalami Abubakar.

The death of General Abacha created a problem for the United States as to how best to address developments in Nigeria. President Clinton was addressing a United Nations conference on the international war on drugs when the news reached him. The White House press secretary Michael McCurry's immediate statement was that "the United States government was interested in what type of opportunity exists for a democratic transition in Nigeria," correspondent Douglas Farah reported. McCurry said the United States had long supported democracy in Nigeria and hoped "an accountable civilian government able to lead the Nigerian people" would emerge from "a very horrific episode in which basic, fundamental rights have been suspended."

The first concern was whether the military leaders that succeeded Abacha could take Nigeria to democracy. The former United States Ambassador to Nigeria, Walter Carrington attested to the fact that General Abubakar was a professional soldier but he too was concerned as to whether hard-liners of the Abacha regime would not make life difficult for him. It would appear that the United States wanted to ensure that initiatives were not hijacked by General Abdulsalami Abubakar and the US decided to change from the personalized policy that had characterized its relations with Nigeria under Sani Abacha. The United States saw a sterling opportunity to go in, urge this new government to re-energize the political process, to bring some integrity to the political parties, and to establish credible democracy. There was, however, a crucial question as to whether Abubakar should start the democratic process all over or just use the five political parties that Abacha had brought into existence.

The disagreements between Nigeria and the United States during the Abacha administration also had its own periods of comedy. For example, when the City of New York decided to name a street corner in Manhattan after Kudirat Abiola, the wife of the detained winner of the June 1993 election who was killed in June 1996, the Nigerian Government and the Congress of Nigerians Abroad had protested, arguing in court that it was an unconstitutional attempt by New York City to conduct foreign policy. When this failed, the Nigerian government retaliated by renaming a street in Lagos after the black American leader of the radical Nation of Islam movement, Louis Farrakhan. The street chosen for the name was the address of many embassies, including that of the United States. This episode was seen by correspondents as retaliation against New York City in a street-naming tug-of-war.

Even after his death, Abacha's human rights records continued to reverberate in the United States. The late general Abacha's relationship with the United States came up again when Senator Moseley-Braun appeared before the American Senate as a nominated American Ambassador to New Zealand. Moseley-Braun who had lost her Senate seat and was being nominated as an Ambassador had been a close associate of the late General Abacha and had served as lobbyist, trying to persuade the United States to ease economic sanctions imposed after the international outcry at Saro-Wiwa's execution in 1995. In May 1996, Moseley-Braun appeared before the Foreign Relations Committee to complain that economic sanctions imposed on Nigeria was unfair. She even went as far as to say that compared with the rest of Africa, complaining about Nigerian abuses was like "opening the refrigerator, seeing an elephant and complaining that a jar of jam is missing." Many Nigerians, especially those living in Chicago, believed that she was unworthy of the position of United States Ambassador. Also Moseley-Braun made a number of visits to Nigeria without notifying the White House, the State Department or even her own chief of staff, who resigned in protest. It was during one of such trips that Abacha presented a letter endorsing President Clinton's re-election. When George Will wrote a column criticizing the trip, Moseley-Braun asked Will to "take his hood and go back wherever he came from." Although she later apologized for the statement, it was believed that her trip to Nigeria more than any other factor, was responsible for her Senate re-election defeat.

The letter written by General Abacha to President Clinton, in which the Nigerian leader expressed gratitude to the President for his assistance to Nigeria but expressed disappointment that the United States had refused removing Nigeria from the list of countries involved in drugs, despite, according to the letter, all the efforts Nigeria was making to free the country from this scourge. As the letter was written just about the time President Clinton was running for re-election, General Abacha also wished President Clinton the best at the polls.[138]

However, one development that came out of the change in America's relationship with Nigeria during the difficult periods of Babangida and Abacha regime was the significant change in the role of the United States Ambassador to Nigeria, Walter Carrington. A Nigerian Social Scientist, Kayode Soremekun, summarised this succinctly:

> One remarkable phenomenon in this testy face-off between Nigeria [and] the United States was the rather transformed role of the United States Ambassador to Nigeria. As the military rule over-reached itself in Nigeria, Walter Carrington ... became more visible on the positive side of the democracy barricade. Indeed at a point in time he was clearly in the vanguard of the opposition to military rule in Nigeria. Analysts that sought to explain his behavior were of the view that his pigmentation was a source of bonding such that he could not but be visible on the side of pro-democracy forces in Nigeria. As attractive as this argument may appear to be, it ignored the fact that, earlier on, particularly under the Bush administration, another US ambassador played a similar role in Kenya. Consequently what best explains Carrington's unusual diplomatic offensive was a new US policy that emphasized the promotion of democracy and human rights.[139]

Carrington confirmed later that it was tasking being America's Ambassador in Nigeria during the Abacha period and that the regime made several attempts to kill him. He specifically mentioned two instances when the Abacha regime attempted to terminate his life – one through shooting of his car and the other through kidnapping. He, however, said that embassy intelligence got wind of these and alerted him.[140] Things were not particularly convenient for the Nigerian Ambassador to the United States during this period, Alhaji Hassan Adamu. He assumed office at a most difficult time in the Nigeria-United States relations and for most of his time in Washington, the relationship did not improve.

The Abdulsalami Abubakar Years

The extent of local tension and external criticism gave Abdulsalami Abubakar very few options as to steps he could take on the issue of human-rights and democracy. By the time he assumed office, there were two sets of "coup" convicts that were in jail. The calibre of these sets of convicts was also important: the first set included the former Head of State, Olusegun Obasanjo and his deputy Yar'Adua who had actually been killed in detention, while the second set included Abacha's own deputy Oladipo Diya and key Ministers in his cabinet. Apart from these set of alleged coup convicts, also in jail was the winner of the annulled election, Chief Abiola. The hanging of the Ogoni activists had also brought Nigeria to the tribunal of international opinion and the country had already been suspended from the Commonwealth. In short, by the time Abubakar assumed office, he had very little option other than to embark on a charm offensive especially on issues relating to human rights and the return of the country to democracy.

From the time he took over and gave indications of reaching out to the international community of issues concerning human rights and democracy, the United States immediately extended hands of support. Within weeks of his assumption of power, a strong American delegation, headed by US Under-Secretary of State, Thomas Pickering and including the Assistant Secretary of State for African Affairs, Susan Rice travelled to Nigeria where they met Nigerian officials and also met Chief Abiola. It was, however while they were still meeting Abiola that he fell ill and was taken to the hospital where he later died.

The death of Abiola in the presence of American officials was a slight embarrassment as there were those who believed that the Americans could have had something to do with the death. In a letter written on 7 July, President Bill Clinton noted how deeply sad he felt about the death of Chief Abiola, who he described as "a distinguished citizen and patriot of Nigeria". While not going too deep into details, he pointed out in the letter that Members of a US delegation led by Under Secretary of State Thomas Pickering and Nigerian officials were with Chief Abiola when he fell ill. He then went on to express his admiration for the "efforts of the new Head of State General Abdulsalami Abubakar to restore public confidence in the Government of Nigeria and to take crucial initial steps to embark on a credible transition to a civilian democratic rule". He concluded his letter by urging the Government of Nigeria "to continue and to expedite this transition and call upon all the people of Nigeria to contribute peacefully and constructively to build a brighter future for the country". When ultimately General Abubakar handed over power to President Olusegun Obasanjo, the chapter closed in America's dealing with Nigeria Military leaders and as will be shown in Chapter 7, the United States has been contributing to the development of democracy and good governance in Nigeria since the re-establishment of democracy.

Conclusion

Addressing the key issues of democracy and human rights was perhaps the most profound challenge that faced the United States in its dealing with military rule in Nigeria. Having pointed this out, however, it is also important to note that America's desire for the establishment of democracy in Nigeria or even the willingness to fight for human rights were not issues that existed under all the military administrations that governed Nigeria. Indeed, the evidence shows that for most of the early periods, during the administrations of Aguyi Ironsi, Yakubu Gowon, Murtala Mohammed/Olusegun Obasanjo and even that of Mohammadu Buhari, issues like human rights and democracy were not profound influences on America's relations with Nigeria. This should not be particularly surprising as it was the period of the Cold War when different considerations underlined America's policy towards Africa and other developing countries. Things however began to change with the end of the Cold War and the simultaneous increase in democratic agitations across the world. The United States, which had been tolerant of dictators in many African countries in the fight against "Communist threats" now found itself championing democratic and human right causes. This explains why the United States had difficult times with Generals Babangida and Abacha. Even though the extent of democratic and human rights violations of these two regimes were worse than most of the military rulers that came before them, it would forever remain one of the tantalising conjectures of history whether America's relationships with the two leaders would have been different if they had administered Nigeria during the peak of the Cold War and had maintained overtly pro-American positions.

End Notes

[126] These administrations were those led by Generals Aguyi Ironsi, Yakubu Gowon, Murtala Mohammed and Olusegun Obasanjo, Mohammadu Buhari, Ibrahim Babangida, Sanni Abacha and Abubakar Abdusalami.

[127] See Isawa Elaigwu, *Gowon: The Biography of a Soldier-Statesman* Ibadan: West Book Publshers, 1985. p. 126.

[128] The issue of the Nigerian civil war being a "British problem" was an issue that came up at different times during the civil war period. For example, the Western Region Commissioner of Agriculture, Prince Alade Lamuye noted it during his discussion with the United States Consul in Ibadan in February 1970. See *Daily Times*, 13 February 1970.

[129] See, Adebayo calls for accurate Reports on Nigeria, *Daily Sketch*, 8 September 1967.

[130] See *New Nigeria*, 4 February 1970.

[131] See *Morning Post*, 9 February 1970.

132. For example it was opposed to any form of total reconciliation to the Biafra secessionists, arguing that they should be taught that secession does not pay and that culprits should be made to be aware of the "effect and consequences of their guilt". See ibid.

133. An example of this was the case of the Governor of Rivers State, Commander Diette Spiff, who physically abused a journalist, Nimierre Amakiri, for writing an Newspaper article critical of his administration.

134. The most profound of this was the death sentence that was passed (and later carried out) on the three people convicted for drug trafficking. The three, Bernard Ogedegbe, Bartholomew Owoh and Lawal Ojulope, were executed on April 14, 1985

135. *National Concord*, 12 June 1993.

136. See details in Kayode Soremekun "International Dimensions of the Democratic Ferment in Nigeria", in *Governance and Democratization in West Africa* CODESRIA Publications, Dakar, Senegal, 1999.

137. See Ikimi i Defence of Nigeria, *Daily Times*, 16 August 1995.

138. See Reuben Abati, Abacha's Letter to Clinton, *The Guardian*, October 11 1996.

139. Kayode Soremekun, " International Dimensions of The Democratic Ferment in Africa: An Insider's View".

140. See, Walter Carrington, "Abacha Almost Killed me", *P.M. News* (Lagos) July 23 2010.

Chapter Five

Convergence and Divergence in Nigeria-United States Policy on the Issue of Majority Rule in Southern Africa

Shola OMOREGIE

Although the political situation in Southern Africa was to become one of the most important issues that underlined diplomatic relations between the United States and Nigeria during the first fifty years of Nigeria's independence, the subject did not come to the fore during the first few years of Nigeria's independence. There are at least three reasons for this. First, Nigeria devoted the immediate post-independence years to defining the focus of its international diplomacy, and beyond the strong desire to remain close to Britain and the Commonwealth, there was no issue that was particularly strong in Nigeria's diplomacy.

Second, the Organization of African Unity (OAU), the continental organization that was to be at the forefront of the struggle for majority rule and the eradication of apartheid in South Africa was not established until 1963 and even for the first few years after its establishment, it offered very little beyond platitudinous condemnation of the illegal apartheid regime in South Africa.

Third, some of the key issues that were to bring southern Africa into the focus of international condemnation, like the Unilateral Declaration of Independence (UDI) in the former Rhodesia, and the Soweto massacre, were yet to occur. Although the Sharpeville massacre had occurred just when Nigeria was a few months into its independence, nothing of major issue occurred again in the region until 1965 when Ian Smith made the unilateral declaration of independence.

All of these made Southern Africa an issue of only minor

importance in the first years of independent Nigeria's relations with the US.

Finally, most African countries, including Nigeria, considered America a bit distant from developments in Southern Africa. Most of the decolonization problems in the region at the time of Nigeria's independence were seen largely as those of Portugal, (then colonizing Angola and Mozambique) South Africa (then illegally holding on to Namibia and implementing apartheid at home) and Britain, (then responsible for developments in Rhodesia). Against this background, southern Africa did not feature much in Nigerian-American relations in the former's immediate post-independence years.

This chapter will focus on the various ways developments in Southern Africa strained the relations between Nigeria and the United States. The central argument advanced in this chapter is that the developments in the southern African region, more than even those in West Africa where Nigeria is situated, constituted the major causes of the conflict in the relationship between the two countries.

This chapter is divided into six sections. The first section provides an overview of the issues in southern Africa and the approaches adopted by both the United States and Nigeria to developments in the region. The second section looks at the divergence of approaches to the situation in Angola, while the third focuses on the situation in Zimbabwe, where there seemed to be a form of consensus of positions. The fourth section examines how Namibia impacted Nigeria-American relations while the politics of majority rule in South Africa is discussed in the fifth section. The sixth section concludes the discussions in this chapter.

One Region, Two Countries, Two Approaches

In the first fifty years of Nigeria's independence, five southern African countries changed the politics of southern Africa. These were Angola and Mozambique, under Portuguese colonial rule but later to be left in limbo after the sudden departure of Portugal in 1974, Namibia, where South Africa maintained an illegal but entrenched hold and the South West African People's Organization (SWAPO) was fighting for independence, Rhodesia, where Ian Smith's minority regime held sway and South Africa itself, where Apartheid was in place. Nigeria fully supported the struggle for independence in all five countries, morally and financially, thus clashing with the interests of the West in the sub-region. Nigeria regarded this support as an article of faith.

Contrary to what is often assumed, it was not under the administration of Murtala Mohammed and Olusegun Obasanjo that Nigeria first took the situation in Southern Africa seriously, even if activities during the earlier periods did not bring the country into collision with other global powers. For example, even the administration of Tafawa Balewa, despite its pronounced conservatism, called for and hosted the first Commonwealth meeting on Rhodesia shortly after the unilateral declaration of independence (UDI) in 1965.

The basis of Nigeria's diplomacy in Southern Africa was always consistent, even if the extent of commitment varied from one administration to the other. It may be necessary here to explain the main position of Nigeria on Southern Africa in order to provide comparison to that of the United States. Basically, Nigeria's position was that all forms of racial discrimination had to end on the African continent. The country branded apartheid as an affront on humanity and a disgrace to all Africans and black people across the world. Being the country with the largest population in Africa and the country with the largest population of Black people in the world, Nigeria made the issue of southern Africa cardinal in all its policies until majority rule eventually came to the entire region.

But Nigeria had another reason to take the situation in Southern Africa more seriously, especially during the period of the country's civil war. Once the civil war broke out in Nigeria, white ruled South Africa, Angola, Mozambique and Rhodesia immediately gave support and encouragement to the Biafra secessionists.[141] The objective of the white minority regimes was to see to the dismemberment of Nigeria and thus prevent the country from having a strong voice with which to intervene in the developments in Southern Africa. The nature and extent of the support brought home to Nigeria the dangers of ignoring the situation in Southern Africa. The country realized that the racist regimes in southern Africa did not wish Nigeria well. This thus reinforced the determination with which the country was willing to address the situation in Southern Africa. Nigeria's former Minister for External Affairs, the late Joseph Garba, summed up succinctly the centrality of southern Africa to Nigeria's foreign policy when he notes:

> No foreign policy issue has more preoccupied Nigerian governments since independence in 1960. Nigeria has made friends with countries with whom she had nothing in common; she has conversely made enemies with erstwhile friends --- all on the account of their attitude towards the Southern African question. We have formulated economic policies that have sometimes been detrimental to our own development because of our commitment to the eradication of apartheid. [142]

On the whole, it can be said that this was also the period that has often been considered as the "golden age in Nigeria's foreign policy. With considerable financial resources and credible leadership, the country was ready and willing to play a major role on the African continent. As Ihonvbere summed it up succinctly:

> The period .... was generally the high point of Nigeria's 'new', 'activist', and 'interventionist' foreign policy and diplomatic practice. Without doubt, it emerged the most important, most prominent, and most influential power in Africa. The West courted it, countries relied on it for financial assistance, and international organisations looked up to it as the most credible and solvent country in Africa.[143]

In assessing Nigeria's contribution to the liberation struggle in southern Africa, there was no doubt that it had the greatest impact that has been made by any country in Africa. Broadly, this can be divided into three categories: financial, military and diplomatic. The financial contribution was two-fold: funds given directly to the freedom fighters in the affected countries and those paid to the OAU Liberation Committee. Nigeria also seconded diplomatic staff to the OAU Liberation Committee. All the liberation movements fighting for independence in all the countries also received financial assistance from the Nigeria

Government. While the exact figures for all the countries may not be available, Robert Mugabe of Zimbabwe was to confirm shortly after his country's independence that Nigeria spent $8 million training Zimbabwe's armed fighters during the war of independence.[144] But apart from the assistance from the Nigerian Government, what was perhaps more profound was the level of solidarity and support demonstrated by the Nigerian people. The Nigeria Government established in December 1976, the Southern African Relief Fund (SARF) and all civil servants were made to contribute 2% of one month's salary for the liberation struggle. The military support given by the Nigerian Government was, however, somewhat minimal as it was felt that direct involvement of Nigerian soldiers in the struggle would have further created escalation. The country, however, supplied the fighters with arms and ammunitions and with logistical assistance for the movement of troops. The diplomatic support came with the centrality that the situation in Southern Africa featured in all Nigeria's official pronouncements. Indeed, any official pronouncement by a Nigerian leader was incomplete without a mention of the situation in Southern Africa.

On its part, the policy of the United States towards Southern Africa was at best ambiguous and at worst hypocritical. In April, 1969, when it was becoming clear that the situation in Southern Africa would play a major role in American foreign policy towards Africa, the State Department under Henry Kissinger commissioned a study to provide analysis of all the various scenarios that might develop in southern Africa. This study was named the National Security Council's Interdepartmental-Group Study on Southern Africa and its main conclusion was that the blacks in Southern Africa were not likely to accomplish the majority rule they desired through armed struggle. This study has received considerable academic and policy attention, most of which have been somewhat negative. The study came out with five possible options of what could happen in Southern Africa, but only three of these were considered important. The first was dubbed the "Acheson Option", and it openly advocated a blatant support for the various white minority regimes in Southern Africa.[145] Option Two, was dubbed the "Relaxation Option" and was based on the premise that greater benefit would come from a relaxation of pressure on South Africa and Rhodesia. Central to this option was a greater assurance of security to the white regimes in these countries that would make them more pliable in their domestic racial views. The third option was tagged the "Status Quo" option and it called for neither the imposition of new sanctions on Rhodesia and South Africa nor a relaxation of old ones.[146] Of all the various options, the United States decided to adopt Option 2. Whether this was the best option opened to the country at the time would remain a matter of opinion but the general assumption was that this policy was in line with Kissinger's general strategy of maintaining "stable" global order that was favorable to American interest, especially against the strain placed on the country's foreign policy machinery by the Vietnam war.[147]

On the whole, at the centre of the policy was the somewhat contradictory policy that all forms of racial discrimination were bad but at the same time, solutions to the problem in southern Africa had to be through negotiation, even though this policy had been known to fail over the years. As will be shown later in this chapter, the entire problem was also colored by the then prevailing Cold War, which added the dimension of American/ Soviet tension to all discussions. Indeed, it is possible to argue that the situation in Southern Africa presented successive governments in the United States with their greatest moral challenge throughout the Cold War period. Because of the advertised love for "Freedom" and "Liberty" which the American founders fought to establish, the country was morally bound to support the struggle for majority rule in Southern Africa. At the time most African countries won their independence, the wave of black emancipation, championed by individuals like Martin Luther King and others was also changing the nature of racial relations in the United States. Consequently, American attitudes increasingly favored support for majority rule in South Africa. However, this was also the peak of the Cold War, when other major issues like the Cuban Missile crisis and other major issues were bringing home to the United States the implications of Soviet advancements in other parts of the world where American interests were paramount. Inevitably, on most of the key issues that emerged in Southern Africa during Nigeria's first fifty years of independence, there were many areas of convergence and divergence in the relationship between the country and the United States.

Angola: The First Major Battleground for Nigerian-American Tension in Southern Africa

Because of Nigeria's avowed support for the liberation movements, US support for the minority regimes and the National Union for the Total Independence of Angola (UNITA) set the stage for confrontation between the two nations. Relations became strained in 1976 when both countries adopted contrasting policy stances on the events in Angola. The United States had been quite worried over the manifest upsurge of Soviet-Cuban presence in Angola in the mid 1970s, and as was usual during the Cold War, decided to scale-up its interest through its policy of containment in Africa to checkmate the Soviets. Coming however, at a time when Nigeria's influence in Africa was at its highest, and its economic fortunes brighter than ever before, thanks to the abundance of petro-dollars, a clash was inevitable. Nigeria supported the People's Movement for the Liberation of Angola - Labor Party (MPLA), while the United States joined apartheid South Africa in supporting the UNITA.

Contrary to what is often believed, Nigeria's support for the MPLA was not immediate nor was it entirely predicated on Soviet support for the liberation movement. Indeed, the Nigerian government was initially opposed to Soviet/Cuban support for the MPLA on the grounds that Africa should not be opened to foreign intervention. Nigeria was in favor of the formation of a unity government that would bring together all the sides and Nigeria's Minister for External Affairs did visit Angola in October 1975 to further advance this line of action. He even went as far as to suggest during the visit that colonial Portugal should postpone the independence of Angola until this was sorted out.[148]

Nigeria's position however soon changed when it was discovered that UNITA was receiving support from the apartheid South African government. Nigerians saw this as an attempt by the West to continue the exploitation of Angolan mineral resources even after independence from Portugal. While

Nigeria was trying to see to the formation of the government of national unity (GNU) where all the disputing parties would be well represented, the United States lent its support to UNITA against the MPLA, which African nations regarded as the legitimate government of Angola. UNITA, apart from the support it received from the racist government of South Africa, was being given $40 - $50 million dollars in annual assistance by the United States, in addition to supplies of Stinger missiles and spare parts. Nigeria felt so strongly about this and rightly saw the United States as an ally of a racist regime. From this moment, Nigeria changed from neutrality to an open support for the MPLA. Indeed, Nigeria believed very strongly that the South African leader, John Vorster, had gone into Angola to protect American interest against what was perceived as a Communist onslaught. The American government was deeply upset at the change of stance from Nigeria and the US President, Gerald Ford, wrote a confidential letter to African leaders, warning them of the dangers of Communism. All the African leaders that had recognized MPLA were advised to withdraw such recognition.

The Nigerian government did not take kindly to President Ford's letter to General Murtala Mohammed denouncing Soviet-Cuban interference in Angola. Murtala described the letter as "overbearing directive and an insult to African leaders". At the OAU Summit in January 1976, General Murtala Mohammed gave a major speech in which he was openly critical of American strategy in Angola. In the speech, he noted:

> Gone are the days when Africa will ever bow to the threat of any so-called superpower. Not content with its clandestine support and outpouring of arms into Angola to create confusion and bloodshed, the United States President took it upon himself to instruct African Heads of State and Government, by a circular letter, to insist on the withdrawal of Soviet and Cuban Advisers from Angola as a precondition for the withdrawal of South Africa and other military adventurers. This constitutes a most intolerable presumption and a flagrant insult to the intelligence of African rulers.[149]

From this moment, the relationship between Nigeria and the United States began the downward plunge where it remained during the entire period of Murtala Mohammed's administration. Indeed, it was not long afterwards that General Mohammed was killed in an abortive coup in February 1976 following which some Nigerian students carried placards implying a link between the incident and the Central Intelligence Agency. That link was never proven and the culprits from the Nigerian Armed Forces were tried and executed.

On Angola, Nigeria took a number of steps to deliberately pull the rug out from under the United States. After learning that South Africa had crossed the Cunene River and was moving towards Luanda, the then Nigeria's External Affairs Minister, Joseph Garba, summoned the American Ambassador to Nigeria, Donald Easum to his office to launch an official protest on the assumption that South Africa would not move towards Luanda without the United States' knowledge. The Ambassador had barely left Garba's office when Garba was summoned to Dodan Barracks by the late General Murtala Mohammed and was instructed to recognise the MPLA.[150]

However, contrary to what is often believed, Nigeria's relationship with the United States under Murtala Mohammed did not actually end on a completely sour note. Indeed, it got to the stage where Nigeria felt it may have overreacted on the Angolan issue and saw a need to ease the tension between the two countries. At the instance of the late Mallam Aminu Kano, who had been a respected figure and a mentor to General Murtala Mohammed, Nigeria decided to mend fences with the United States. Joseph Garba requested a meeting with Henry Kissinger. The United States was glad to receive the request and Kissinger broke an engagement on the West Coast to attend the meeting in October 1975 where both sides exchanged views frankly.[151] Not long afterwards, Murtala was killed in an abortive coup in February, 1976.

When Angola obtained its independence under the Government MPLA and then slid into a civil war, the relationship between Nigeria and the United States over Angola shifted to another level as both sides began supporting rival factions in the conflict. However, it is also important to say that from this moment, Angola came down in the level of importance in the Nigerian-American relations as both sides seemed to have agreed to disagree on the subject. As the war went on, Nigeria continued to criticize UNITA and its sub-regional backer, apartheid South Africa more than the country was criticizing the United States for supporting the rebel force. The extent of the financial resources available to the MPLA government through its control of the country's oil resources also meant that Nigeria did not need to assist the Angolan Government militarily.

The end of the Cold War caused another major shift. With worry about Soviet activities removed, the United States was willing to see developments in Angola in a new light. After an election that was widely viewed as being free and fair and also one that was endorsed by both the United States and the United Nations, Jonas Savimbi and UNITA still continued the war against the MPLA government. This resulted in the American withdrawal of support for his rebellion. This was a coda to the story, as Angola had fallen completely off the radar completely in American-Nigerian relations by this time.

One aspect of the diplomatic relationship between Nigeria and the United States over Angola during the Kissinger period was a perception of a slight difference in outlook between the State Department in Washington and the US Embassy in Nigeria. Indeed, there were grounds to suspect that the State Department felt that America's Ambassador to Lagos, Donald Easum, was getting too friendly with Nigeria to the detriment of the United States. After Garba made a passing remark that Easum had been a "good man", Kissinger was alleged to bluntly reply "good for whom, you or us?" Easum was subsequently removed from office as the Assistant Secretary of State from Africa on the grounds that he was profoundly pro-Africa.[152] Also whilst disagreements lasted between Nigeria and the United States over apartheid in South Africa, there were also some American academics that were sympathetic to the Nigerian cause and were constantly reminding the American government that Nigeria might impose some form of economic pressure on American companies doing business in both Nigeria and apartheid South Africa.[153]

One of the most ironic dimensions of Nigerian-American relations - and also one not often recognized – is that despite initial disagreements, both countries actually took a number of united positions that ultimately helped end the conflict in

Angola. Apart from the fact that both countries were later on the same side after America ceased to support Savimbi, the United States also took a major stand against illegal diamond sales, thus undermining a major source of income for UNITA and other rebel movements in Africa. As far back as October 1999, a United States Democratic Congressman from Ohio, Tony Hall, had introduced the Consumer Access to a Responsible Accounting of Trade Act (CARAT), which required diamonds coming into the United States to be accompanied by a Certificate of Origin.[154] The United States government was to take this more seriously after it became clear that there was a link between illegal diamond sales and Al Qaeda activities against American interests. However, another country that was always lurking in the corner of American-Nigerian relations was Zimbabwe, where Ian Smith's Unilateral Declaration of Independence (UDI) of November 1965 had occasioned a bitter war of liberation against the illegal regime and where armed groups fighting for majority rule were also contending, even if only occasionally, in inter- and intra-ethnic squabbles.

The Struggle for Zimbabwean Independence and Nigerian-United States Relations

Not long after the Angolan disagreement, the leaderships in both Nigeria and the United States changed. In Nigeria, General Murtala Mohammed was killed during the abortive coup of 1975 and General Olusegun Obasanjo assumed the leadership of the country, while in the United States, Jimmy Carter was elected president, thus ending the Republican Administration of Nixon and Ford. This was to mark the beginning of a new phase in the relationship between the two countries and Zimbabwe was the beneficiary of this new relationship. Under Jimmy Carter, the United States recognized Nigeria as a stabilizing force in Africa and was willing to consult with Nigeria on African issues. The two governments appeared to have similar interests in Southern Africa.

It needs to be pointed out that for Nigeria, handling the Zimbabwean problem was somewhat difficult because unlike other countries struggling for majority rule in Southern Africa, there were no agreements among the countries in the region on one policy position. For example, there were leaders, like former President Kenneth Kaunda of Zambia, who supported Joshua Nkomo, while there were those who pitched their tent, like the late Samora Machel, with Robert Mugabe. Thus, in coming up with a position Nigeria also had to ensure that it balanced the regional situation.

In various pronouncements, both Presidents Carter and Obasanjo criticized the situation in Southern Africa. During his visit to Nigeria in March 1978, Carter condemned the "racist" policy in Southern Africa. This was a reversal of policy that the Apartheid regime in South Africa found most disturbing, such that the former South African Prime Minister, John Vorster, condemned President Carter for criticizing his country in Nigeria, a country Vorster described as being under a "military dictatorship with no press freedom".[155] During an earlier visit to the United States in October 1977, Obasanjo had told an American business audience that:

> The intransigence of the minority regimes (in Southern Africa) has created a situation whereby we have to use every weapon in our armory to bring about majority rule in Rhodesia, Namibia and South Africa. We are compelled in these circumstances to insist that those whose economic activities in these territories help to keep the minority regimes afloat cannot be our friends and should not be our friends and should not expect to profitably do business with us ... We are screening all foreign contractors and business firms with a view to discriminating against all those who have business relations with Rhodesia and South Africa. Such business firms are, however, free to discontinue their relationship or at least do nothing to expand it, if they feel their bread is better buttered on our side.

At the time both Nigeria and the United States took the developments in the region that would become Zimbabwe seriously, the military situation had reached a decisive phase. By the mid 1970s, the liberation movements ZANU and ZAPU had, through their respective armed wings, ZANLA and ZIPRA, fought the Rhodesian security forces to a standstill. Military assistance was coming to the guerrillas from the OAU Liberation Committee and from friendly neighboring states. With the independence of the former Portuguese colonies of Angola and Mozambique, both countries began imposing the UN sanctions that Portugal never implemented against the Rhodesian regime. This thus left the illegal regime in Rhodesia with only the apartheid regime in South Africa as the main source of support. On the diplomatic front, the countries in the region had formed an informal organization known as the Frontline States. Because of the level of its support for the liberation struggle in Southern Africa, Nigeria also became a member of the Frontline States.

But Nigeria realized that the fear of the United States in southern Africa as a whole was mainly because of Soviet influence. While Nigeria was not as fearful as Soviet influence in the region as America, the Obasanjo administration also felt that it was necessary to put the Soviets on the alert as well and to assure them that their actions were being watched. In short, where Southern Africa was concerned, the Obasanjo administration considered both the Soviets and the West under surveillance. In a speech made at the July 1978 OAU summit in Khartoum, Sudan, Obasanjo said:

> To the Soviet and their friends, I should like to say that having been invited to Africa in order to assist in the liberation struggle and the consolidation of national independence, they should not overstay their welcome. Africa is not about to throw off one colonial yoke for another ... To the Western powers, I say they should act in such a way that we are not led to believe that they have different concepts of independence and sovereignty for Africa and for Europe. Paratroop drops in the twentieth century are no more acceptable to us than the gunboats of the last century were to our ancestors. Convening conferences in Europe and America to decide the fate of Africa raises too many specters which should be best forgotten both in Africans' and Europeans' interests.[156]

Unlike the case of Angola where Nigeria felt there was no European country that could be held responsible for the affairs of the country after Portugal's uncoordinated departure, Nigeria realized that there was still a country (Britain) that still claimed legal and administrative rights over Rhodesia. Thus, from the outset, Nigeria tried to consider Britain's position, even if it didn't agree with it, on all issues relating to Rhodesia.

The first major diplomatic cooperation between Nigeria and the United States on the subject of Zimbabwe was the Anglo-American Proposal on Rhodesia of 1977. The proposal called for transition from white to black majority rule during 1978, with a British administrator supervising elections in which adults of all races would have the right to vote. During this period, both the Rhodesian army and the guerrilla armies would be replaced by a U.N. military force, and eventually by a new army for independent Zimbabwe, the African name for Rhodesia. The US, Britain and other nations would provide a development fund of between US$1 billion and US$1.5 billion to help revive the country's battered economy. This proposal was championed by the British Foreign Secretary, David Owen and the US Permanent Representative at the United Nations, Andrew Young. British officials emphasized that according to the Anglo-American security proposals, the new army would comprise not only the guerrillas but also "acceptable elements" of the Rhodesian forces. Moreover, they pointed out, the Rhodesian police would remain in place under the transitional leadership. Overseeing this delicate grouping of white-led police and black-controlled army units would be UN forces perhaps composed of contingents from Nigeria, Kenya and Finland. British and American officials argued that once a transitional government embracing moderate African elements was in place in Salisbury, the guerrilla armies would be under increasing pressure not to fight on for total control.

Although Nigeria had some reservations about the Anglo-American proposal, the country still decided to give it the benefit of the doubt. While addressing the United Nations General Assembly, General Obasanjo pointed out that the proposal was not perfect, but it was hoped that in the implementation of the details, some of the rough edges could be perfected. It is not impossible that Nigeria decided to give the proposal a chance because of the implicit trust that had developed between the new administration and the leadership in the White House. In the end, however, the Smith regime rejected the Proposal. It is also worth noting that the Carter administration joined Nigeria and most other African nations in rejecting the internal arrangement that brought Bishop Abel Muzorewa to power as the leader of the hyphenated state of Zimbabwe-Rhodesia.

After the Anglo-American proposal failed and movement started towards the Lancaster House Agreement, both Nigeria and the United States were also in agreement with many of the decisions that were taken. Indeed, it was somewhat of an irony that Nigeria felt more comfortable dealing with the United States on issues relating to former Rhodesia than the country did with Britain. The Nigerian leadership during this period believed that Britain was not particularly straightforward on the issue of Rhodesia and that it was the lack of support for its questionable policies from the Carter administration that constrained Whitehall from carrying out some of its hidden agenda in Rhodesia.

When Zimbabwe finally became independent, the United States was particularly appreciative of Nigeria's role. President Carter noted:

> We were particularly gratified to cooperate with Nigeria in helping to see established the new democracy in Zimbabwe. This must be followed by a sustained commitment to see the same development of a government based on majority rule and an end to racial discrimination in Namibia. We were cooperating not only with this great country but also through the United Nations and we hope to see the consummation of our efforts in the early future. The elimination of apartheid, the elimination of racial discrimination, is a goal that we share with deep commitment and with fervent effort.

Thus, with the independence of Zimbabwe, Namibia became the next centre of attention in the liberation struggle, and as will be shown in the next section, here again, Nigeria and the United States found themselves at the centre of attention.

Shortly before Zimbabwe became independent, democratic rule came to Nigeria and Shehu Shagari became the President. In the policy towards Southern Africa, there were those in the United States who felt that the return of civilian rule to Nigeria would help destroy one of the principal myth upon which South Africa's racial policies were constructed. Specifically, it was argued that Nigeria's return to civilian rule would show that democratic rule was possible in a highly pluralistic society.[157] Also in anticipation of incoming civilian rule, American scholars and policy practitioners anticipated three possible directions Nigeria foreign policy towards Southern Africa could take: the first was a continuation of the policy of deep interest in Southern Africa and a continuation of mounting deep pressure on the United States and the West to take more pro-active roles in ensuring black majority rule in Namibia and South Africa; the second was to turn inward and concern itself with domestic issues whilst only paying cosmetic and occasional attention to Southern African issues; and the third was to become more active and provide greater military support for the liberation struggle in Southern Africa.[158]

Nigeria, the United States and Namibia

In a rather curious way, the effort to bring about majority rule in Southern Africa seemed to have been taken one-step-at-a-time. Although the general condemnation of apartheid continued, it seemed that the effort of the international community had been to take each of the countries in turn. The most immediate implication of this for the United States/Nigerian relations was that it often reflected the changing nature of the leaderships in the two countries. After the somewhat boisterous relationship between Obasanjo and Carter that assisted in bringing independence to Zimbabwe, President Carter lost the 1980 election and was replaced by Ronald Reagan who found an instant ally in British Prime Minister Margaret Thatcher. Not long afterwards too, the leadership in Nigeria also changed as President Obasanjo handed over power to Alhaji Shehu Shagari in a transition from military to civilian governments. It was thus under a different framework that the politics for majority rule in Namibia had to be negotiated.

The nature of the problem in Namibia was quite different from that of Zimbabwe as the country with whom the international community had to negotiate – South Africa – was the bastion of racist rule in the continent and was concerned at the rapidity with which neighboring countries were falling to African rule. Consequently, by the time international attention was focused on Namibia the problem was not only the change of leadership in the United States but also the recalcitrance of a country that saw itself increasingly under siege and thus was more unwilling to co-operate with the international community.

Possibly against the background of the pronouncements during the election campaign and possibly because he came from a political party that was perceived as being unsympathetic towards Africa, the Nigerian government was expecting a difficult time from President Ronald Reagan even before he came to power. Nigeria's Foreign Affairs Minister during the period had committed what many consider as a diplomatic blunder when he said Nigeria preferred a Carter victory in the Presidential election. Although there were various attempts to retract this statement, it was believed that the blunder had already been registered in the minds of the Republicans. After the election, a key actor in the formulation of Nigeria's foreign policy during the period, Bolaji Akinyemi, who held the position of the Director-General of the Nigerian Institute of International Affairs, wrote an opinion piece in Nigeria's foremost newspaper, *The Sunday Times* where he addressed some of the key issues that had been raised by Reagan during the election campaign touching on the situations in Namibia and Southern Africa.

Bolaji Akinyemi presented Nigeria's position on the crucial question of "linkage" which Kissinger established and which the incoming Reagan administration was determined to adopt in its fight against Communist advances in Southern Africa. Akinyemi noted that Soviet policies in Africa, unlike those of the United States, were in conformity with Nigeria's position.[159] He pointed out that Nigeria would not subscribe to the linkage policy that wanted the exit of the Soviet as a condition for Namibia's independence for at least three reasons: first, it was the Soviets that repelled South Africa from taking over Angola; second, it was due to Soviet help that the OAU concept of territorial integrity had been defended where that concept had been under threat; and third, the Soviet Union was an important country that had provided financial assistance and material support to liberation movements in southern Africa.

From the moment Reagan assumed power he was quite definite that it would not be business as usual and that Cold War politics would be the determining factor in all his policies. Consistent with this view, he developed a "linkage policy" on the issue of Namibian independence. Broadly, the whole idea of the linkage policy was Namibian independence was tied to the withdrawal of Cuban troops from Angola. At this period there was sizeable number of Cuban troops in Angola assisting the MPLA government in repelling attacks from South Africa. The Reagan administration gave a clear endorsement to the belief by the apartheid government that the unconditional independence of Namibia would open South Africa to Communist onslaught, especially as it was known that the South West African People's Organization (SWAPO) was billed to take over the leadership of Namibia. In the calculation of both the Reagan administration and the apartheid regime, this would open South Africa to Communist siege.

Nigeria obviously did not share this sentiment. As far as the Nigerian government was concerned, Namibian independence was not negotiable. The Shagari administration seemed to have given in to the Reagan philosophy, as the administration also gave some form of endorsement to the link Reagan was making as a condition for Namibian independence. It was, however, not long before the Shagari administration was overthrown and replaced by another military regime headed by General Muhammadu Buhari, which continued the radical position that was started by the Murtala and Obasanjo administration. Namibia advanced no closer to independence, however, until the situation in South Africa changed.

From the time significant changes began in South Africa and the country was willing to alter its stance on Namibia, the country ceased to feature prominently in American-Nigerian relations. Both countries began to give encouragement to South Africa to continue with the process towards the independence of Namibia. However, while Nigeria was cautious and watched every development with considerable trepidation, the United States was quite demonstrative with the way it encouraged the South African government.

On the divergence of position over Namibia, the former

American Ambassador to Nigeria, Ambassador Princeton Lyman noted:

> We want independence for Namibia. But saying it will not make it so... We are castigated for our assessment of the Angola-Namibia connection. But no one else has proposed an alternative – one that involves all the parties who are involved – that will untangle this combination of illegal occupation, cross-border violence and civil war, that runs from Pretoria, through Windhoek to Luanda and that involves outside men and arms that we cannot ignore."[160]

But while the Namibian issue was still going on, bringing majority rule to South Africa continued to be a recurring factor in Nigeria-United States relations.

Nigeria, the United States and South Africa

Both Nigeria and the United States appreciated that South Africa was the real prize in the struggle for majority rule in Southern Africa and both also seemed to realize that the struggle for the independence of the country was going to be far more difficult than the cases of Angola, Mozambique, Namibia and Zimbabwe. Indeed, it would appear that neither Nigeria nor the United States expected majority rule in South Africa to come easily. A document the United States government had commissioned much earlier had concluded that Blacks in South Africa would not attain the majority rule they desired quite easily. This report, which seemed to have been predicated on the military might of South Africa and the apparent weakness of the guerrilla movements, did not take into consideration the possibility of internal change in dynamics of the apartheid regime. On its part, Nigeria too believed that the walls of apartheid, unlike that of the Biblical Jericho, would not come down at a mere trumpet blast. Nigeria realized that the apartheid machinery was too strong for the guerrilla movement to remove. It was, however, the expectation of the country that with the independence of all the states surrounding South Africa, the country would become more vulnerable to external pressure, thus forcing the apartheid regime to come to the negotiating table. In short, Nigeria realized that the attainment of majority rule in South Africa would come not through armed struggle and that diplomacy would have to be the only way out. Thus, there was a sort of belief from both Nigeria and the United States that negotiation was the answer. This was, however, never really discussed between the two countries.

The confluence of positions ended there, however. The Reagan administration that took over from President Carter found a ready ally in the British Prime Minister, Margaret Thatcher to maintain the position that apartheid South Africa should be given the opportunity to reform. Nigeria vehemently rejected this position, and Nigerian/US relations were at their lowest ebb during the Reagan administration. After General Babangida overthrew the Buhari administration, Nigeria's deep commitment to majority rule in Southern Africa continued, as did the low tone of the relationship with the United States.

Since Nigeria could not militarily intervene in South Africa largely because of logistical issues, the West African nation concentrated attention to supporting the liberation struggle and also to fighting apartheid through international organisations, especially the United Nations. It was the latter that brought Nigeria into collision with the United States. Since the general belief of the Nigerian government was that the United States was among the key countries supporting apartheid in South Africa, some of the criticisms levelled against South Africa extended to the United States. When Nigeria assumed the position of the Chair of the UN Special Committee Against Apartheid, established in 1962 by General Assembly resolution 1761 (XVII) of November 6, 1962, there were several occasions when the country had to specifically condemn actions taken by the United States. For example, in February 1982, when the United States relaxed arms embargo against South Africa, Nigeria openly condemned this action, with the Chairman of the UN Special Committee on apartheid, Alhaji Yusuf Maitama Sule who was also Nigeria's permanent Representative to the UN saying that this step could further encourage South Africa's intransigence. He described it as "regrettable".[161] But although relations between Nigeria and United States during the Reagan period were not particularly friendly, there were still high-level visits. For example,

Agricultural Secretary John R., Block and Commerce Secretary visited Nigeria not long after the administration took over. Also Vice President George H.W. Bush visited Nigeria in November 1982, while General Vernon A. Walters visited twice in 1984 and 1985 as President Reagan's Special Representative.

Nigeria also used its economic strength to force American companies to undertake policies they may not have adopted otherwise. For example, when in 1976 the Federal Government of Nigeria decided to ban foreign companies with interests in South Africa from operating and gaining contracts in Nigeria, the First National City Bank of New York and the Chase Manhattan Bank announced the cessation of syndicated loans to the South African government and its agencies. Also in April 1978, the banking Committee of the United States House of Representatives voted to stop all US Export/Import bank loans to South Africa. Another strategy adopted by the Nigerian government was to attempt to make a distinction between the State Department/White House and the Congress. The Nigerian government praised the American Congress anytime it passed a resolution that fell in line with Nigeria's position on South Africa. Also the wording of Nigeria's responses to developments was often phrased in such a way as to make a distinction between elected representatives in the government. For examples, in October 1986, after the Congress voted to impose sanctions on apartheid regime in South Africa, the Nigerian government noted that by that development, "the American people, through their elected representatives have now joined the mainstream of world opinion in its fight against the racist regime".[162]

The situation changed a bit after the end of the Reagan years. Although his successor, George Bush had been his Vice President, there was a slight change in America's relations with Africa. Indeed, as noted in Chapter 4, both George Bush and President Babangida met to discuss bilateral issues. In short, from the time George Bush came to power and with the increasing changes in Southern Africa, the extent to which South Africa could be a factor in the tension between Nigeria and the United States decreased significantly. But there was another reason why things slowed down on the Southern African end — the increasing weakness of the Nigerian economy. With the downturn in the economy, the extent to which the country could pursue a forceful foreign policy was drastically reduced. It would, indeed, remain one of the tantalizing conjectures of diplomatic politics if Nigeria would have been able to pursue its clear anti-American stance over Southern Africa if the hard-line leaders at the helms of affairs in Nigeria during the time have had to contend with a weak economy.

For the United States, there was an explanation for the divergence on the politics of Southern Africa. This has been well expressed by the country's former Ambassador to Nigeria, Ambassador Princeton Lyman, in a speech he made at the Nigerian Institute of International Affairs, (NIIA) on 30 April, 1987. He pointed out:

> There is a popular misperception, not unanimous by far, but still much too popular, that the United States is not seriously opposed to apartheid. This perception, quite frankly, misses the point... There are lots of reasons why we are opposed to apartheid; it runs counter to our values; it touches on very crucial domestic issues in the United States of racial equality; and it is a source of the instability that threatens the entire Southern Africa. Strip away the moral lessons and there would still be the realpolitik of the danger that apartheid poses to our interest. There cannot be continued economic progress in South Africa with apartheid; there cannot be peace in southern Africa. Without peace, others will put in arms, extend their influence, seem to turn the peoples of the region against the West. Turmoil, war, arms from our competitors: None of this works to the interest of the United States as a world power ... When you add the power of morality to this array of self-interest, our opposition to apartheid is overwhelming.

He then noted what he considered as the crux of the differences between Nigeria and the United States on the issue of apartheid in South Africa:

> [Thus] the issue between us is how to bring about the end of apartheid. ... If apartheid ends in an orgy of destruction and through the pushing aside of reasonable leaders by the purveyors of violence, then apartheid will surely end but the result will be one of devastation, suffering and perhaps dictatorship. Who will

pay the price of recovery? And who will keep those who come to power by the gun from keeping power by the gun. These are not questions we can ignore simply because we want apartheid to end. Nor will African countries ignore them when they arise. The difference between us is that we do not feel we can ignore these questions now.

In his conclusion, he argues that on southern Africa, the relationship between Nigeria and the United States have been long on rhetoric and not much on cooperative analysis and action.

Throughout the periods Nigeria had disagreements with the United States over southern Africa, the fora where many of the disagreement played out was on the floor of the United Nations, where Nigeria often ended up openly criticising the stance of the United States. This was an issue that the United States did not feel comfortable about. While the United States recognised and respected Nigeria for being non-aligned, it did not feel comfortable with the desire to concentrate criticism on the US while allowing the Soviet Union to escape untouched. For example, the former US Ambassador to Nigeria noted that the Non Aligned Movement never named Soviet Union in the UN resolutions condemning foreign forces or human right violations in Afghanistan, even though the only foreign forces there then were Soviet or to criticise Vietnam for its occupation of Cambodia. However, the former United States Ambassador to Nigeria, Princeton Lyman, noted that in the last General Assembly, there were 15 resolutions tabled on Southern Africa which singled out the United States for criticism and that Nigeria voted 15 times out of 15 to condemn the United States by name.

Conclusion

Most academic and policy analysts consider the situation in Southern Africa as the most important diplomatic issue between Nigeria and the United States throughout the first fifty years of Nigeria's independence. As shown in this chapter, there were areas of convergence and those of divergence. However, what seemed certain in all these was that both countries were acting to protect their respective national interests. For example, while Nigeria was unequivocal in its stance that Apartheid was repugnant and should be eradicated by whatever means possible, the United States conceded the injustice of the Apartheid philosophy but insisted that it should be stopped through negotiation, even after it became clear that the idea of negotiation was not working. However, because of the huge economic investment in the Southern African region, the American Government realized that it had to strike a balance between many tendencies. Ironically, the way independence eventually came to South Africa, the bastion of racist rule in Africa, was such that gave both Nigeria and the United States vindication in their discordant strategies. The United States could argue that the ultimate round-table discussion that saw the freeing of Nelson Mandela and the eventual independence of South Africa was a vindication of its strategy that peaceful negotiation was more effective than revolutionary militancy and that round table discussion was able to achieve within months what force failed to accomplish in more than three decades. Nigeria, on its part could argue, quite legitimately that peaceful negotiation was only considered by the Apartheid regime after an effective armed struggle, coupled with international sanctions that had weakened the resolve of the apartheid regime. Nigeria had chaired the UN General Assembly Special Committee against Apartheid for over two decades. It used this means to harness international pressure on the Apartheid regime, including the imposition of sanctions which the United States congress supported, thanks to the tireless efforts of Senator Edward Kennedy and others.

For Nigeria, Southern African liberation was a subject of considerable interest, especially during the mid 1970s to the first half of the 1980s. The country felt it stood up while countries like Britain and the United States were sympathetic to the Apartheid regime. It is, however, ironic to many Nigerians that most Southern African countries especially South Africa, have targeted Nigeria and Nigerians for wanton vilification. They are also surprised that it was the Americans, British and others that are reaping better benefit for a society whose establishment Nigerians believe that these countries contributed very minimally to free from the burden of Apartheid.

End Notes

141. See Olayiwola Abegunrin, Nigeria Foreign Policy Under Military Rule 1966 – 1969, Westport: Praeger, 2003, p. 35.

142. Joseph Garba, Diplomatic Soldiering: Nigerian Foreign Policy 1975 – 1979, Ibadan; Spectrum Books, 1987, p. 93.

143. Julius Ihonvbere (1994: 45 – 46).

144. *Nigerian Tribune,* (Ibadan) 11 August 1984.

145. This was named after the United States former Secretary of State Dean Acheson, who openly advocated this position.

146. National Security Council Memorandum 39, prepared by the US National Security Council Interdepartmental Group for Africa, 1969.

147. See Bassey Atte, *Decolonization and Dependence: The Development of Nigerian-US Relations 1960 – 1984,* Boulder: Westview, 1987. p. 183.

148. For more discussion on this, see, Bolaji Akinyemi, "Mohammed/Obasanjo Foreign Policy, in Oyeleye Oyediran (Ed) *Nigeria Government and Politics under the Military, 1976 – 1979,* (Lagos: Macmillan Press, 1979, p. 155.

149. See, Murtala Obasanjo, "Africa has Come of Age" Extraordinary Summit of the OAU, Addis Ababa, Ethiopia, 10 – 11 January 1976, (Lagos: Ministry of Information, 1976.

150. See Joseph Garba, *Diplomatic Soldiering: Nigeria Foreign Policy 1975 – 1979,* Ibadan: Spectrum Books 1987.

151. Joseph Garba op-cit, p. 29.

152. Ibid.

153. One such scholar was Professor Jean Herskovits, who sent the text of her testimony before the sub-Committee on Foreign Relation of the United States Senate to the Nigeria Foreign Affairs Minister, Joseph Garba, in May 1976.

154. For more on this, see, Abiodun Alao, *The Tragedy of Endowment: Natural Resources and Conflict in Africa,* Rochester: University of Rochester Press, 2007, p. 146.

155. See Olayiwola Abegunrin, op-cit, p. 73.

156. Quoted from Olayiwola Abegunrin, op-cit, p. 73.

[157.] See Bolaji Akinyemi and John Stremlau, Nigerian-American Relations: A Report on Nigerian-American Dialogue, (A Dialogue sponsored by the Nigerian Institute of International Affairs and The Rockefeller Foundation) Bellagio, Italy, October 9 – 12 1978.

[158.] Ibid.

[159.] See Bolaji Akinyemi, "Reagan's African Policy and Nigeria", *Sunday Times* 14 December 1980.

[160.] Princeton Lyman, "Nigerian –United States Relations", delivered at the Nigerian Institute of International Affairs, April 30, 1987.

[161.] Press Release No. 349 Executive Office of the President, Lagos March 4, 1982.

[162.] Press Release No. 1590, Federal Ministry of Information and Culture Lagos, October 3 1986.

Chapter Six

The Military Dimension in the Relationship Between the United States and Nigeria

Abiodun ALAO

Defence and security issues have always been crucial in Nigerian-American relations, and apart from trade and consular matters, defence and security, broadly defined, seem to be the most prominent on-going matters in the diplomatic relations between the two countries in the last fifty years. A number of reasons seem to underline the importance of defence and security issues in Nigerian-American relations. First, there have been key security issues in Nigeria that have attracted the attention and concern of the United States, and consequently, Washington has been particularly interested in exploring discussions with Nigeria around these areas. Second, the United States' role as a global superpower since the Second World War and Nigeria's position as a key strategic military power in Africa almost guarantee that Nigeria would feature prominently in American considerations. This is particularly the case because the US has woven its strategic policies in the West African sub-region around Nigeria. Third, the US has always wanted to make Nigeria a strategic military training centre for African countries which had historically been tied to their erstwhile colonial masters for their training needs. While Washington realised that it might not be able to rival European military institutions like Sandhurst, it also wanted to attract the cream of the African armed forces to come to its military academies and Nigeria, having one of the most advanced military establishments on the continent was a strategic area to start. Fourth, Nigeria occupies a principal position as a major source of oil for the United States. Indeed, the country is the fifth largest oil supplier to the US and with the growing importance of the country in global oil supplies and the instability in some of the largest oil producing countries, it has become vital for the United States to take the affairs of the sub Saharan region of West Africa seriously. Finally, America's arms procurement companies have always targeted Africa as a primary market for their wares and again, Nigeria has been a source of considerable interest. Indeed, the military-industrial complex that was a key component for most of the Cold War era always paid special attention to Africa.

The objective of this chapter is to look at the nature of defence and security issues that have emerged in Nigerian-American relations in the last fifty years. The chapter is divided into six major sections, with the first looking at the role the United States has played in the provision of training for military personnel in Nigeria. This section includes the controversy over the activities of the Military Professional Resources Inc (MPRI) and United States Africa Command (AFRICOM). The second focuses on the nature of arms sales by American companies to Nigeria. The third discusses the military objectives of the United States to defend key sources of oil supplies in Nigeria and the Gulf of Guinea, while the fourth looks at the relationship between the United States and Nigeria in the desire to ensure peace and stability in Africa. The fifth section discusses the involvement of Nigerians serving in the American armed forces, while the sixth concludes discussions in the chapter. The other key issues that come under defence and security in the relationship between the two countries including the involvement of the United States in the Nigerian Civil War and the war on terror are separate discussions in this book.

United States and the Training of Nigerian Military Personnel

While historically Nigeria had no military links with the United States before independence, things began to change almost immediately afterwards. The United States actually began to rival Britain as the country of natural choice for Nigeria's defence training,[163] and there has also been significant diversion of interest and attention to the country in the last few decades. In

1970, a training programme was initiated for the Nigerian armed forces in the United States and many Nigerian military officers, including those who were later to become heads of state, like Buhari and Babangida, benefitted from this training. Not long after this programme was initiated, senior military officers from the US National War College, led by Rear Admiral Jackson, visited Nigeria and met with the Chief of Army Staff, Brigadier Hassan Usman Katsina and senior officers of the Nigeria Defence force.[164]

Broadly, there are four ways that both the United States and Nigeria have been connected in the area of military training. These are: (a) the training of Nigerian military officers in American military institutions, (b) joint military operations between Nigerian and American military officers, (c) through the gifts given to the Nigerian military by the United States and (d) through the usage of American defence hardware in Nigerian military institutions.

a. The Training of Nigerian Military Personnel in American Military Institutions

For the first few years of independence, Nigeria relied mostly on Britain, and to an extent, other Commonwealth countries like India, for its military training. Institutions like Sandhurst and Moors were the institutions that registered in the minds of many Nigerians. By the middle of the first decade, however, American military institutions had started making inroads into military training in Nigeria. In a way, turning away from Britain showed Nigerians that the proposed Anglo-Nigerian Defence Pact, which was abrogated because of protests from Nigerians, especially university students, had been completely thrown overboard.

But offering military training for Nigerian officers created subtle dilemma for the United States. While in theory the United States wanted to provide military training for Nigerian personnel, it was also conscious of the human rights records of the Nigerian armed forces. Thus, although military links existed between Nigeria and the United States during the era of military leadership, these were minimal and nothing was done to give it the publicity that was to be given in later years to the same links during the period of the civilian rule. Indeed, during the Abacha administration, there was a complete embargo on all forms of military links between Nigeria and the United States.

After the return of civilian rule in 1999, the training of Nigerian military personnel in the United States increased significantly. This new interest also coincided with the period when America realised the growing importance of Nigerian oil. From this period, there has been increasing American involvement in the Nigerian military itself.

In 2000 and 2001, the United States trained five Nigerian battalions for peacekeeping operations in Sierra Leone under "Operation Focus Relief." In 2003, the United States gave Nigeria four Coast Guard naval vessels to assist the Nigerian Navy in its ability to conduct search and rescue operations, environmental protection of coastal resources, tackle illegal fishing, smuggling and oil bunkering (stealing), and patrol waterways.[165]

A major issue that has emerged in Nigeria's military relations with the United States has been the controversy over the African Crisis Response Initiative (ACRI), one of the five initiatives that the United States tried to sell abroad.[166] The United States claimed that the purpose of the ACRI was to enhance the capacity of African countries to participate effectively in peacekeeping operations and in humanitarian responses. In short, the US saw it as an attempt to translate a political mandate into a military presence on the ground. In the words of Ambassador Hooks:

> ACRI reflects the concern about the conflicts that have troubled the African continent in recent years and the desire on the part of the United States government to help African countries ... as they seek to address the problems that take place on the continent ... therefore, the goal of the programme is to enhance the capacity of African nations to build a more stable future for themselves and for the continent as a whole.[167]

There was considerable opposition to the ACRI in Nigeria, however, and both the government and the population expressed their profound objection to the initiative. The main government objection was that such an initiative undermined African security and that the continent had demonstrated that it had the capacity to respond to conflicts in its own backyard. The government argued that key countries in the continent like Nigeria and South Africa had demonstrated effective crisis response capacity with Nigeria intervening in Liberia and Sierra Leone and South Africa being deeply involved in bringing dialogue to conflicts in Zimbabwe, Angola and the Democratic Republic of Congo (DRC). The population, however, had other reasons for opposing the ACRI, the most important being the fact that the United States had been at the centre of many of the security problems facing Africa and that it would be hypocritical for the same country to attempt preaching peace and stability to Africans. It was also argued that the country had been responsible for the supplies of arms worth more than US$250 million to African troubled spots.[168] But while Nigeria and South Africa rejected the ACRI proposal, a number of African countries signed up for it. Between July 1997 and 2001, ACRI conducted battalion initial training in Senegal, Uganda, Malawi, Mali, Ghana, Côte d'Ivoire, and Benin. ACRI has conducted battalion follow-on training for Senegal, Ghana, Uganda, Malawi and Mali. Future follow-on training is scheduled for all ACRI partner nations. Initial and follow-on training in Ethiopia has been deferred until resolution of the Ethiopian/Eritrean conflict. (Follow-on training in Uganda and Cote d' Ivoire was placed on hold due to the conflict in the Democratic Republic of the Congo, in the case of the former, and a coup, in the case of the latter). To date, ACRI has provided training and non-lethal equipment to almost 6,000 peacekeepers from seven African militaries.[169]

It is not clear whether Nigeria actually wanted to have a defence pact with the United States shortly after the return of democracy to the country in 1999. The American Ambassador to Nigeria at the time, Ambassador William Twadell, noted that the United States "refused" to sign a Defence Pact with Nigeria because it might be interpreted as a form of "neo-colonialism".[170] He said that the United States had informed Nigeria "in clear terms" that it had no interest in signing any Defence Pact but that the US "will work to protect the country's nascent democracy".[171] He also made it clear that even if there were to be a Defence Pact, it would only be relevant if the country was attacked by an external force and not operative during a military coup. Given the unwillingness of the American administration to sign a

Defence Pact with Nigeria, the task of forging closer military tie between Nigeria and the United States had to be repackaged in a different form.

But what seems to be the most controversial of all the military training between Nigeria and the United States has been the agreement between the two countries under which an American military training team, the MPRI, was invited to train the members of the Nigerian Army.[172] The agreement was signed during the administration of President Obasanjo and it was meant to be part of the broader Security Sector Reform programme of the administration.[173] The complete details of the arrangement with the MPRI are not very clear, except that this team was to come to Nigeria and assist in "re-professionalising" the Nigerian army. The MPRI's first assignment was to do an audit of the Nigerian armed forces.[174] It is also known that the Nigerian government would contribute US$3.5 million in implementing the defence plan.

The MPRI agreement turned out to be very controversial. The grounds of objections were numerous. First, there were those who opposed the agreement because they saw it as a form of foreign domination of Nigeria by the United States. While it was not disputed that the Nigerian armed forces needed some form of "re-professionalising" there were debates as to whether the MPRI was best suited for this assignment. Some even saw a similarity between an oversight of the US military personnel in Nigeria and the IMF's role in monitoring and influencing the economic policies of nations worldwide. Second, there were those who objected to the expenses. The sum Nigeria was asked to contribute to the training (US$3.5m) was seen as a waste of resources at a time when many Nigerians were still struggling to make ends meet and where basic infrastructures like water and electricity were collapsing. Third, objection also came from those who felt that such an agreement with the Americans would mean a switchover to US weapon systems , compelling Nigeria to discard the equipment from North Korea, the Soviet Union (now Russia), and other countries from its arsenal. The whole controversy became more serious when the former Chief of Army Staff, General Victor Malu, who seemed to have acquiesced to the whole MPRI involvement, fell out with President Obasanjo and roundly condemned the entire initiative. The more the US tried to adhere to the initiative, however, the more the continent became skeptical. As would be expected, the level of co-operation by the Nigerian military with the MPRI was very low. This was not helped by the belief that General Malu lost his job because of his criticism of the MPRI initiative.[175]

But just as the MPRI controversy was winding down, another controversy arose in American/Nigerian military relations over the introduction of the AFRICOM by the administration of US President George W. Bush. In theory, this was supposed to be a unified command responsible for all African countries, except Egypt. In former President Bush's assertion, AFRICOM was meant to:

> strengthen our security cooperation with Africa and create new opportunities to bolster the capabilities of our partners in Africa, ... Africa Command will enhance our efforts to bring peace and security to the people of Africa and promote our common goals of development, health, education, democracy, and economic growth in Africa.[176]

AFRICOM was established in October 2007 as a temporary sub-unified command under U.S. European Command and was formally activated on October 1, 2008. This again became highly controversial and it was immediately condemned by most African countries on the ground that it negated African independence. The American government did all that it could to explain that the intention was honourable and was not meant to undermine the continent's security.[177] The deputy Commander, Civil-Military Activities, US African High Command, Ambassador Mary Yates and the Deputy Commander, Military Operations of the Command, Vice Admiral Robert Moeller said the Command was not created to undermine Nigeria.[178]

Specifically, the American government claimed that the decision to situate the command in West Africa was not to station a force close to oil rich West African nations but a desire to help African states establish their own security. To further advance this position, the Deputy to the Commander for Military Operations for AFRICOM, Vice Admiral Robert Moeller and

Ambassador Mary Carlin Yates, Deputy to the Commander for Civil Military activities came to hold meetings with Nigerian officials in an effort to clarify what they saw as "misconceptions" about the AFRICOM.

Nigeria's attitude to the entire AFRICOM controversy deserves some discussion. After an initial condemnation of the initiative and an assurance to Nigerians and Africans that Nigeria would not have anything to do with it, the former Nigerian President, the late Umaru Yar'Adua, went to the United States and did what many saw as an ultimate diplomatic turn around. During the visit, the late Nigerian President noted while he was with President Bush:

> We have discussed on security issues ... and peace and security on the African continent. We shall partner AFRICOM to assist not only Nigeria but also the African continent to actualise its peace and security initiatives. It is an initiative to have standby forces in each of the regional economic groupings in Africa.[179]

This position immediately created confusion and the Minister for Foreign Affairs, Ojo Madueke, clarified Yar'Adua's position, pointing out that what the President meant was support from the United States for the African High Command that was planned for the continent and not an externally sponsored initiative like the AFRICOM.[180]

> President Yar'Adua's statement on the proposed AFRICOM is consistent with Nigeria's well-known position on the necessity for Africa to avail itself of opportunities for enhanced capacity for the promotion of peace and security in Africa; Nigeria's position on AFRICOM remains that African governments have the sovereign responsibility for the maintenance of peace and security in the continent, especially in the context of the proposed African Union Stand-by Force and in this regard, the need for support and assistance by Africa's development partners, such as the United States, in the provision of training, funding and logistics for African militaries was duly acknowledged.[181]

The President also came up shortly afterwards to further explain his position:

I did not accept AFRICOM in my discussions with Bush. I asked for assistance and told Bush that we have our plans to establish bases for African countries. We asked for [weapons training] and training to establish our bases to be managed by our people.[182]

As soon as Obama became the President, Nigeria made clear its position that he should dump the entire AFRICOM initiative and support the African Standby Force. The former Minister of Foreign Affairs, Ojo Madueke further reiterated this while attending Obama's inaugural.[183]

b. Joint Military Operation

But apart from direct military training, there has also been joint training. For example, in 2004, a group of United States naval personnel underwent training with their Nigerian counterparts in Calabar. The chief aim of the exchange program, called the "Joint-Combined Exchange Training" (JCET), was to ensure that both nations kept their own military skills up to date and develop intercultural skills. The exercise took place at the Army's amphibious training school, near Calabar, capital of Cross River State. The JCET is an established program and training exercises continue to be conducted around the world, including partnerships with many other African countries. It provides training and cultural immersion for both countries.[184]

There are also collaborations with the Navy. The Nigerian Navy's on-going acquisitions of platforms and collaborations with the United States are part of capacity building for its personnel. This is a collaborative effort between the US Navy and navies in the Gulf of Guinea to build capabilities to protect of off-shore assets while building local capacity to cope with threats and other security challenges in Nigeria's waters. Past exercises have covered Port Security Planning, Oil Platform Protection and Leaders' Training.

The United States has also trained several battalion-sized contingents of Special Forces of the Nigerian Army since 2000. Five battalions numbering a total of 4,000 troops have been trained in-country by a 225-man contingent drawn from the 3rd Special Forces Group from Fort Bragg, North Carolina. The Nigerian Army commenced military training cooperation with the US Special Forces nearly a quarter of a century ago. Between 8 May 1986 and 23 December 1986, C Company, 3rd Battalion, 10th Special Forces Group trained the core of the Nigerian Army's Airborne forces. They also trained amphibious forces in riverine operations, tactics, maintenance and patrols. Until now, detachments of Special Forces troops who have already been in action in the Niger Delta, the Bakassi Peninsula, the Mandara Mountains and during the Boko Haram insurgency have hitherto operated as company-sized contingents integrated into amphibious and other infantry battalions.

In February 2010, USS Samuel B. Roberts (FFG 58) departed Lagos, Nigeria after a seven-day port visit. During the visit, the ship was able to get underway and conduct joint training at-sea with two ships from the Nigerian Navy. Additionally, the crew of the Roberts provided military-to-military training and familiarization in basic damage control, first aid, anti-terrorism force protection, non-lethal weapons, visual communications, and visit board, search, and seizure (VBSS).

Members of the VBSS team took advantage of the unique underway opportunity to board the Nigerian naval ships Barutu and Nwamba while the three ships were at sea during a two-day underway. This was the first instance of such cooperation in which Nigerian ships sailed with U.S. Naval ships.

While in port, 12 Nigerian sailors had a chance to board the Roberts and learn basic damage control and line handling techniques such as wearing a self-contained breathing apparatus, a device used to help sailors breathe while fighting fires. After the training and familiarization, sailors participated in a community relations project. They painted and did electrical work at the Lagos Island Maternity Hospital and donated hygiene and recreation supplies to both the hospital and Lion's Village Orphanage as a part of "Project Handclasp." Sailors also played a friendly game of soccer and volleyball against members of the Nigerian Navy, shopped at a bazaar, coordinated by the American Embassy, and hosted a reception onboard where Congressional representatives Jack Kingston, Gregory Meeks, Melvin Watt and Bob Goodlatte attended.

c. Gift of Military Hardware

In April 2000, US Defense Secretary William S. Cohen, visited Nigeria and announced a US$10.6 million military aid package, the first such program since the United States suspended all aid to Nigeria in 1993. The package includes US$4 million to help train pilots and refurbish Nigeria's aging fleet of C-130 airplanes, used mostly to transport troops for peacekeeping missions in a region that has been plagued by civil wars, ethnic strife and military coups. Nigerian troops formed the bulk of the regional peacekeeping forces that have fought extensively in Liberia and Sierra Leone. Another US$3.5 million paid for a private U.S. company to implement a plan to install civilian control over the military, redesign the military's three branches and devise a strategy for dealing with officers who lose their jobs as the bloated forces are trimmed.

In Fiscal Year (FY) 2008, for example, the United States delivered more than half a million dollars worth of military equipment to Nigeria, provided the Nigerian government with US$1.3 million in Foreign Military Financing (FMF) to buy more U.S. weaponry, and spent almost US$1 million to train Nigerian military officers in the United States. In FY 2009, the U.S. government provided Nigeria with US$1.35 million in FMF funding and spent almost US$1 million dollars on military training programs for Nigerian military officers. And in FY 2010, the Obama administration's budget request called for the United States to give Nigeria another US$1.35 million in FMF funding and to increase spending on military training programs for Nigeria to US$1.1 million.

In addition to arms sales and military training, the United States delivered four surplus U.S. Coast Guard Balsam-class coastal patrol ships in 2003 through the Excess Defense Articles program of the U.S. Defense Security Assistance Agency. These ships had a total value of more than US$4.1 million at the time they were delivered to Nigeria. Nigeria is also one of the countries that are eligible to receive additional U.S. security assistance through the Trans-Saharan Counter-Terrorism Partnership program. And Nigeria receives further U.S. security assistance through ACOTA, the Anti-Terrorism Assistance program, and the International Narcotics Control and Law

Enforcement (INCLE) program. The level of funding for Nigeria is not available for most of these programs. But we do know that Nigeria was scheduled to receive an estimated US$720,000 in assistance through the INCLE program in Financial Year 2009 and that the Obama administration requested US$2 million in INCLE funding for Nigeria for Financial Year 2010.

The United States also remains engaged with the Nigerian military on health and humanitarian assistance. The U.S. embassy's Office of Defence Cooperation has implemented humanitarian assistance programs all over the country, most recently renovating and equipping Misau General Hospital in northern Bauchi State. In addition, the US Department of Defence has pledged approximately US$300,000 to set up a very modern medical research reference laboratory in the Mogadishu barracks in Abuja that will focus on vaccine research for HIV/AIDS, as well as provide a range of care from testing and diagnosis to anti-retroviral therapy and treatment of opportunistic infections. There are about four million HIV-AIDS carriers in Nigeria. The U.S. aid package include: To refurbish fleet of C-130 transport aircraft US$4.0 million; Plan to create greater civilian oversight of military and restructure army, navy and air force (Nigeria is adding another US$3.5 million); Computer simulation centre for teaching peacekeeping skills 2.0; Training of Nigerians in the United States 0.6; Classroom equipment for military 0.5 TOTAL US$10.6 million. In 1999, the United States gave Nigeria US$425,000 under the International Military Education and Training (IMET). This increased to US$600,000 in 2000. Also the sum of US$10 million in Foreign Military Funds has been set aside to assist the Nigerian military in re-establishing the effectiveness of military training facilities and help restore the Nigerian fleet of C130 aircraft to support regional peacekeeping.[185]

d. Usage of American Defence hardware in Nigerian Military Institutions

The Nigerian Army Training and Doctrine Command in Minna, which has the responsibility for developing, conducting and evaluating army training and doctrine has, since 1985, been using the United States-designed Systems Approach to Training.

The Military Dimension in the Politics of oil in Nigeria -United States Relations

Oil has become one of the most important components in Nigerian-American military relations. While this was not envisaged at the time of independence, it had, by the end of the Nigerian civil war, played crucial part in the military agenda between the two nations. As noted in Chapter 8, oil is the backbone of Nigerian – US economic relations. Since 10% of the World supply of oil is in West Africa – a percentage equal to that of North America[186] – US interest in the region is keen. In order to understand the military dimension of oil politics between the two countries, it is important to put the oil demands and supply between the two countries in context. America is significantly energy-dependent. Although the country has considerable oil reserves, the total is far less than required. However, the main source of oil supply to the United States, the Middle East, has long been volatile, and the US has sought other sources since 1973, making Africa attractive. For Nigeria, on its part, oil has been the main source of external revenue. However, the source of the country's oil supply, the Niger Delta, has been at the centre of persistent clash between militants and successive central governments in Nigeria until very recently. Consequently, America's demand for oil, and Nigeria's desire for stability in ensuring continuous flow of revenue from the same resource combine to make the military a crucial subject of mutual interest to both countries. In looking at military considerations of both countries in the politics of oil, the discussions can be broken into two broad sections. The first is on the link between them on the politics of security in the Nigeria Niger Delta region, while the second is on the larger military politics surrounding the Niger Delta.

The United States now obtains between 22 and 24 per cent of its total oil imports from Africa, depending on periodic variations in production levels, particularly fluctuations in Nigerian oil production as a result of attacks on oil facilities by MEND and other political unrest in the Niger Delta. As a result, the United States now imports more oil from the African continent than from the entire Middle East, and is expected to get an even larger percentage of its oil imports from Africa in the coming years. In December 2000, the National Intelligence Council of the U.S. Central Intelligence Agency concluded that Africa would be supplying 25 per cent of America's total oil imports by 2015. Most oil industry analysts now believe that this estimate was too conservative and that Africa will actually be supplying a considerably greater percentage of U.S. oil imports throughout the next decade.

Despite the inauguration of President Barack Obama in January 2009, U.S. government policy on the procurement of African oil is largely governed by the National Energy Policy Report—the final report of the National Energy Policy Development Group (NEPDG)—which was issued on May 17, 2001. The NEPDG, chaired by Vice President Dick Cheney, was a high-level body appointed by President Bush in February 2001, and its final document is often referred to as the "Cheney report." In the most general terms, the report calls on the federal government to undertake numerous initiatives to substantially increase the nation's supply of energy, including energy derived from petroleum. As is well known, these initiatives include measures aimed at increasing oil output from domestic U.S. sources, most notably by commencing drilling on the Arctic National Wildlife Refuge (ANWR). But because America's need for energy is expected to expand substantially in the years ahead, the report also calls for increasing U.S. reliance on foreign sources of energy.

In light of Africa's unique ability to increase its oil output in the years ahead, the Cheney report highlighted Africa's potential to supply an ever-increasing share of America's energy needs. "West Africa is expected to be one of the fastest-growing sources of oil and natural gas for the American market," the report states. Moreover, "African oil tends to be of high quality and low in sulphur, making it suitable for stringent refined product requirements." Particular mention is made of the oil potential of Nigeria and Angola. Nigeria's 2001 production is estimated at 2.1 million bbl/d in the report, and that country is said to harbour "ambitious production goals as high as 5 million barrels of oil per day over the coming decades." Angola is also described as a "major source of growth," with the potential "to double its exports over the next ten years." On this basis, the Cheney report calls for vigorous action by the United States to promote increased oil output in Africa and to channel these additional supplies to markets in the United States. To accomplish this, American oil companies are encouraged to increase their investments in Africa and African countries are encouraged to welcome and facilitate such investment.

The Bush administration also sought to enhance U.S. access to African oil in order to reduce—to some degree, at least—American dependence on the ever-turbulent Middle East. While it is impossible to escape dependence on the Middle East altogether, the Cheney report notes, it is important to reduce U.S. vulnerability to supply disruptions caused by Middle Eastern instability as much as possible – a strategy known as "diversification." "Concentration of world oil production in any one region of the world is a potential contributor to market instability," the report notes. Accordingly, "encouraging greater diversity of oil production...has obvious benefits to all market participants." In accordance with this outlook, the Cheney report calls for vigorous U.S. efforts to increase imports boost from all potential alternatives to the Middle East, but West Africa is viewed with particular favour in this regard because many of its most promising new fields are located offshore, in the Atlantic Ocean, and thus safely removed from the strife and disorder of the African mainland. "Technological advances will enable the United States to accelerate the diversification of oil supplies," the report notes, "notably through deep water offshore exploration and production in the Atlantic Basin," particularly West Africa."

The direct linkage between growing U.S. dependence on oil imports from Africa—and particularly from Nigeria—is based on the assertion that U.S. national security—and our continued enjoyment of the "American way of life"—requires unimpeded access to African oil. Commenting on this development, the former U.S. ambassador to Chad, Donald R. Norland, told the Africa Subcommittee of the U.S. House International Relations Committee in April 2002, "It's been reliably reported that, for the first time, the two concepts – 'Africa' and 'U.S. national security' – have been used in the same sentence in Pentagon documents." Michael A. Westphal, Deputy Assistant Secretary of Defence for African Affairs, also noted this linkage in a Pentagon press briefing on April 2, 2002. "Fifteen per cent of the United States imported oil supply comes from sub-Saharan Africa," he declared, and "this is also a number which has the potential for increasing significantly in the next decade." Walter Kansteiner, the Assistant Secretary of State for Africa, further acknowledged the national security implications of African oil during a visit to Nigeria in July 2002. "African oil is of strategic national interest to us," he declared, and "it will increase and become more important as we go forward."

As a result, the "Carter Doctrine," proclaimed by President Jimmy Carter in January 1980 has been extended to Nigeria, the rest of Africa, and — indeed — the entire world. In his final State of the Union Address, President Carter designated the free flow of Persian Gulf oil as a "vital interest" of the United States and declared that this country would use "any means necessary, including military force," to defend that interest. To implement this policy, widely known as the "Carter Doctrine," the U.S. Department of Defence established the U.S. Central Command (Centcom) to oversee U.S. military operations in the Gulf area and built up a substantial military basing infrastructure in the region. Later presidents subsequently cited the Carter Doctrine as the basis for U.S. combat operations during the Persian Gulf War of 1991, the war in Afghanistan from 2001 until the present, and the invasion of Iraq in 2003.

On the Future U.S. Security Assistance to Nigeria for Military Operations in the Niger Delta, on 12 August 2009, during her trip to Africa, U.S. Secretary of State Hillary Clinton met with Nigerian Foreign Minister Ojo Maduekwe. Following the meeting she applauded the efforts of the Nigerian government to establish "security in the Niger Delta," and stated, "We support the Nigerian Government's comprehensive political framework approach toward resolving the conflict in the Niger Delta." She went on to say that "the process, as it was explained to me by several of the ministers who were present, is incorporating the region's stakeholders as absolutely essential, focusing on the region's development needs, separating the militants and the irreconcilables from those who deserve amnesty and want to be part of building a better future for that part of Nigeria. And we have offered, again, our support and that of the international community."[187]

In answer to a reporter's question, Secretary Clinton said that she had also met with the Nigerian Defence Minister, "and he had some very specific suggestions as to how the United States could assist the Nigerian Government in their efforts, which we think are very promising, to try and bring peace and security to the Niger Delta. We will be following up on those. There is nothing that has been decided. But we have a very good working relationship between our two militaries. So I will be talking with my counterpart, the [U.S.] Secretary of Defence, and we will, through our joint efforts, through our bi-national commission mechanism, determine what Nigeria would want from us for help, because we know that this is an internal matter, we know this is up to the Nigerian people and their government to resolve, and then look to see who we would offer that assistance."

As this statement indicates, there is little doubt that the Obama administration will provide even more security assistance to the Nigerian government in the future. Moreover, it is clear that this security assistance will be intended specifically for the Nigerian government to use for military operations in the Niger Delta.

The United States, Nigeria and Conflict Resolution in Africa

The United States had always intervened in conflict situations all over the world based on its perceived moral responsibility to do so. According to President Bush:

> I understand the United States alone cannot right the wrongs, but we also know that some crisis in the world cannot be resolved without American involvement, that American action is often necessary as a catalyst for broader involvement in the community of nations. Only the United States has the global reach to place a large security force on the ground in such a distant place quickly and efficiently and thus, save thousands of innocent deaths.

However, the reality of its involvement in Africa conflicts is firmly grounded in Cold War politics. Once the cold war was over, it felt no strong need to intervene, at least militarily to resolve lingering African crisis. This disposition was further reinforced by the Somali debacle where 18 American Rangers were killed and their corpses dragged through the streets of Mogadishu in 1993. This accounted for the refusal of the United States to intervene to stop the Rwandan genocide.

United States' efforts in conflict resolution in Africa had, for the most part, precluded the use of military troops. In West African conflicts, especially, it prefers to support the Nigerian-led ECOWAS initiative while it concentrates on delivering humanitarian assistance. Even in Liberia, with which it had a special affinity, the US never intervened until 2003, during the second round of the war, and even at that, not militarily. It only deployed a task force of 2000 marines off the coast of Liberia to "boost ECOWAS' efforts in establishing peace in Liberia, to provide general logistic support to ECOMIL, and to limit its duration".

Since then the US has adopted the approach of strengthening the capacity of African peacekeepers to undertake peacekeeping and humanitarian operations in conflict areas. In 2004, the Global Peace Operations Initiative (GPOI) was created to address the disparity between the persistent demand for trained peacekeeping forces and their inadequate availability, especially for missions in Africa. In 2005 alone, GPOI trained and equipped 27,025 military personnel from 37 countries to participate in UN peacekeeping operations. That number has increased exponentially since then. Nigeria is a key beneficiary of this support.[188]

In November 2000, teams of Special Forces soldiers and military medical personnel were deployed to create more stability in West Africa. Operation Focus Relief, a US State Department initiative, was designed to improve the effectiveness of the Nigerian military in helping United Nations initiatives in West Africa. The brunt of the training, military officials acknowledged, was geared toward handling the Revolutionary United Front, a group of vicious Sierra Leonean rebels that had battled UN peacekeepers and the Sierra Leone government over diamond fields in the country. About 250 members of the 3rd Special Forces Group Airborne from Fort Bragg, North Carolina, conducted trainings in mortars, light anti-tank weapons and M60 machine guns for Nigerian troops..

Training had been halted for about 10 days in October 2000 when some 80 unknown Nigerian soldiers arrived unexpectedly to take part in the mission. The operation was suspended while US State Department officials checked if any of the new soldiers had been accused of past human rights abuses. The United States only would train soldiers who have passed the human rights abuses background check. The Nigerians, who had been criticized in the past for tolerating human rights abuses, were receiving instruction on how to handle civilians and prisoners. The training culminated in mid-December 2000, when 750 Nigerian soldiers held a coordinated company-level attack and defence simulation. The US$20 million training program was part of US$66 million in military aid and training the United States extended to Nigeria.

Nigeria's commitment to regional peace and security remains exemplary in a troubled continent. Nigeria has provided the largest number of peacekeeping troops in Africa. It has fielded troops to trouble spots in West Africa and to Darfur, and played an important role in returning stability to Sierra Leone and Liberia. Secretary Clinton further stated in this regard:

> We seek to enhance Nigeria's role as a U.S. partner on regional security, but we also seek to bolster its ability to combat violent extremism within its borders. Nigeria is a partner in counter-terrorism efforts, and it is in this context that Nigerians have expressed dissatisfaction with their inclusion on the Transportation Security Administration's "Countries of Interest" list. Nigerians perceive this as collective punishment for the actions of a wayward son, when in fact they shared our outrage at the attack and have been providing assistance to the ongoing investigation. Let me be clear, our friendship and relationship with Nigeria is strong and continues to be based on a wide range of important bilateral issues.

During her August 2009 visit to Abuja, Secretary Clinton agreed to establish a U.S.-Nigeria Bi-national Commission that would allow the United States and Nigeria to engage on key bilateral issues including regional security and counterterrorism, and advance discussions on governance and transparency issues, Niger Delta post-amnesty progress, and economic development.

Nigeria, United States and Security Sector Reform in Nigeria

Another area where the US has assisted Nigeria since the dawn of democracy in Nigeria has been in the area of security sector reform. Having been deeply involved in politics for more than three decades, the government realised that the Nigerian army had to be professionalised to respect democratic control. This was indeed paramount in the mind of the Obasanjo administration. Security Sector Reform as the government envisaged it meant:

a. Making the entire defence establishment accountable and subject to a freely elected legislative body of civilian representative;
b. Enabling the citizens of the nation to decide through democratic process, which civilian they want to serve them as Head of State and Commander in Chief of all the armed forces;
c. Ensuring that the military is non-partisan and does not compete for power with civilian political parties;
d. Ensuring that the military accept the principle of civilian control and the rule of law as inseparable from their military professionalism.

Since the return of democracy to Nigeria, there had been many training activities for members of the Nigerian Armed forces by officers of the United States Defence forces. In June 2001, the US agreed to train three new battalions of the Nigerian army. This training programme, codenamed Operation Focus Relief 111 would focus on 1 battalion, Kebbi, 20 Battalion Serti and 222 Battalion, Ilorin. Earlier training had been given to the battalions in Sokoto and Ibadan.[189] In October 2001, the United States and Nigeria entered into a joint pact to fight terrorism. Also as part of strengthening democracy through assistance in security sector reform, the US agreed to train members of the Nigeria Police in riot handling.[190]

Nigerians Serving in the United States Armed Forces

A subject that is often ignored in the Nigeria-United States military relations is the involvement of Nigerians who have enlisted in the American armed forces. As would be expected, this has raised a number of questions, including the motivation for the commission and where their loyalty would lie in the eventuality of a war between the two countries. There have been various reasons alluded for the enlistment of Nigerians in the United States armed forces. The most popular (and arguably most erroneous) explanation is that most of these people have joined the force to get a faster access to acquiring citizenship. There is the belief that it is easier to acquire American citizenship once a foreigner volunteers to join the army. While, of course, there could have been people who joined the American defence forces for this purpose, there are far more important reasons why others have sought and obtained enlistment.

Various discussions held with Nigerians who fall into this category has shown that there are different reasons for their motivation. Broadly, there could have been five main reasons: First are those who joined mainly in search of adventure. Indeed, some of those who fall into this category are those who are young and wanted to see the world. Second are those who sought enlistment out of prestige. To be associated with the armed forces of the most powerful country in the world is a sufficient motivation for many Nigerians. Third, are those who have joined out of the genuine desire for revenge against those perceived as terrorists who have caused havoc to American interests. Many of those who fall into this category are those who joined the American military after the terrorist attacks on 9/11. Indeed, some of those in this category claimed that they felt sufficiently aggrieved that they intended to avenge the mass destructions that claimed innocent lives. Fourth are those who joined because they could not get any other gainful employment. With economic meltdown coming at a period of recruitment into the American military because of diverse external engagements it is almost certain that some people of Nigeria descent could have joined the American forces for the desire of gaining employment. Finally, there could have been those who joined mainly to ensure a faster track to American citizenship. Many of the Nigerian nationals who have joined the American military have performed creditably well and some have even paid the supreme sacrifice.

Conclusion

Nigeria's defence and security links with the United States have followed largely the nature of diplomatic links between the two countries. During periods when diplomatic relations were friendly, there were more links and conversely, periods of strain, as in the 1990s, resulted in suspension of these links. There are, however, a number of ironies in the military links between the two countries and this shows the fluid nature friendship in international relations. The period when there was low diplomatic (and military) links between the two countries was during the Murtala and Obasanjo administration. It is, however, much of an irony that it was under the same administration of Obasanjo (this time as a civilian leader) that Nigeria granted some of the most significant and arguably, most controversial security concessions to the United States. In looking at the future of the relationship, it seems certain that stronger military links will continue to develop between the two countries. This is not only because the consolidation of democracy in Nigeria makes it easier for the United States to justify close military links, but also because there are growing developments in the West African region that make the military situation of the region of mutual interest to both Abuja and Washington.

End Notes

[163.] Although British institutions like Sandhurst and to an extent, Moors still retain the prestige military institution, especially as the number of Nigerian officers who went to the institutions began to dwindle, American military institutions also began rising into prominence.

[164.] Senior officers who attended the meeting included, Colonel Mohammed Shuwa, Col. Olufemi Olutoye, Col. Martin Adamu, Col. C. M. George, Col. F. A. Sheilu and Lt. Col. George Innih from the Army, Commodore Nelson Soroh, the Deputy Chief of Naval Staff and Col. John Obada, the Acting Chief of Air Staff.

[165.] www.defencetalk.com/forums/navy-maritime/u-s-nigerian-military-skills-exchange - training- program-266.

[166.] The other programmes were International Military Education and Training (INET), African Centre for Strategic Studies (ACSS), Joint Combined Exchange Training (JCET) and the Expanded IMET (E-IMET).

[167.] Andrew Fadason, Africa and ACRI, *New Nigeria*, 14 June 2000.

[168.] Ibid.

[169.] For more on ACRI, see, P. Omach, *The African Crisis Response Initiative: Domestic Politics and Convergence of National Interests* and Emmanuel K. Aning "African Crisis Response Initiative and the New African Security (Dis)order", *African Journal of Political Science* Vol. 6, No. 1, 43-67, 2001.

[170.] Ambassador Twadell made this declaration while visiting the Nigerian Eastern Naval Command in Calabar with the Commander in Chief of the US Naval Force in Europe, Rear Admiral Michael Haskins. See *Vanguard*, (Lagos) 24 March 2000

[171.] Ibid

[172.] The MPRI is based in Alexandria, Va., and is operated by senior retired military officers. The consulting firm has done extensive contract work for the Pentagon, including training and organizing the Croatian army in the mid-1990s.

[173.] Discussed later in this chapter.

[174.] In the audit, the MPRI found that more than 75 percent of the army's equipment was not operational and that training had virtually stopped, said two sources familiar with the document. The study found that the air force's pride, its 22 MiG-21 and 15 Jaguar fighter jets, were grounded, as were all but two of the eight C-130 transport planes, the sources said. And, the audit found, the navy had 19 admirals but only nine seaworthy ships.

[175.] Said Adejumobi, "Guarding the Guardian? The Obasanjo Regime and Military Reform in Nigeria", *Development Policy Management Network Bulletin*, Vol. XIII, N° 3, September 2001 pp.17-19.

[176.] Vince Crawley, U.S. Creating New Africa Command to Coordinate Military Efforts, www.africom.mil/printStory.asp?art=1484

[177.] Francis Obinor, Fears over AFRICOM unwarranted, *The Guardian* January 11 2008.

[178.] *Punch* Nov. 30 2007.

[179.] Paul Ohia and Constance Ikokwu, "Yar'Adua in White House Ready to partner US on Africom" *ThisDay*, 14 December 2007.

[180.] *Daily Independent*, December 16 2007.

[181.] Waheed Bakare, "Nigeria's Citizens' Diplomacy and Africom's Blunder", *Punch* 29 May 2008.

[182.] Constance Ikoku and Juliana Taiwo, "Yar'Adua Denies Approving AFRICOM, *ThisDay* (Lagos) 15 December 2007.

[183.] *The Guardian* (Lagos) January 29 2009.

[184.] http://www.defencetalk.com/forums/navy-maritime/u-s-nigerian-military-skills-exchange-training-program-2666/

[185.] *This Day*, (Lagos) 13 June 2000.

[186.] http://www.lookoutmtn.com/Documents/Sources_of_United_States_Oil_Supply.pdf.

[187.] US Department of State "Remarks with Nigerian Foreign Minister Ojo Maduekwe" www.state.gov/secretary/rm/2009a/08/127823.htm.

[188.] The US, through its Transportation and Logistics Support Arrangement (TLSA) of GPOI contributed $11.5 million in 2005, $5 million of which went to construct portions of 34 base camps in Darfur. In 2007, it gave out $32 million to TLSA to support initiatives including: $12 million in equipment to ECOWAS, $6.8 million for the training and equipping of Ugandan troops supporting AMISOM, and $6 million to support Nigerian deployment to AMIS (American.gov, 2007).

[189.] *The Guardian*, (Lagos) 27th June 2001.

[190.] *The Punch* (Lagos) 21-12-2002.

Chapter Seven

Relationship under the New Democratic Dispensation: The Nature and Dynamics of Nigeria/US Relations from 1999 to 2010

Funso ADESOLA & Ronke Iyabo AKO-NAI

After decades of military rule, the return of democracy in Nigeria was welcomed by the United States, albeit with some trepidation. Against the background of failed and questionable transition agendas by the military, the White House was not completely convinced that the Abubakar Abdulsalami transition programme would be pursued to its logical conclusion. Indeed, former President Bill Clinton was to confirm in his memoirs that he woke up in the middle of the night while he was on an official trip to Nigeria – to wonder whether or not the swearing-in of a new Nigerian President would come to pass.[191] To ensure the successful conduct of the election, therefore, the United States provided US$5 million in aid. President Clinton followed this up with a statement congratulating the people of Nigeria and promising the United States continued support to the government and people of Nigeria.[192] Coming after the incident where key US officials were believed by many Nigerians to have been connected with the controversial death of the late Mashood Abiola, the government was eager to demonstrate its long term interest to democracy in Nigeria. Although the American government knew the election was not particularly free and fair, it was still the belief of Washington that the outcome still represented the wishes of most Nigerians, even if the actual figures were somewhat questionable.

With the assumption of office of an elected civilian administration in Nigeria, some of the key issues that affected the relationship between Nigeria and the United States during the Abacha administration dissipated somewhat, especially those issues surrounding human rights. In this chapter, we discuss the relationship between Nigeria and the United States since the return of democracy. The central argument we propose is that, although there has been a significant improvement in the relationship between Nigeria and the United States since the end of the Abacha regime, the link between the two countries still has key issues that are yet to be effectively resolved, and that the principles of democracy that both countries hold so dearly have ironically contributed to this delay, especially the fight against corruption. This chapter has been divided into sections that correspond to the administrations of successive American and Nigerian Presidents to facilitate discussion. There are accordingly four sections in the chapter: the first looks at the Clinton era while the second discusses the administration of George W. Bush. The third section discusses the Obama administration while the fourth concludes the discussions in the chapter.

The Clinton Era

Democracy came to Nigeria when President Bill Clinton was in the final phases of his administration and also just about the time the President was recovering from the Monica Lewinsky scandal.[194] Indeed, the immediate dangers had been surmounted and the concern was limited largely to how the whole scandal could affect the future electoral chances of Vice President Al Gore and the Democrats. Against this background, President Clinton devoted some attention to international diplomacy, especially in Africa, where there had been considerable sympathy for him during the difficult days of his impeachment.[195] Also apart from the perennial problem of the Middle East, there were no other major international challenges facing the United States at the time. The fallout from the Abdulmutallab "underwear shoe bomb" episode had largely dissipated and, in the area of international diplomacy, there were largely procedural issues that were not particularly contentious. This was an advantage which, as would be shown later, was not enjoyed by Clinton's immediate successors.

The first indication of a new dawn in the US/Nigerian relationship was the visit of the newly elected President of Nigeria, Olusegun Obasanjo in October 1999. This trip seemed to set a new tone for involvement between the nations in a new environment of democracy in Nigeria. Clinton identified the key issues, specifically promising to assist Nigeria in the areas of expansion of law enforcement, cooperation to stimulate trade and investment between the two countries and to help Nigeria recover some of the assets of the previous regime. He also identified other wider American policies that would help Nigeria, including the Africa Growth and Opportunity Act,[196] support for debt rescheduling through the Paris Club with encouragement that other countries to do the same, and the continued support an end to regional conflicts in Africa. A crucial issue that was to come up many times in the course of the next decade also arose during Obasanjo's visit. This was the assistance that could come from the United States in the area of recovering money stolen from Nigeria by previous administrations. Here, President Clinton said he would be working with Attorney General Janet Reno and the Nigerian government including with Attorney General Reno to recover some of the money looted from Nigeria. President Clinton also noted that he had increased America's bilateral aid to Nigeria fourfold more than before and that he was expecting Congress to pass the bill which included this fund.

A return visit was paid by President Clinton to Nigeria in August 2000, during which key issues like debt relief, the spread of Human Immunodeficiency Virus (HIV)/Acquired Immunodeficiency Syndrome (AIDS) and regional conflicts were discussed. The visit was also used by President Clinton to announce a US$100 million aid package to Nigeria. This aid was specifically aimed at improving primary education and health care. The visit was also symbolic for the opportunity that the visiting President had to address the joint session of the Nigerian National Assembly.

The timing of the renewed friendship between the US and Nigeria limited what President Clinton could do, as his term was nearing its end. Clinton did his best in a short period to ensure that the future relations between the two countries were based on a solid footing. Mainly he focused on securing as much support as possible to help Nigeria strengthen its fragile democracy. But while this was mainly to ensure political stability and economic development of Nigeria, it was also believed that it served America's interest as a political stable Nigeria was important in ensuring the stability of West Africa – a region of growing importance to the United States. Furthermore, Nigeria's political stability also meant that the country would be in a better position to continue its peacekeeping activities in the region. But there were also more direct interests around which Bill Clinton's Nigeria's diplomacy also hinged. The first was the primacy of the country in the global oil politics. It is worth noting that as of this time, world oil prices were topping $30 a barrel, and Clinton wanted the Organization of Petroleum Exporting Countries (OPEC) to boost output to bring the price down to the low to mid-$20s. Another area where Clinton also felt that support for Nigeria could help solve American problems was on the issue of global drug trade. It is worth pointing out that, as of this time, Nigeria was a well-known source of drug supply to the United States.

Nigeria, for its part, also saw the Clinton era as a period to ensure that the isolation of the past was removed while also ensuring that the country gained as much as possible to consolidate its new democracy. Among the specific areas where Nigeria needed American support during this period were in the efforts to get debt relief, increase in trade, the re-establishment of Air-link, better consideration in visa issuance and aid. While all these could not be achieved during the short time that Clinton remained in power, it is worth noting that American aid to Nigeria increased from $7 million to $108 million over 1999 and 2001.

Clinton was always interested in encouraging democracy in Nigeria. During the visit to the country in 2000, he recalled the progress that had been made in the advancement of democracy. Setting his speech against the background of the visit he made to the country two years earlier, President Clinton noted:

> When I came here 2 years ago, one of the biggest obstacles to a new relationship with the entire continent was the fact that

the democratic hopes of Nigeria's people were being smothered by military misrule and corruption, with your finest leaders being killed, banished, or in the case of President Obasanjo, forced to languish in prison. My greatest hope then was that some day I could come to Africa again, to visit a Nigeria worthy of its people's dreams. Thanks to President Obasanjo and the people of Nigeria, I have the high honor today to visit the new Nigeria and to pledge America's support for the most important democratic transition in Africa since the fall of apartheid. All of us in the American delegation know that after so many years of despair and plunder, your journey has not been easy. But we are also committed to working with the people of Nigeria to help build stronger institutions, improve education, fight disease, crime, and corruption, ease the burden of debt, and promote trade and investment in a way that brings more of the benefits of prosperity to people who have embraced democracy.[197]

On the whole, it can be said that Bill Clinton's diplomacy towards Nigeria is enveloped in its overall diplomacy towards the African continent. Indeed, Nigeria was a microcosm of its overall African diplomacy. On the whole, the key policies that dominated his attention were HIV/AIDS, the debt crisis, direct financial assistance, aid, peacekeeping, economic justice, fair trade, human rights and democracy, environmental sustainability, disaster mitigation and conflict resolution. As Adewale Banjo has noted, the key features of Clinton diplomacy in the continent include: more multilateralism and less bilateralism; highlighting of developmental issues, preference for support for renewed regionalism in Africa, redefinition of America's military role in Africa, increased power and influence of America's Non-Governmental Organizations (NGOs) in Africa and the retention of political conditionalities for granting aid.[198] On their part, many Nigerians saw in Clinton a leader that reminded them of the affectionate disposition they enjoyed during the Carter era. These were the legacies that were set for his successor, George W. Bush, when he assumed office in January 2001.

The Administration of George W. Bush

The circumstances under which President George W. Bush came

to power did not particularly endear him to many Africans. In the first instance, there was the general feeling that Africans, both at home and in the diaspora preferred Democrats to Republicans. The nostalgic sentiments Africans, particularly Nigerians had of former Democratic Presidents like Jimmy Carter and even Bill Clinton were nothing comparable to the subtle resentment they had for Presidents like Ronald Reagan, who was seen as being anti-Africa, especially for his policies on Apartheid and even for his successor, George H.W. Bush, who also pursued policies similar in many respects to Reagan.[199] The mere fact that George W. Bush was the son of the first President Bush created the impression for some that he would be of the same political stock as his father. The election itself was another factor that could have reduced the affection with which his new administration was received. Indeed, there were many in Africa who believed that the election had been manipulated for the new President Bush by his brother, the Governor of Florida, the State that produced the controversial result in the 2000 election.

Moving specifically to Nigeria, there could have been some concerns in key circles in the country as to how the new President would relate to the country. First, the new President could have been aware of the deep friendship between President Obasanjo and President Carter, whom his father helped defeat in the 1980 election, especially given the diplomatic gaffe made at the time by Nigerian leaders that the country preferred a Carter victory. But while the younger President Bush may have had some hang-ups against Nigeria, the strategic importance of the country to the United States made any personal sentiments to be of secondary importance in his consideration.

The era of George W. Bush's administration was particularly important in relationship between Nigeria and the US because of its length. Indeed, Bush joined only two other US Presidents who had stayed in office for two full terms since Nigeria achieved independence, the other two being Ronald Reagan and Bill Clinton.. Bush's years in power spanned the administrations of two Nigerian Presidents, Olusegun Obasanjo and the late Umar Yar' Adua.

An event that was to colour most of America's policy with the outside world occurred very early in President Bush's administration. This was the infamous September 11, 2001 attack on American cities of New York and Washington. This reduced, to a large extent, the amount of concern the American government had for African issues.

It is possible to argue that President Bush did not accord Nigeria the recognition that the country expected. For example, Olusegun Obasanjo, then Nigeria's President, visited the United States in May 2001, just few months after Bush assumed office, but there was no reciprocal visit by Bush until July 2003, when the President included Nigeria in his five-nation African tour. The visit to Nigeria was also an opportunity by the President to address the Sixth Sullivan meeting of African and African American leaders that was held in Abuja, Nigeria between July 12 and 17 2003.[200] Apart from the fact that the visit also fed on the Sullivan meeting, many Nigerians were not happy that President Bush only met President Obasanjo very briefly on the last day of his five-nation tour.[201] Discussions during this meeting centred mainly on Nigeria's fight against HIV/AIDS and the American President expressed his interest in Nigeria's recognition of the problem as a major health concern. However, in-between Obasanjo's first visit to the United States and Bush's whistle stop-over in Nigeria, the two leaders had used the opportunity of a G8 Summit in Paris, France, to hold bilateral discussion in June 2003.

The next major meeting between the two leaders was in December 2004, when President Obasanjo again visited the United States in his dual capacity as the President of Nigeria and the Chairperson of the African Union. Although the two leaders discussed wider African issues like the situation in Darfur, Sudan and Cote d'Ivoire, there were also major discussions on the issue of trade and economic opportunities.

Obasanjo and Bush again met in January 2006, when the American President and his wife visited Nigeria. Most of what dominated discussions during the visit were largely health and larger continental issues. The meeting was again followed by another visit by President Obasanjo to Washington D. C. in March 2006. During the meeting, attention was largely focused on wider regional issues, especially the situation in Darfur. Indeed, the main domestic issue that came up in their discussion was the situation in the Niger Delta, on which President Bush said his Nigerian counterpart had discussed with him his strategy for dealing with the problem.

A major issue that emerged between President Bush and President Obasanjo was the Charles Taylor issue. The full story of what happened is still not known as there were, obviously different versions. Charles Taylor, the Liberian warlord turned President, had left his country and was living in exile in Nigeria under an agreement that had been brokered by African leaders to bring peace to the West African nation.[202] However, complications entered the equation after President Taylor was accused by the International Court, the Special Court for Sierra Leone (SCSL), of complicity in the civil war in the neighbouring Sierra Leone. Specifically, the Liberian leader was accused of trading in blood diamonds and of human rights violations. However, it was difficult to serve the arrest warrant on the Liberian leader and despite domestic pressures even from Nigerians, Obasanjo refused to hand over Taylor to the International Court. It was, however, believed that President Bush, for a number of reasons, was determined to get Taylor to stand trial for war crimes. In circumstances that still remain unclear, Taylor was arrested in Nigeria for allegedly trying to escape the country, thereby violating the terms of his asylum. He was thus arrested and transferred to Liberia. Taylor has always refuted this allegation and has persistently argued that he was set up by his Nigeria counterpart.[203]

Bush's diplomacy in Nigeria shows how many bilateral contacts between Presidents can produce most minimal results in terms of direct relationship between two countries. It seems both leaders had different desire in what the content of the relationship should be, and neither was willing to tell the other that he was going in a different direction. While Nigeria obviously wanted its regional and continental importance recognized, what it desired from the United States was more of economic assistance and aid. However, President Bush saw Nigeria's relevance more in the area of assisting America to solve key African problems and not as a recipient of America's assistance.

But if Bush showed minimal interest in Nigeria, the country received considerable interests from other American sources, meaning that the United States still remained very prominent in Nigeria. One of the key actors in this respect was the former American President, Jimmy Carter whose Carter Centre has been deeply involved in activities in Nigeria. The Centre has been involved in the treatment of diseases like schistosomiasis. Indeed, with the assistance of the centre, the Nigerian Ministry of Health was about to record a zero case of Guinea worm in 2009, as against almost 700,000 cases reported in 2006. President Carter was also able to establish a close working relationship with another former Nigerian leader, Yakubu Gowon. Also, the founder of Microsoft, Bill Gates, visited Nigeria in 2009 through its Bill and Melinda Gates Foundation. The visit was to assist Nigeria in its fight against Polio. Continuing in the field of health, the United States and Nigeria jointly commissioned a state-of-the-art laboratory for the manufacturing of drugs for tuberculosis in Idu, Abuja.

In looking at President Bush's diplomacy towards Nigeria, it seems clear that it was weak in content and commitment when compared to that of his predecessor. Beyond the platitudinous promise of support to Nigeria to strengthen its democracy and the rehashing of the statement that Nigeria is fundamental to political stability in Africa, there was no serious assistance to the country during the Bush era. The main area where some form of direct benefits came to Nigeria was, as noted above in the areas of health, especially in the fight against diseases like polio, guinea-worm tuberculosis and HIV/AIDS.

It was also during the period of President Bush that democracy came back to Nigeria with the swearing in of President Olusegun Obasanjo as the elected President of Nigeria. President Obasanjo enjoyed the support of the US government in spite of his military background. It was expected (at least by Washington) that Obasanjo was a committed Democrat – who would be acting as a bastion of Western reform system. In this, he was expected to revamp the dwindling economy and set political liberalization tone for his country.[204]

It was on the strength of this that Obasanjo's administration enjoyed the goodwill of the US government. In 2006, Ngozi Okonjo-Iweala, his Finance Minister, secured the US's Treasury Department assistance to persuade the Paris Club to forgive

Nigeria's foreign debt worth of US$18 billion. Coupled with that, the Economic and Financial Crimes Commission (EFCC) which was established in 2003 also enjoyed US financial support. The body worked against official corruption. One of its achievements was its celebrated prosecution of Tafa Balogun – the police chief who was convicted of embezzling some US$98 million out of public funds.[205] In the eight years of Obasanjo's civilian administration, Nigeria earned US$223 billion, two and half times the amount earned over the previous eight years. Also US$400 billion had been wasted since independence – so said the EFCC.[206]

The US has repeatedly acknowledged the strategic importance of Nigeria since independence. This is not only because of Nigeria's status as a US strategic oil supplier in the African continent, but also partly because of Nigeria's willingness to take on regional challenges – thereby enabling the US to sidestep, what to many, is its historic obligation to help in containing the turbulence in the region.[207]

For instance, under Obasanjo, Nigeria intervened to reverse military takeovers in Guinea Bissau and Sao Tome and Principe. It made efforts but achieved little in reconciling the warring factions in Somalia and Zimbabwe. As mentioned earlier, Nigeria provided succour for Charles Taylor (former Liberian President) thereby prepared the ground for war-weary Liberia elections that eventually ushered in Ellen Johnson Sirleaf. This was in itself of strategic importance to the US – in that it warded-off an outbreak of another war that might have required US intervention.[208] Effort was also made by Nigeria to ensure the transformation of a weak Organisation of African Unity (OAU) into a promising African Union (AU).

In fact, in 2003, Washington set aside the European Union (EU), Human Rights Watch, the International Republican Institute and Nigerian civil society groups that that years' election was fatally flawed. This was quickly followed by a state visit of President Bush to Abuja – Nigeria's seat of government – shortly after Obasanjo's inauguration. In like manner, a few warnings against electoral fraud were issued by the US Mission in Abuja as a lead-up to the 2007 elections. Beyond that, the US's White House and the State Department were simply reticent, but issued critical statements after the elections were over.²⁰⁹

In the US's strategic calculations, Nigeria's stability in relation to West African sub-region stability mattered to the US. But given the volatility of the Middle East, it seems that Nigeria's oil supply was a more important consideration.²¹⁰

In the wake of violence by the irate Niger Delta youths over the despoliation of their environment by the activities of the oil prospecting firms and the alleged connivance of the Federal Government (of Nigeria) with the oil multinationals – to the detriment of the oil bearing communities of the Niger Delta, the US government felt concerned. This is because expatriates were harassed, abducted, maimed or killed by the irate militant youths. This has led to the disruption of the operation of these oil prospecting firms – to the utter embarrassment of the Nigerian government and interests woven around oil prospecting in Nigeria. Washington, therefore, offered Nigeria a number of joint training and equipment programmes to curb the violence. It donated four boats and sold seventeen others to the government to patrol the creeks of the Delta.²¹¹

Apart from the Niger Delta debacle, the US was also interested in how to obviate Nigeria's economic woes. For instance, Nigeria was scheduled to get debt relief of about US$35 billion owed the group of eight (G8) – the world's most industrialised nations. The debt relief is contingent on political and economic reforms as well as the fight against corruption. On this, President Bush has said "Nobody wants to give money to a country that is corrupt and where leaders take money and put it in their pockets". In order to be in the good books of these donors, therefore, President Obasanjo intensified efforts on his anti-corruption crusade. In the process, top government officials were removed from office on account of corruption charges. This group included Tafa Balogun – former Inspector General of Police; Fabian Osuji – former Education Minister; Adolphus Wabara (he was later exonerated) – former Senate President and Mobolaji Osomo – former Housing Minister.²¹²

Furthermore, the US keenly monitored Nigeria's political developments. For example, when it was increasingly becoming clear that President Obasanjo was trying to shield Atiku Abubakar, his former Vice President who defected from the ruling People's

Democratic Party (PDP) and became the Presidential aspirant of the opposition Action Congress (AC), the US made a strong case to allow him contest the April 2007 polls;[213] the same way that the US objected to extensions of Obasanjo's tenure, after two-terms, running concurrently. In fact, the US was emphatic on the issue, saying:

> The United States Embassy in Nigeria wishes to make the following statement in response to continuing media inquiry regarding our position on the on-going process of amending the Nigerian Constitution. Our view is very clear that executive term limits should be respected in the interest of institutionalising democracy and opening political space. This allows for new leaders to be groomed and it supports the rule of law. A regular turnover of power ingrains and institutionalises a democratic process.[214]

At some point, American troops had been placed on a red alert as the US government was monitoring the potential situation in Nigeria – Africa's most populous nation – said General William Ward, the Commander of African Crisis Response Initiative (AFRICOM).[215]

To wean itself off the Middle Eastern oil suppliers, the US purchases 10 per cent of Nigeria crude oil and hopes for more. This is part of the US rationale of supporting President Obasanjo in spite of the shortcomings of his administration, i.e., flawed 2003 elections, official ostentation and flagrant abuse of human rights. However, the 'last straw' of the Obasanjo administration that impacted Nigeria's relations with the US was the 2007 election saga. The flawed 2007 election was dysfunctional to the US's interest in Nigeria.[216] It was speculated that once the most populous African country and the largest US energy supplier implodes, arising from post election crisis, it will affect one of the main arteries of oil supply to the US and spell doom for the US; since the Persian Gulf has already been turbulent.

It is the outcome of the 2007 flawed elections that ushered in Umar Yar'Adua's administration. Hence, Yar'Adua's administration had to face legitimacy and credibility problems from the very start. Meanwhile, there was the continuing allegation that President Obasanjo hand-picked Yar'Adua –

who had not sought the nomination, in the first place. Certain elements saw the 2007 elections as 'selection' and Yar'Adua was Obasanjo's 'anointed' candidate for the Presidency. [217]

In another breath, during the Bush years, the US played a pivotal role in recognising Nigeria (and Senegal) as foundation member(s) of New Partnership for African Development (NEPAD) and invited them to the G8 Summit holding at the Italian Island of La Maddalena between June 8 and 10, 2009. Food crisis, drug trafficking, organised crime, regional crises, immigration, the economy, energy issues, climate change and terrorism were the burning issues that Nigeria and Senegal were invited to hash out with the world's most industrialised nations.[218] American philanthropists have also ventured into Nigeria. For instance, Nigeria together with four African countries (Togo, Ethiopia, Burkina Faso, and Cote d' Ivoire) have benefitted from Carter Centre Guinea Worm Eradication Programme.[219]

On the whole, it would appear that with democracy established in Nigeria, the Bush administration focused attention on an area where the country could be of assistance to Africa, with Nigeria playing a pivotal task. This was where American assistance for diseases like Malaria, AIDS and tuberculosis came into the equation. As President Bush noted during the visit of President Obasanjo and UN Secretary General Kofi Annan to the White house:

> Suffering on the African Continent has been especially great. AIDS alone has left at least 11 million orphans in sub-Sahara Africa... In a part of the world where so many have suffered from war and want and famine, these latest tribulations are the cruelest of fates. We have the power to help. The United States is committed to working with other nations to reduce suffering and to spare lives, and working together is the key. Only through sustained and focused international cooperation can we address problems so grave and suffering so great. I thank President Obasanjo [who] last month led the nations of Africa in drafting the Abuja declaration which lays out crucial guidelines for the international effort we all envision.

The Obama Period

In his relationship with Nigeria, as indeed with any other African country, President Barrack Obama assumed office with considerable advantage. Being a black of African descent was something that thrilled most Africans and the brilliance with which he ran his campaign was of tremendous interest to many people in the continent. When eventually he assumed office as the President of the United States, many people in Africa believed that an unprecedented dawn was at hand in America's relationship with the African continent. While they knew that the new President would not openly show preference to the continent, they were also of the thought that Obama would not ignore the continent of his father, especially going by the nostalgic sentiments he had expressed about Africa in his memoires.[220]

Interestingly, Nigeria had been in Barrack Obama's calculation even before he became the President. He had made it clear on the floor of the Senate whilst still an Illinois Senator that he would be a strong advocate of debt relief for Nigeria if the country could hand over Charles Taylor who had then been indicted by the International Court. He noted:

> I strongly believe that Nigeria is a worthy candidate for debt relief and a key U.S. partner in West Africa. When Charles Taylor is turned over, there is no doubt in my mind that I will be a forceful advocate for debt relief for Nigeria, No nation should be permitted to wilfully ignore an indictment issued by the special court. Moreover, there are credible reports that Mr Taylor has broken the terms of his exile, is a threat to the Liberian peace process and continues to meddle in the internal affairs of Liberia – just before a few months before the Liberian elections.

Many Nigerians were also interested in Obama's involvement in the American Presidential race. Two non-government organisations (NGOs) sprang up in Nigeria to drum up support for the notion that a Democrat Senator Obama could win the American Presidency. One of these organisations was led by Ndi Okereke-Onyuike – President of the Nigerian Stock Exchange and the second NGO named 'Obama Nigeria Initiative' was led by Adelabu Onibiyo – a member of the Lagos State House of

Assembly. Though it is unacceptable under American legislation for the Presidential candidates to receive finds from abroad, the two organisations targeted the large Nigerian community in the US and encouraged people to vote for Obama.[221]

Not long after Obama assumed office, indications began to emerge that he was not particularly impressed with Nigeria. The first indication of this was his reluctance to include Nigeria into the list of the countries he visited during his first trip to the continent. The impact of this was all the more difficult for Nigeria to countenance when the President visited neighbouring Ghana. The general impression indeed was that Nigeria was really lagging behind Ghana in the area of democracy and good governance. However, while some Nigerians were surprised at what they saw as a slight, there were some who believed that the country should not have expected anything different. Writing in one of the national dailies, a Nigerian, Jibola Asolo may have captured the feelings of many Nigerian when he points out that:

> Statements "we are the giant of Africa" or "Nigeria is the greatest nation in Africa" not only serve as unwarranted and perplexing affirmations of national gratification, but they only underscore the myopic irony that afflicts us. How are we the giant of Africa when we cannot even conduct relatively free and fair elections? How are we the giant of Africa when corruption is the national pastime? ... That the first black American President is visiting Africa, and has no intention of making a stop-over in the world's most populous black country should really serve as a moment of reflection for us as a nation. It should shame us as a people.[222]

Obama's trip to Ghana was used, as a yardstick by many to measure the extent of recognition the new President would give to Nigeria. In his speech in Ghana, titled "A New Moment of Promise", President Obama vowed that the American government would support governments that uphold freedom, justice, the rule of law and the fight against corruption. Obama's choice of Ghana was predicated on its progressive democratic credentials. In his words, "America would allow each country practice a form of democracy that suits it but it has a responsibility to support those governments who act responsibly and to isolate those who don't".[223] On the occasion of the visit, John Kufuor, immediate past Ghanaian President, had this to say: "We feel we're the centre of the world at this moment. It should send a message to the world that Ghana is a Mecca for them to converge. It should encourage investors to come".[224] It could be argued that Ghana 'stole' the moment away from Nigeria because many observers expected that the latter's demographic strength; its distinguished global peacekeeping credentials that is unrivalled by any country in Africa; its strategic economic nexus in the US economy and its hegemonic clout in West Africa should have been factored into the choice of country(ies) in the Obama's African visit. Evidently, all of these were dwarfed or spoiled by official corruption, flawed elections, incessant and disturbing trends of religious violence and ethnic agitations.

But apart from his refusal to include Nigeria in his schedule, it is believed that some of his pronouncements during the visit were to underscore the obvious lapses in Nigeria's governance system. Despite the refusal to visit Nigeria, both countries had their first official contact in August 2009, when the new Secretary of State, Hillary Rodham Clinton, visited Abuja as part of a seven nation trip to Africa.

The relationship between the two countries since the ascension to office of President Obama has also had its own period of uncertainties. The first of these came with the illness of the late Nigerian president, Umaru Yar' Adua. In November 2009, the Nigerian President took ill and was flown to Saudi Arabia for treatment. As there was no official communication as to the welfare of the President, rumours inevitably went around and there were concerns in the United States as to the implications of the impasse on Nigeria. What further compounded the whole problem was that the state of the Nigerian President was not known as of the time when a Nigerian, Umar Farouk Abdulmutallab made an attempt to bomb an America Airliner. Although the details of this are discussed in the next chapter, it is important to note here that the Abdulmutallab affair was the most difficult incidence in Nigeria-American relations since Nigeria's independence. Another period of uncertainty, but no doubt of much lesser scale, was when a Nigerian Ambassador designate to the United States, had to be rejected for a criminal offence committed by his son. It was, however, not long afterwards that a new Ambassador was sent to replace him.

Situations began taking a new phase when in March 2009, a new Ambassador, Adebowale Adefuye, was appointed as Nigeria's Ambassador to the United States. Although there were still uncertainties about the health condition of the President, there were also issues of urgency in the American-Nigerian relations. The new Ambassador arrived in the United States with four primary objectives: to improve Nigeria's relations with the United States; correct the traditional stereotype against Nigerians in the United States; provide the best form of support for the Nigerian populations in the United States; and to mobilize Nigerians in the United States to support national development.[225]

While still acting as the President, Vice President Goodluck Jonathan paid an official visit to the United States in April 2010. This was the first opportunity the American population had to meet the person who was later to become Nigeria's leader. During the three day visit, the Acting President met President Barack Obama, Vice President Joe Biden, Assistant Secretary of State for African Affairs, Johnnie Carson, Congressional Black Caucus leaders and members, the President of the World Bank Robert Zoellick, UN Secretary General Ban Ki-moon and the Executives of Exxon Mobil and Chevron.

One of the most prominent developments in American-Nigerian relations during the Obama period has been the signing of the US/Nigeria Binational Commission. The objective of the commission is to establish a mechanism for sustained bilateral high level dialogue to promote and increase diplomatic, economic and security cooperation between the two countries. Going into specifics, the Commission is intended, among other goals to:

a. Promote and coordinate the diplomatic, economic, military, commercial, technical, social, and cultural cooperation between the two countries;
b. Address areas of mutual interest and/or concern and develop strategies for tackling these issues with assistance and coordination from both Governments;

c. Assist in the implementation and follow-up of Agreement and all other legal instruments already concluded between the Governments;
d. Create favourable conditions to carry out cooperation programmes and projects as may be decided by mutual consent, and help to resolve any difficulties that may arise in carrying out any such programmes and/or projects; and
e. Evaluate the development of cooperation between the two countries as well as initiatives from each Government aiming to expand cooperation to new areas.

The cardinal focus of the Commission is for the US government to work with Nigeria in the area of good governance, electoral reform/preparations, transparency and anti-corruption. Energy (electricity supply) reform and investment in Nigeria; as well as food and agricultural development are the other areas that the Commission is focused on. No doubt, the reform regime will latently benefit US investors and businesses. The Commission also seeks to promote cooperation for the Nigerian Niger Delta people. Sectors of the cooperation include security and counterterrorism. Underlying this is US oil/energy security and the protection of the US oil multinationals operating in the turbulent Nigerian Niger Delta. This became tellingly so since the Bush administration declared that access to African oil supplies would henceforth be defined as a "strategic national interest" to the US. This is a sign of good things to come as the US is known to establish such commissions only with valued and strategic partners. Expectedly, the set of issues to be addressed by the commission include: Good governance, transparency, and integrity; energy and investment, food security and agriculture, and Niger Delta and regional security cooperation. Not long after Vice President Goodluck Jonathan visited the United States, Nigeria's President Umaru Yar'Adua died.

The death of President Yar'Adua drew a sympathetic response from the United States. In a Statement from the White House, President Obama recognized the late President's "profound personal decency and integrity, deep commitment to public service and his passionate belief in the vast potential and bright future of Nigeria".[226] President Yar'Adua's contribution to peace in Africa was also recognized.

What is most likely to be a defining issue in the future of Nigeria-American relations is the way Nigeria conducts the 2011 elections. Already, the country has a long history of election malpractices and the United States has made it clear that it would expect the new administration to conduct a credible election. Consequent on this, President Jonathan made the election a key issue. Among the steps taken so far has been the removal of the former electoral Commissioner, Maurice Iwu and his replacement with Attahiru Jega.

The War on Terror

United States has always realized that the nature of its composition and the peculiarities of its history make religion a crucial issue in Nigeria. With its ethnic groups divided even if somewhat crudely, along religious lines and with a fairly long history of tension and violence, Nigeria has always been a country of interest in global discussions on religious radicalisation and political violence. The country witnessed its first major case of religious violence during the 1970s, when the late Mohammed Marwa, widely known as Maitatsine, staged major riots that engrossed the Northern city of Kano and resulted in the death of more than 10,000 people.[227] A series of other religious violence followed during the 1980s and 1990s and many of these were in the northern parts of the country. These conflicts were later to affect inter-group relations in Nigeria, especially when there were major debates as to whether Sharia should be incorporated into the Nigerian constitution. Although the United States was concerned about the violence associated with radicalisation in Nigeria, this was largely for the sake of Nigeria and there were no reason for Washington to be concerned with what was, purely seen as an issue of domestic concern.

A new layer of Islamic radicalisation in Nigeria that was to attract more interest from the United States came during the early 1980s, when the successful revolution of the Iranian people against their Shah led to an awakening of Islamist tendencies in Northern Nigeria. The emergence of an Islamic government under the leadership of Ayatollah Khomeini and the subsequent humiliation it meted out to the US provided inspiration to Muslims the world over and youths in particular saw in Islam a viable alternative to the bi-polar systems of capitalism or communism. The Islamist revival began in the 1980s, as young Muslims, radicalized by revolutions, began introducing variance of Islam that were of more radical dispositions. The whole atmosphere of global terrorism changed in 1992, when Al-Qaeda launched the first in its series of attack on American interest. This was through the attack on hotels in Aden, Yemen. Subsequent attacks were to take place around the world, including the ones on the World Trade Centre, the American embassies in Kenya and Tanzania and ultimately 9/11.

For most of the early years of Al-Qaeda attacks on the United States, the politics of global terrorism was a difficult one for both countries to handle in their bilateral discussions. While Nigeria was against the activities of Al-Qaeda, it had to make its response quite carefully as any provocative condemnation could have implications on domestic policies at home, especially as it was widely known that there were some Nigerians who did not have much sympathy for the United States and were, in fact supporters of Al-Qaeda's motives, if not the extent of its actions. On its part, the United States realised that the Nigerian government could not be so demonstrative of its condemnation of the attack because of the nature of its internal composition.

The Al-Qaeda attacks on United States embassies in Kenya and Tanzania were to be a major turning point in the relationship of both the United States and Nigeria to global terrorism. To Nigeria, the attack was seen as taking terrorism too far. While, of course, the country was against terrorism, the incidence of it in Africa was widely condemned. The Nigerian government felt that Al Qaeda had exploited Africa's geo-strategic and political weakness of the continent in its war against America. On its part, the United States identified Nigeria as a country that could help in the fight against terrorism in Africa but also as a country that should be closely watched as a potential source of attack on American interest. This was largely because of the prevalence of religious conflicts in the country and the extent to which radical Islamic tendencies were known to have penetrated the country.

When the terrorist attack on the United States occurred in September 2001, reactions of Nigerian radical groups were somewhat confusing. The best known radical leader in the country during the period, Sheikh El Zakzaky, condemned the attack but was also quick to condemn what he saw as President Bush's efforts to consider Muslims all over the world as evil. He saw the September 11 attack as an attempt by the enemies of Islam to use adherents of the religion to destroy it. He said the attack was used as a cover to invade, destroy and take control of the resources of the oil-rich Muslim nation-states, using violent Muslims to launch an attack on the US and provide a pretext for such an invasion. On his part, Mujihad was of the opinion that the context of the attack and America's controversial foreign policy in the Middle East made the attack understandable, if not, in fact, justifiable. While it will be inaccurate to draw ethnic inferences from national responses to the attack on the United States, it appeared that greater support came for it from the northern parts of the country while support, even from South-Western Muslims was significantly reduced.

The entire atmosphere was to change in December 2009, when a young Nigerian, Umar Farouk Abdulmutallab, was arrested whilst trying to bomb Northwest Airlines Flight 253, flying into Detroit from Amsterdam. Because of the extent of concerns generated by the incident, there is the need to put a number of things in perspective. Farouk's journey towards terrorism is an unusual one. He was the son of a former Federal Commissioner (Minister) in Nigeria, Umaru Mutallab who was also a former chairman of a Nigerian bank. Consequently, he enjoyed the trappings of a wealthy upbringing, privately educated in a highly regarded international boarding school. He later went to University College London, where he studied Engineering. Although he was known to have been very religious, it is believed that it was while he was at University College London that he got radicalized and got converted to extremism. After graduating from UCL, he moved first to Egypt, and then Dubai in the United Arab Emirates where he studied for an MBA before dropping out and telling his family he did not want to have anything to do with any of them again.

The moment the father realized the potential dangers that could emanate from his son's radicalization, he alerted British and American authorities but apart from taking note of the information, nothing much was done to put the suspect under close watch, until the abortive December 2009 attempt. The suspect reportedly told officials he had traveled to Yemen for training by Al-Qaeda, although British counterterrorism officials dismissed the claims. President Barack Obama's top security official Janet Napolitano on December 27 stated "Right now we have no indication it's part of anything larger", warning it would be "inappropriate to speculate" that Al-Qaeda had sent Abdulmutallab on a suicide mission. On December 28, President Obama called it an "attempted terrorist attack" and promised to "to use every element of our national power to disrupt, to dismantle and defeat the violent extremists who threaten us, whether they are from Afghanistan or Pakistan, Yemen or Somalia..." That same day, Al Qaeda in the Arabian Peninsula claimed responsibility for the attack. The group released photos of Nigerian Umar Farouk Abdulmutallab smiling in a white shirt and white Islamic skullcap with the Al Qaeda in Arabian Peninsula banner in the background. On January 8, 2010, President Barack Obama took responsibility for security lapses exposed by the attack, declaring in televised remarks "We are at war against Al-Qaeda", noting "our adversaries will seek new ways to evade them, as was shown by the Christmas attack" By February 2010, the suspect told federal investigators that cleric Anwar al Awlaki gave him orders to carry out the attack. Al-Jazeera reported that Awlaki issued a statement that:

> Brother Mujahed Umar Farouk – may God relieve him – is one of my students, yes ... We had kept in contact, but I didn't issue a fatwa to Umar Farouk for this operation.

The United States swiftly reacted by listing Nigeria on its "Terror Watch List". This is a list of countries that the US sees as supporting terrorism or terrorists. Nigeria joined the 14 other countries – Pakistan, Lebanon, Yemen, Syria, Sudan, Somalia, Algeria, Cuba, Saudi Arabia, Iran, Iraq, Afghanistan and some radical organizations – on the list. While the Nigerian government and the general public expressed outrage at the US action which some black Americans referred to as 'profiling,' the US government defended its actions on the need to take measures that would protect aviation and by extension the whole world since citizens from the whole world travel by air daily. It said the action was without prejudice to Nigeria and was based on objective reality rather than an attempt to embarrass Nigeria.

Nigeria expressed its disappointment and concern over its undeserved placement on the countries of interest list and viewed this action as having the potential of undermining longstanding and established US-Nigeria bilateral ties.[228] Also, the Nigerian National Assembly issued a two week ultimatum to the US government to remove Nigeria from the list. The legislators however failed to state the action they would take if the US fails to act after the expiration of the ultimatum. In any case, it was argued that with a very weak and dependent economy, Nigeria was in no position to stand up to the US. After several pleas and diplomatic entreaties from the Nigerian government and right groups, the United States agreed to remove Nigeria from the terror watch list on the following conditions:

- That the Nigerian Government must make a public condemnation of acts of terrorism wherever they occur in the world.
- That Nigeria takes urgent steps to address security lapses at its airports.
- That Nigeria be a party to an agreement to deploy air marshals on all US-bound flights originating from Nigeria, and
- That the anti-terrorism bill pending before the National Assembly be passed into law.[229]

Nigeria's name was subsequently removed from the list after it was adjudged to have substantially complied with the conditions listed above.

Conclusion

Since the return of democracy to Nigeria, the relationship between the country and the United States has been easier to contextualise. Although there were efforts by both sides to ensure an improvement in the relationship between the two countries, there were sometime vibes that do come from the United States which Nigeria sometimes found unacceptable. For example, there was a State Department declaration that Nigeria would cease to exist as an entity by 2015. This opinion divided Nigeria, with many in government criticising the American report as being alarmist and not based on any objective assessment of the situation in the country and others, especially outside the government agreeing that there were justifiable grounds for the State Department's position. Again, in 2010, a former American Ambassador to Nigeria, Mr. John Campbell, published an article in the *Foreign Affairs Journal,* under the aegis of the Council for Foreign Relations entitled "Nigeria on the Brink, What Happens if the 2011 Elections Fail?". This article was to draw an instant response from the Nigerian Ambassador Adefuye.[230]

The 2011 elections in Nigeria was seen as one of the defining issues in the future of Nigeria-American relations, oil supply and security. Already, the country has a long history of election malpractices and the United States has made it clear that it would expect the new administration to conduct a credible election. Consequent on this, President Goodluck Jonathan made the election a key issue. Among the steps taken was the removal of the former electoral Commissioner, Maurice Iwu and his replacement with Attahiru Jega. On the whole, since 1999 when Nigeria returned to democratic rule, the US has been actively concerned and interested in the sustenance of democratic rule and the building of critical state institutions. It was in the forefront of efforts to strengthen the capacity of INEC to conduct free and credible elections. Even though Nigeria's democracy has been very fragile and characterized by frequently rigged elections, sectarian and religious violence, human rights violations and abuses, and general economic hardships, the US had continued to invest so much hope in Nigeria's democratic stability partly because of its selfish interests, and the security of the West African sub-region. The United States has shown keen interest in the peaceful resolution of the Niger Delta crisis and has often spoken out strongly in favour of democracy in Nigeria in critical times when the country's democracy was being threatened. Such support, no doubt, has been quite critical to the sustenance of the country's democracy and sends a very clear message that military coups and unconstitutional takeover of governments would no longer be tolerated. It was heartening that the United States was very instrumental to the seamless transition of power from late President Yar'Adua to the Vice and now President Goodluck Jonathan.

End Notes

[191.] Bill Clinton (2004), *My Life*, Knopf Publishing Group, (Random House). P.

[192.] See the Statement issued by the White House on January 11, 1999.

[193.] Critical elements in the American body polity like the former American President, Jimmy Carter and the former Secretary of State, Colin Powell, observed the Presidential election and confirmed that the election was flawed.

[194.] The Monica Lewinsky scandal was the sex scandal between the former United States President Bill Clinton and a then 22-year-old Intern, Monica Lewinsky. After initial denial, President Clinton later admitted to an "inappropriate relationship" with Miss Lewinsky. This resulted in the impeachment of the President by the House of Representative on the charges of perjury and obstruction of justice. He was, however, acquitted on all impeachment charges by the Senate.

[195.] Although opinions were divided among Africans, it was widely believed that many people in African supported Bill Clinton during the Lewinsky scandal. It will never be known the extent to which the former President realised the support had had in Africa during the scandal, even though he had recognised the specific role played by the former South African President, Nelson Mandela.

[196.] This was to remove trade barriers to opportunities for Africans. As of this time, the Senate was yet to approve the Act.

[197.] Remarks Following Discussions With President Olusegun Obasanjo of Nigeria and an Exchange With Reporters in Abuja, Nigeria, August 26, 2000

[198.] Adewale Banjo (2010), "US Development Diplomacy in Africa: From Bill Clinton to George Bush", *African Journal of Political Science and International Relations*, Vol. 4, No. 4, April.

[199.] To avoid confusion between President George H.W. Bush (in office January 1989-January 1993) and his son, President George W. Bush (in office January 2001-January 2009), all references in this chapter to "President Bush" will refer to the son.

[200.] The Sullivan gathering was named after the late Reverend Leon Sullivan, who had the conviction that Africa's challenges can be solved by determined and optimistic addressing of the continent's challenges.

201. The countries President Bush had visited before coming to Nigeria included Senegal, South Africa, Botswana and Uganda.

202. There had been several attempts to end the civil war which failed. Ultimately there was the Accra Accord signed in --- which called for a Transition Government. It was organised by ECOWAS with full support of the African Union. Under the terms, President Charles Taylor left office to end the war raised by the Liberian United for Reconciliation and Development (LURD) and the Movement for Democracy in Liberia (MODEL).

203. This could be seen from his testimony at the International Court.

204. Jean Herskovits (2007), "Nigeria's Rigged Democracy", *Foreign Affairs*, Vol. 86, No. 4. July/August. PP. 116 – 117.

205. Ibid.

206. Ibid. P.118.

207. Ibid.

208. Ibid.

209. Ibid. P. 128.

210. Ibid.

211. Michael Mukwuzi and Oluokun Ayorinde (2007), "Dangerous Militants", *TheNews*, (Lagos, Nigeria), April 2. PP. 20 – 29.

212. Solomon Ibharuneafe (2005), "Road to Debt Forgiveness", *Newswatch* (Lagos, Nigeria), July 4, P. 34.

213. Aliyu Askira (2007), "Go, Just Go… Or Else", *The Week* (Lagos, Nigeria), Vol. 25, No. 9, April 2, P. 18.

214. Fola Adekeye (2006), "Death to Traitors", *The Week* (Lagos, Nigeria), Vol. 23, No. 18, May 15, PP. 11 – 12; Ademola Adegbamigbe (2006), "Third Term takes shape", The News, (Lagos, Nigeria), February 20. PP. 18 – 22; and Jeffrey Tayler (2006), "Third Term and US Interest", *Tell*, (Lagos, Nigeria), May 1. PP. 50 – 51.

215. News Item (2010), "Third Term takes shape", Nigerian Compass, (Lagos, Nigeria), March 19. P. 1

216. Herskovits, op.cit. P. 116.

217. Ibid. P.121.

218. Ranti Adedeji (2009), "Two African Countries for G8 Summit", *Broad Street Journal*, (Lagos, Nigeria), March 2. P. 43.

219. Folasade Adebayo (2008), "Guinea Worm…Going…Going", *Tell*, (Lagos, Nigeria), May 5. P. 14.

220. Before assuming office, Barrack Obama had written two books which detailed aspects of his life. *The Audacity of Hope: Thoughts on Reclaiming the American Dream and Dreams from My Father.*

221. Ololade Adewuyi (2008), "Rooting for Obama", *Tell*, (Lagos, Nigeria), August 11. P. 57.

222. Jibola Asolo, "Ruminations on Obama's Planned Visit". *ThisDay*, 18 November 2009.

223. Ololade Adewuyi (2009), "Africa's Moment of Promise", *Tell*, (Lagos, Nigeria), July 27. P. 35.

224. *Ibid.*

225. Adefuye had previously served as Nigeria's High Commissioner to Jamaica and as Deputy High Commissioner to the United Kingdom.

226. Statement from the White House, May 5 2010.

227. The name "Maitasine" was given to Marwa because he often ended his public preaching with the Hausa word *Wanda bata yarda ba Allah tatsine* (meaning "May God curse whosoever does not agree with me".

228. *Reuters,* January 6, 2010.

229. *The Punch* (Lagos), February 12, 2010.

230. Ade Adefuye, "A Bad Taste: Response to John Campbell article on Nigeria". Press Release by the Nigerian Embassy, Washington DC- Professor Adefuye.

Chapter Eight
Trade and Economic Relations

Bolaji KEHINDE and Temilade ABIMBOLA

As with most diplomatic relations, trade and economics lie at the centre of the US-Nigerian friendship. Indeed, what began as ordinary relations at the time of Nigeria's independence in 1960 had by 2010 become one of the most important and most dynamic economic relations between the United States and any African nation, with every prospect of steady increase in the years ahead. Even on the occasions when there were tensions in the relationship, as was the case during the Abacha era in Nigeria, trade and commercial activities continued, such that calls for sanctions on the regime for its human-rights records were almost completely ignored by the United States. But while the issues of trade and commercial relations have appeared in many of the preceding chapters, the objective of this chapter is to focus exclusively on the trade and economic relations between Nigeria and the United States during the first fifty years of Nigerian independence. While it is impossible to discuss all the ramifications of the trade between both countries, this chapter considers the salient issues that underline relations between both countries and offers a broad perspective of the possible future directions of trade and commercial relations between both countries.

There are seven main sections in this chapter. In the first section, we look at the broad principles underlining Nigeria's economic diplomacy. The second section looks at Nigeria's economic relations with the United States during the First Republic. By coincidence, this is also the period before oil came in to completely re-focus Nigeria's economic fortune and its external relations. In the third section, we discuss the transformation wrought on Nigerian-American relations by the oil boom. The fourth section examines the trade relations between the two countries since the return of democracy to Nigeria. The rough edges in the Nigerian-American trade relations are discussed in the fifth section. Section six concludes discussions in the chapter.

Determinants and Contents of Nigeria's Economic Diplomacy

Before going deep into the specificities of Nigeria - US economic relations, some general comments may be appropriate. Broadly, economic relations entail the development, formulation and implementation of commercial policy, movement of labour and capital, balance of trade and exchange of payments, among others. Within these core themes are the rubrics dealing with issues such as import licensing, exchange control, adjustment of balance of payments and other trading and commercial activities between nations. Pivotal political and economic-based strategies such as those to do with poverty alleviation, humanitarian assistance, economic aids (such as agricultural, infrastructural development, social cohesion to support nation building) are all other forms of economic relations directly pertinent to our discussion of the Nigeria-USA economic relations. We hasten to point out that bilateral economic relations are rarely devoid of political, diplomatic and cultural ideas common to the two states. In addition, international economic relations add another dimension to the foreign policies of both countries. As will be shown later, one can also assert that despite changing economic relations, one can discern an underlying framework for discussing Nigeria - US relations. The economic policy between Nigeria and the US can be contextualized in terms of their mutual foreign policy positions and the internal political situations that emerged in the course of their 50 years of association.

As with most nations, Nigeria defines economic diplomacy as a way of reaching out economically to other countries and the general international community, especially international organisations, multinational corporations and similar institutions. Like other developing countries, however, the primary motive of Nigeria's economic diplomacy has always been to strengthen the country's economic base. As a developing country, the key issues that have always recurred in the country's economic diplomacy have included attracting foreign investment, negotiating trade concessions, partnering in development projects and rescheduling debts.

The issues that have determined Nigeria's economic diplomacy have also been similar to those that have underlined the same situation in other developing countries. Perhaps the most important of these is the structure inherited at the time of independence. In the case of Nigeria, the clearly pro-western pattern of economic relation bestowed by British colonial rule had meant that the country, at least at the time of independence, was clearly pro-western in its economic diplomacy, despite the advertised stance of political non-alignment. Another determinant of Nigeria's economic diplomacy has been the political situation in the country at any given moment. As will be shown later in this chapter, on the occasions where there has been domestic political stability, there has been a coherent economic diplomacy and the country has benefitted significantly. Third, Nigeria's economic diplomacy has been determined by its domestic economic strength. This, as will again be shown later, has threaded through Nigeria's economic diplomacy, especially in the relationship with the United States of America.

Trade and Economic Relations in the Immediate Post Independence Period

On the whole, Nigeria's early economic relations were quite modest. By 1960, imports were valued at N432 million. They increased to N756.0 million and N8.132 million in 1970 and 1978 respectively. The bulk of the imports were finished and semi-finished goods. However, from 1974, food imports became noticeable in Nigeria's external trade. The country had an unfavourable trade balance from 1960 to 1965, partly because of the aggressive drive to import all kinds of machinery to stimulate the industrialization strategy pursued immediately after independence.[231]

At the time of Nigeria's independence and throughout the first few years, the economic relationship was characterized by "aid" coming from the direction of the United States. A five man US delegation visited Nigeria in June 1960 to investigate possible economic cooperation. A key point that emerged from the recommendations of the US trade mission included the provision of US$225 million in economic development aid over five years. In June 1961, Nigeria's Finance Minister, Festus Okotie-Eboh, led a delegation to the United States to finalize discussions regarding US aid to Nigeria. In January 1962, USAID also announced an allocation of US$1.9 million to assist Nigeria in expanding its economy, creating industry and stimulating investments and in 1963, the United States provided US$42 million out of the estimated $201 million needed to finance dams on the River Niger.[232] Indeed, the United States became involved in Nigeria's economic development during most of the early years and this continued until around 1974, when assistance was phased out because of a substantial increase in Nigeria's per capita income resulting from rising oil revenue. It is believed that by 1974, the United States had provided Nigeria with approximately US$360 million in assistance, which included grants for technical assistance, development assistance, relief and rehabilitation, and food aid. These disbursements continued into the late 1970s, bringing total bilateral economic assistance to roughly US$445 million.

Despite this, however, trade went on between the two countries, with Nigeria exporting groundnut, cocoa and other primary commodities in exchange for finished American products. Nigeria's regions were planning to take advantage of this trade through increased focus on agricultural products, with the western region focusing on cocoa, the north on groundnuts and the east on palm products. At this time, the whole issue of revenue allocation that was to be one of the most controversial issues in Nigeria politics was yet to emerge. With the discovery of oil, however, the pattern changed in Nigerian/US relations and the consequences continue to shape the situation between the two countries till today.

Oil in Nigerian/US Relations

For Nigeria, the discovery of oil was perhaps the most important economic development in the history of the country, as it immediately catapulted the nation from a struggling agricultural economy into a prominent place in global economic politics. The importance of oil to the Nigerian economy has been the subject of several studies such that it will not serve any purpose relating it here. It only needs to be pointed out that since its entrance into national prominence it has become, perhaps, the most important factor in the Nigerian economic and political life. The resource now accounts for more than 95% of Nigeria's external earnings. The country is also Africa's largest and the world's seventh largest producer of the resource. For the United States, oil has both economic and strategic importance. The country is the highest consumer of oil in the world, with a daily appetite of almost 20,000,000 barrels per day. This is far less than the annual production of the country and the United States has had to depend significantly on outside supply. The strategic dependence emanating from this consumption rate has also meant that oil is a crucial element in foreign policy objectives. In short, put in very crude economic terms, Nigeria has a significant deposit of oil and the United States needs oil. The American need for the resource has become all the more important because of the general instability in the Middle East which is also a major source of oil for the country. This has thus increased the importance of Nigerian and other African sources of oil in the United States' strategic calculations. Indeed, the former Assistant Secretary of State for African Affairs, Walter Kansteiner, noted that while Africa is currently producing 15 per cent of US oil needs, the supply from the continent may soon rise to 25 per cent.[233] This was further confirmed in the May 2001 National Energy Policy Report, when then US Vice-President, Dick Cheney, recognized the fact that West Africa is the fastest-growing source of oil and gas for the American market.[234]

But, quite ironically, oil came into Nigerian life at a time when diplomatic relations between Nigeria and the United States were not very cordial. Nigeria was unhappy with the tacit role the United States played in the civil war, which had been prosecuted without recourse to borrowing thanks to Nigeria's new found oil wealth. The timing, however, meant that the realization of the importance of oil to the economy happened at a time when relations with the United States were cautious and tentative. It was not long, however, before this was transformed and within a very short time oil had become the most important factor in Nigerian-US relations.

A number of American oil companies are involved in Nigeria, the most prominent being Exxon Mobil and Chevron. Exxon Mobil has a lot of facilities in Nigeria and recently the company made history when it laid the first ever set oil and gas grade pipes made in Nigeria in its Edop-Idoho Offshore field. Chevron is the third-largest multinational oil corporation in Nigeria. The company's records shows that it is spending more than US$3 billion annually and it operates under a joint venture arrangement with the Nigerian National Petroleum Corporation. Chevron has extensive interests in deep-water oil resources off the coast of Nigeria, including the Agbami and Usan projects. Although the exact number of staff employed is not known, especially as many are on casual contracts, it is believed that Chevron provides jobs for more than 3,000 employees and up to another 3,500 workers are under contract.

American Imports from Nigeria: A Look at Oil Compared to Other Products

Nigeria is the fifth-largest exporter of oil to the United States, with more than 1 million barrels of crude oil being exported to the country daily. Indeed, the trade in oil makes Nigeria the United States' largest trading partner in sub-Saharan Africa. Although militant activities in the Niger Delta sometimes reduce the flow, the export still remain significant and Nigeria has constantly maintained its position as being among the top seven oil exporters to the United States. The table below illustrates the volume and value of these exports.

Table 1: Petroleum Products (Including Crude Oil) Export to the U.S.A: 2003- 2006

s/no	Year	Net Weight (kg)	Value (Naira)
1	2003	41,667,580	1,101,160,349,957
2	2004	50,545,699	1,874,472,799,873
3	2005	51,091,522	2,511,320,846,702
4	2006	1,417,409,160	3,170,569,236,589

Source: *National Bureau of Statistics, Nigeria Foreign Trade Summary, 2003-2006 Various Editions, Abuja: NBS.*

Tailing crude oil exports are other petroleum products as shown in the table below:

Table 2: Petroleum Products (Excluding Crude Oil) Export to the U.S.A: 2003- 2006

s/no	Year	Net Weight (kg)	Value (Naira)
1	2003	3,745,996	49,762,718,934
2	2004	1,405,298,466	168,363,432,091
3	2005	2,260,214,597	145,023,550,498
4	2006	3,699,721,204	174,474,562,943

Source: *National Bureau of Statistics, Nigeria Foreign Trade Summary, 2003 2006 Various Editions, Abuja: NBS.*

Although oil dominated the scene since its introduction into the Nigerian economy, there are other commodities that continue to be important in Nigerian-American relations. For example, rubber-products, cocoa, gum, cashews, coffee and ginger constituted over US$70 million of United States imports from Nigeria in 2007. In 2008, Nigeria took significant steps towards implementing trade reforms and improvements in the environment for business and trade. The government of Nigeria removed import bans on several products of interest to the United States, including corn, wheat flour, crude vegetable oil, and several food and consumer products. It also reduced tariffs on many other products and streamlined its system of tariffs by placing all import tariffs into five broad categories. The U.S.-Nigeria Trade and Investment Framework Agreement (TIFA) is part of a comprehensive U.S. effort to support the Nigerian Government's efforts to advance trade and economic development. Below are some of the figures that capture the whole picture of the economic relationship between Nigeria and the US.

Table 3: Summary of U.S Trade with Nigeria: 1985- 2010 (Figures in Millions of USD)

s/no	Year	Exports	Imports	Balance
1	1985	675.7	3,001.9	-2,326.2
2	1986	408.8	2,530.3	-2,121.5
3	1987	295.2	3,573.5	-3,278.3
4	1988	356.8	3,278.6	-2,921.8
5	1989	490.3	5,283.9	-4,793.6
6	1990	553.2	5,982.1	-5,428.9
7	1991	831.4	5,168.0	-4,336.6
8	1992	1,001.1	5,102.4	-4,101.3
9	1993	894.7	5,301.4	-4,406.7
10	1994	509.0	4,429.9	-3,920.9
11	1995	602.9	4,930.5	-4,327.6
12	1996	818.4	5,978.3	-5,159.9
13	1997	813.0	6,349.4	-5,536.4
14	1998	816.7	4,194.0	-3,377.3
15	1999	627.9	4,385.1	-3,757.2
16	2000	721.9	10,537.6	-9,815.7
17	2001	955.1	8,774.9	-7,819.8
18	2002	1,057.7	5,945.3	-4,887.6
19	2003	1,016.9	10,393.6	-9,376.7
20	2004	1,554.3	16,248.5	-14,694.2
21	2005	1,619.8	24,239.4	-22,619.6
22	2006	2,233.5	27,863.1	-25,629.7
23	2007	2,777.9	32,770.2	-29,992.3
24	2008	4,102.4	38,068.0	-33,965.6
25	2009	3,687.1	19,128.2-	15,441.1
26	2010	4,039.7	30,515.9	-26,476.2

Source: US Department of Census, accessed in http://www.census.gov/foreign-trade/balance/c7530.html#2010.

Challenges to the Relationship

The political situation between the countries became particularly difficult on a number of occasions. The first of these came during a period of disagreement over Angolan independence, when the Murtala administration reacted strongly to the letter written by President Ford to African leaders. However, as recorded by General Joseph Garba,

TRADE AND ECONOMIC RELATIONS

> The realities of bilateral economic relations outweighed political and diplomatic disagreements in our relations. American technology had a role to play in Nigeria's policies of rapid economic development. Nigeria, with a lot of oil to sell, had become (then) the second largest supplier to the United States. There was therefore, a mutual interest in developing strong bilateral economic cooperation.[235]

Garba went on to say that businessmen as well as US Government officials focused on petroleum. At the end of 1975, the petroleum industry accounted for 94% of the United States direct investment in Nigeria. Chemical and allied products accounted for only .02 per cent, primary and fabricated metal investment was only .005 per cent, while investment in machinery was almost non-existent.[236] Because of Nigeria's petroleum, trade with the U.S had grown to such a height that by 1980, Nigeria would enjoy a favourable trade balance of nearly US$1 billion.

Much more serious challenges to economic relations arose first after Babangida nullified election results and later when the Abacha regime killed Ken Saro-Wiwa and other activists. During all the period, trade continued, albeit at much reduced levels. This changed significantly after majority rule was restored in May 1999.

Trade and Democracy: Developments Since the Return of Civilian Rule to Nigeria

Since the return of democracy to Nigeria in 1999, there has been a significant increase in Nigeria's trade relations with the United States. By a pleasant co-incidence, the African Growth and Opportunity Act (AGOA), which was designed to offer tangible incentives for African countries to continue their efforts to open their economies and build free markets, was signed into law in 2000, just a year after the return of democracy to Nigeria. This has further increased American-Nigerian trade relations.

In recent times, Nigeria has emerged as the United States' largest trading partner in sub-Saharan Africa, largely due to the high level of petroleum imports from Nigeria, which supply 8% of U.S. oil imports--nearly half of Nigeria's daily oil production. Nigeria is the fifth-largest exporter of oil to the United States.

Two-way trade in 2008 was valued at more than US$42 billion, an 18% increase over 2007 data. Led by machinery, wheat, and motor vehicles, US goods exports to Nigeria in 2008 were worth more than US$4 billion. In 2008, US imports from Nigeria were over US$38 billion, consisting predominantly of oil. However, rubber products, cocoa, gum arabic, cashews, coffee, and ginger constituted over US$70 million of US imports from Nigeria in 2007. The US trade deficit with Nigeria was US$21 billion in 2007. Nigeria is the 50th-largest export market for U.S. goods and the 14th-largest exporter of goods to the United States. The United States is Nigeria's largest trading partner after the United Kingdom. Although the trade balance overwhelmingly favours Nigeria, thanks to oil exports, a large portion of US exports to Nigeria is believed to enter the country outside of the Nigerian Government's official statistics, due to importers seeking to avoid Nigeria's excessive tariffs.[237]

The United States is the largest foreign investor in Nigeria. The stock of US foreign direct investment (FDI) in Nigeria in 2006 was US$339 million, down from US$2 billion in 2004. US FDI in Nigeria is concentrated largely in the petroleum/mining and wholesale trade sectors. Exxon-Mobil and Chevron remain the two largest US corporate players in offshore oil and gas production.[238] In March 2009, the United States and Nigeria met under the existing TIFA to advance the on-going work program and to discuss improvements in Nigerian trade policies and market access. Among the topics discussed were cooperation in the World Trade Organization (WTO), market access, export diversification, intellectual property protection and enforcement, commercial issues, trade capacity building and technical assistance, infrastructure, and investment issues.[239]

Anti-liberalizing policies hamper foreign direct investment in most developing countries. Nigeria's oil industry appears to be an exception to the global trend characterized by increasing state ownership and resource nationalism in the oil and gas sectors. Globally, approximately 85% of the oil traded is controlled by state oil companies owned by host governments and prefers to work with foreign oil companies only for the expertise, technical services and investment capital that they offer.[240] This has contributed to increase in Foreign Direct Investment in the country. FDI from the US in 2009 accounted for as much as 15.6 per cent of total FDI. Other contributory factors are the liberalization of the economy, reform of public institutions, predictable political transitions, and enactment of extractive industries transparency and other corporate governance-friendly laws.

Reliance on oil has also drastically increased trade deficits for the United States. The United States is the major importer of Nigeria's crude petroleum. The stock of U.S Foreign Direct Investment (FDI) was US$190 million in 2006. The US goods trade deficit with Nigeria was US$30.0 billion in 2007, an increase of US$4.4 billion from US$25.6 billion in 2006. US goods exports in 2007 were US$2.8 billion, up to 24.8 per cent, from the previous year. Corresponding US imports from Nigeria were US$32.8 billion, up to 17.6 per cent. Nigeria was at that point the 50th largest export market for US goods. The stock of US foreign direct investments in Nigeria was US$339 million in 2006 (latest data available), down from US$1.2 billion in 2005. US FDI in Nigeria is concentrated largely in nonbank holding companies and the wholesale trade sectors.[241]

In 2008, the US goods trade deficit with Nigeria was $34 billion, an increase of US$4 billion from US$30 billion in 2007. US goods exports in 2008 were US$4.1 billion, up 47.4 per cent from the previous year. Corresponding US imports from Nigeria were US$38.1 billion, up 16.2 per cent. As at 2009, Nigeria was the 44th largest export market for U.S goods.[242]

When Nigeria announced the Structural Adjustment Programme in June 1986, the United States became more involved in the economic affairs of Nigeria: Among others:

- The US provided a credit cover for Nigeria into the Summer of 1986 through Export-Import Bank when almost all countries had ended it;
- The US joined other countries in an extraordinary US$250 million bridge loan to underwrite the SFEM when disbursement of the World Bank loan was delayed;
- The US officially endorsed Nigeria's decision not to draw on the IMF loan and urged creditors to reschedule Nigeria's debt without the added help of IMF resources;
- The United States rescheduled all its own official debt on

almost exactly the terms requested by Nigeria and the government also urged American commercial banks to do the same;

- The US government announced during the visit of Secretary of State George Shultz in January 1987, the organisation of a trade and investment mission and are taking other steps to encourage investment in Nigeria.

Rough Edges in United States-Nigerian Trade Relations

Although the relations between Nigeria and the United States have been remarkable since the independence of the country, there are also a number of rough edges that need to be highlighted. As would be expected, most of these have to do with oil and its role in the relationship between the two countries. First, there is the belief in Nigeria that, despite the friendship between the two countries, the United States might be doing things that are not necessarily in Nigeria's long-term interest. One such area is over the politics of the Joint Development Zone (JDZ) between Nigeria and Sao Tome, which allows Nigeria to make investment in Sao Tome. There was the belief in Nigeria that the United States, in its desperate desire to secure hydrocarbon assets for US companies, wanted to use the Sao Tome authorities to scuttle the investment drives being made by some Nigerian companies.[243] Indeed, a report signed by the Attorney General of Sao Tome requested that US authorities investigate contracts awarded to Houston-based ERHC Energy. The report, which indicted the Nigerian government, alleged that Nigerian controlled ERHC made improper payments to officials and their families during the award of oil blocs in the JDZ.[244]

The second has to do with the activities of American oil companies operating in Nigeria. Exxon-Mobil and Chevron, the two largest, are at the centre of many of the controversies in the Niger Delta. The main allegation that has been levelled against the two companies is that, in their bid to maximize their economic profit in Nigeria, they have ignored completely the interest of the local population. Three main allegations arise:

1. Pollution emanating from the process of exploration. While it must be conceded that some pollution may be caused by sabotage of oil pipelines, the environmental damage to

the Niger Delta wrought by large scale exploration and oil extraction is extensive.
2. Connivance with the Nigerian security apparatus to brutalise the indigenous population of the oil producing region and lack of respect for local culture and tradition.
3. Allegations of improper financial deals that involve oil and gas enterprise in Nigeria and how this gets connected with the United States of America. There have always been allegations of corruption in the management of the Nigerian oil business. One of the most prominent of this was the widely publicised Halliburton Scandal. In 2003, it was revealed that Kellogg Brown & Root, a company eventually acquired by international conglomerate Halliburton, gave approximately US$180 million in bribes to Nigerian officials. It was alleged that these bribes were an attempt to obtain a lucrative contract to develop Nigeria's liquefied natural gas project. After six years of legal wrangling, Halliburton finally admitted guilt and agreed to pay US$492 million in fines to the United States government for violating the Foreign Corrupt Practices Act. Many Nigerians feel, however, that this whole situation shows how American companies can collude with key players on the Nigerian side to do things that may be detrimental to Nigeria's larger interest.

Conclusion

It is expected that economic relations will continue to increase and yield corresponding benefits to Nigeria and the United States. In this wise, the Nigeria-United States Bi-National Commission, which is a strategic partnership between Nigeria and the United States to sharpen joint collaboration between the two countries, has been inaugurated. It is aimed at achieving measurable progress on issues that are of mutual interest to the two nations, namely: good governance and transparency; regional cooperation and development; security issues and counterterrorism; energy reform and investment; and food security and agricultural development. The Commission provides a framework to work towards mutually beneficial relationships. However, a lot will depend on how organized the

Nigerian government and private sector are to negotiate a more favourable trade framework for the country.

US Government documents have asserted that trade relations are being impeded by the Nigerian government in a variety of ways. According to the Department of Trade, 'some importers complain that tariffs are excessively high and that the Nigerian government sometimes uses arbitrary reference prices for valuation purposes. This problem is aggravated by Nigeria's dependence on imported raw materials and finished goods and affects both foreign and domestic manufacturers.' It also claims further that 'potential investors must contend with poor infrastructure, complex tax administration procedures, confusing land ownership laws, arbitrary application of regulations, corruption and crime'. US authorities further claims that 'Nigeria port practices continue to present major obstacles to trade. The country's long list of items prohibited for import, coupled with incorrect declaration of goods by importers, results in 95 per cent of containers being physically examined. There is need therefore for the Nigerian government to correct these anomalies.' In conclusion, it is hoped that vestiges of political and institutional uncertainties still remaining in Nigeria will be removed through continued consolidation of democracy and provision of an atmosphere conducive to economic growth, respect for contracts, and the institutionalization of the rule of law, in order to enable international trading partners to support local investments, particularly in the non-oil sector of the economy.

End Notes

231. (Ekpo and Umoh, 2011).

232. Detailed discussion of American aid to Nigeria during this period is provided in Chapter 1.

233. Stephen Boit, "Oil, Africa and the US: The Dangers", West Africa 2-8 December, 2002, p. 11.

234. *ibid.*

235. Garba, 1987: 164).

236. Garba: 165).

237. (United States Bureau of African Affairs, 2011).

238. (United States Bureau of African Affairs, 2011).

239. (United States Bureau of African Affairs, 2011).

240. (Hong, 2007: 5).

241. (United States Trade Department 1).

242. (United States Trade Department 2).

243. See, Samuel Ibiyemi, "US Wants Nigeria out of Sao Tome", Financial Standard, (Lagos), December 26, 2005.

244. *Ibid.*

Chapter Nine

The Nigerian Diaspora in America

Adebayo OYEBADE

Perhaps the most enduring legacy of the trans-Atlantic slave trade was the establishment of an African Diaspora in America. The descendants of the enslaved Africans who were forcibly removed from Africa and transported to the Americas between the 17th and 19th centuries are today known in the United States as African Americans. By the time the American Civil War began in 1861, about 3.5 million enslaved Africans and another half-a million free ones lived in the United States. The first African Diaspora in America was in the making.

In the late 20th century, a new African Diaspora in the United States began to gradually take shape. Available records show that as early as the immediate post-civil war period, a few African students were already studying in the United States. For instance four Liberian students arrived at Lincoln University, Pennsylvania, in 1871, and others followed thereafter.[245] From the post-World War II period, more Africans, though still in small numbers, were coming to the United States mostly to study in its colleges and universities. By the 1960s and the 1970s, the number of Africans coming to the United States had increased tremendously. It has been noted that between 1960 and 1990, the African immigrant population increased forty-fold.[246] Although, many still came for educational purposes, there were many others who came to pursue other ventures including business. Generally, African immigrants in America before the 1980s carried non-immigrant status and did not often seek United States' permanent residency. Indeed, the vast majority returned to Africa after their period of sojourn in the United States.

The dynamics of African immigration to the United States changed during the last two decades of the 20th century. New African arrivals to America not only planned to acquire permanent residency, but also American citizenship. At the forefront of this new corps of African immigrants who intended to make America home were Nigerians. From the 1980s, the hitherto buoyant Nigerian economy began to go downhill. By the 1990s, political repression and economic downturn threatened the livelihood of the average Nigerian. Those who had the opportunity, irrespective of socio-economic status at home, simply emigrated to America and Europe, attracted by the allure of greener pastures abroad. Greater opportunities for immigration to America became available for many more Nigerians when in 1995 the United States' government instituted the yearly Diversity Immigrant Visa Program, often referred to as "Green Card Lottery," which provides permanent residence and work status to 50,000 immigrants each year. As a result of worsening economic situation and contracting opportunities for social mobility at home, most Nigerian immigrants made the conscious decision to remain in the United States and raise their families there. Sometimes, their children identify themselves with the larger black community as African Americans.

Demographic Dynamics

According to United States Census Bureau data, 1.7 million foreign-born African immigrants lived in the United States in 2000. As shown in the table below, Nigerians made up the lion share of this number with a population over 165,000. This made Nigerians the single largest African immigrant group in the United States. Indeed, Outside Nigeria itself, and followed by the United Kingdom, the Nigerian Diaspora in the United States constitutes the third largest Nigerian community anywhere.

Table 1: Number of Immigrants from Sub-Saharan Africa by 2000

Country	Population
Cape Verde	77,103
Ethiopia	86,918
Ghana	49,944
Kenya	17,336
Liberia	25,575
Nigeria	165,481
Sierra Leone	12,410
Somalia	36,313
South Africa	45,569
Sudan	14,936
Other African countries	1,250,292
Total	1,781,877

Source: Table is culled from U.S. Census Bureau, 2000 Census.

With such a large Nigerian population in the United States, there is clearly a Nigerian Diaspora in America. A considerable number of these Nigerian are also American citizens, thus they are also Nigerian Americans. While there are undocumented Nigerians, the vast majority of Nigerian immigrants are legal residents. Many have permanent residency, as Green Card or student visa holders.

Nigerians are widely spread through-out the United States, perhaps more than other African immigrant groups. While they reside in the towns and cities of all sizes in all the fifty states, they are found in large concentrations in the metropolitan areas of the states of Texas, New York, Maryland, Virginia, Georgia, Illinois, Ohio, and California. The largest Nigerian communities are found in Houston, Dallas, New York City, Baltimore, Atlanta, and Washington D.C. Metropolitan area. Reasons for settling in a particular place vary but in many cases, at least at the initial stage, it is determined by the presence of relatives or friends in a particular city.

Nigerians are engaged in diverse occupations in practically all professional areas, both in the service and production sectors. Often highly trained, many Nigerians hold high-paying, prestigious job, as academics, engineers, doctors, lawyers, bankers, architects, and other professional positions.

Some are successful in privately owned businesses like medical clinics, travel agencies, auto dealership, law offices, and others. However, there are many Nigerians who are engaged in low-paying, unprofessional odd jobs, which, for some, is a temporary measure. Some, especially youths but also adults, combine work with schooling. Certain professions are generally associated with the Nigerian community. For example, nursing is very popular among women, a profession to which many turned including those who had been trained in Nigeria in other unrelated professional disciplines such as law. In many urban centres such as New York City, Houston, and the Washington D.C. metropolis, taxi driving is popular among men, even those with a university education.

Unlike in the past, Nigerian immigrants to the United States are increasingly diversified. Immigrants are no longer predominantly those in pursuit of educational opportunities; professionals across the spectrum now constitute a large portion of the Nigerian population in the Diaspora. Academics, in particular, have moved in droves to American institutions as teachers, researchers, scientists, and administrators, to the extent that an intellectual "brain drain" detrimental to Nigeria's educational system is feared.[247] Recent immigrants have also tended to be whole families, rather than individuals, an increasing phenomenon to which the Green Card lottery has contributed significantly. With the complete family in America, most Nigerian immigrant parents, whether consciously or unconsciously, have made the United States their permanent home rather than a temporary place of sojourn.

Education: A Hallmark of Nigerian-Americans

Education is highly valued by Nigerians and is generally seen as a necessary ticket to socio-economic advancement. This thirst for education is no less true of Nigerians in the Diaspora. Early Nigerians immigrants to the United States were mostly in pursuit of education. Later groups were also often persuaded by educational needs. Nigerian students in American colleges and universities have historically constituted one of the largest immigrant student groups in the United States.[248] According to recent Institute of International Education (IIE) data on educational exchange, in the 2009/2010 academic year, Nigeria was the twentieth leading place of origin for foreign students in the United States. In that academic year, Nigerian students in the United States numbered 6,568, representing an increase of up to 5% from the previous academic year.[249] The table below shows progressive increase, except in 2005/06 and 2006/07, in the number of Nigerian students in the United States between 1996 and 2010.

Table 2: Historical Trend of Nigerian Students in the United States, 1996-2010.

Year	No. of Students from Nigeria	% Change from the Previous Year
2009/10	6,568	5.0%
2008/09	6,256	0.5%
2007/08	6,222	4.7%
2006/07	5,943	-4.0%
2005/06	6,192	-2.3%
2004/05	6,335	3.2%
2003/04	6,140	5.6%
2002/03	5,816	29.3%
2001/02	4,499	17.8%
2000/01	3,820	6.1%
1999/00	3,602	25.2%
1998/99	2,876	18.1%
1997/98	2,436	11.5%
1996/97	2,184	NA

Source: IIE, Open Doors: Report on International Educational Exchange

With a long tradition of educational attainment, Nigerian immigrants in the United States are the most educated of all racial groups including white and Asians. This fact is reflected in the United States Census Bureau statistics for 2006 shown below.

Table 3: Academic Qualifications of Nigerians Compared to Other Groups, 2006

Degree	% of Nigerians with degree	% of all groups with degree
Bachelor's	37	17
Master's	17	7
Professional	5	2
Doctorate	4	1

Source: U.S. Census Bureau, 2006 American Community Survey.[250]

At Home Abroad: The Nigerian Cultural Presence in America

More than at any period in the history of the Nigerian Diaspora in America, contemporary Nigerian immigrants to the United States are more at home in their adopted land of sojourn. This is not just because improved communications technology — cheaper and more efficient telephone system, increased popularity of social media, and ready access to email — has made it easier for them to connect with home. More importantly, the considerable expansion of the Nigerian immigrant community in the last two decades has produced, to a large extent, the transplantation of Nigerian culture into urban America. This transplantation of Nigerian culture has occurred in a number of ways which will be discussed below.

Religion

Religion is of considerable importance to Nigerians, whether they are Muslims, Christians, or practitioners of one of the many traditional religions. Many Nigerians in America profess Christianity or Islam, and longed to practice their religion the way they did at home. As the Nigerian community rapidly expanded from the 1980s, indigenous Nigerian religious institutions began to multiply.

The proliferation of Nigerian churches in the United in the last twenty-five years is perhaps, the most evident sign of the transplantation of Nigerian culture into America. Nigerian churches are of various denominations and they exist in practically all the major American cities. The largest and the fastest growing of the churches is the Redeemed Christian Church of God (RCCG). Founded in Nigeria and with headquarters in Lagos, the RCCG moved to the United States in 1992 and established its first parish, Winner's Chapel, in Detroit, Michigan.[251] With fervent evangelism and aggressive church planting, the church, as of 2008, had about 400 parishes in the United States and Canada.[252] Some of the largest parishes have as many as 2,000 members, mostly Nigerians.[253] In 2006, the church established its headquarters, called Redemption Camp, spread over a 600 acre land in Floyd, Texas. Other major indigenous Nigerian churches are, among others, the Deeper Life Ministry, Mountain of Fire, and Christ Apostolic Church.

The most thriving Nigerian churches in America are those of Pentecostal evangelical persuasion such the RCCG. Primarily, they seek to provide their members spiritual nourishment through worship services. For many Nigerians, the churches offer an opportunity to feel at home in their religious life. They could worship in the way they were used to in Nigeria characterized by loud singing, ecstatic praises, and drumming and dancing, forms of worship that were unavailable in most American churches.

Nigerian churches do more than provide spiritual benefits. Many of the well established ones offer special programs of social benefits for their members such as counselling and seminars on marriage, immigration, and financial management, for example. For many, church was not simply a place to receive spiritual nourishment on Sundays and during other weekly services; it represented a social rendezvous as well where exchanges could be made in Nigerian languages, and where social events such as house warming, birthday celebration, and marriage and naming ceremonies provide socialization opportunity. Invariably, the church plays a significant part in the lives of many immigrants.

Nigerian churches are not the only religious institutions that provide avenues for fostering group identity. Nigerian Muslim organizations, though not as numerous as Christian churches, are active in promoting the interest of their members. An umbrella organization, the National Council of Nigeria Muslim Organization in the USA, was established in 1976 in

Washington, D.C. One of its objectives was "to foster mutual understanding among all brothers and sisters in Islam in general and Nigerian Muslim associations in particular."[254] Beginning with three chapters, NCNMO now has thirteen member chapters in the major cities of states of New York, Illinois, Texas, Florida, Pennsylvania, Maryland, Rhode Island, New Jersey, Georgia, North Carolina, Massachusetts, Indiana and, Minnesota.[255]

It must not be construed that despite the ready availability of Nigerian religious establishments, Christian or Muslim, in the United States, every religious-minded Nigerian immigrant subscribe to them. For instance, many church-going Nigerians elect to be members of American, rather than Nigerian churches. Also to be noted is the presence of Yoruba traditional religion in America. However, this is popular only in the African American communities especially in major cities such as Miami, Atlanta, Chicago, Philadelphia, Washington, D.C., San Francisco and New York, where religious and cultural centres dedicated to the worship of traditional Yoruba deities exist. Interest in Yoruba religious practices first became popular in the 1960s during the era of the Black Power movement. Increasing number of American blacks has continued to propagate this tradition, many becoming practitioners of Òrìsà worship, and even priests of Òrìsà temples. Perhaps, the epitome of Yoruba culture in contemporary Black America is the Oyotunji African village, a small community of African Americans in South Carolina, which practices Yoruba culture and religion.[256] Yoruba traditional religion has continued to be an important part of the African American religious tradition.[257] Ironically, beyond traditional ceremonies such as naming and marriage engagement, which are, in any case, often mixed with Christian practices, Nigerian Yoruba immigrants in America generally do not partake in Òrìsà worship.

Cuisine, Fashion, and Music

The Nigerian community in the United States is closely identified with retail stores, many owned by Nigerians themselves and by other Africans. There is hardly any American major city with a sizable Nigerian population where these stores are not available. These outlets in New York, Chicago, Atlanta, Houston and many other US cities offer a variety of traditional African, and specifically, Nigerian wares including assorted, ready-made traditional attires such as *adire* (hand-dyed clothing), beauty products, household commodities, CDs and DVDs by African artists, and, particularly, a wide selection of foodstuffs, from *gari* (cassava flour) and *elubo* (yam flour), to palm oil, vegetables, and herbs and spices. Some carry delicacies such as *moin-moin* (bean cake), *chinchin* (cookies), and *suya* (roasted meat). The Nigerian store is an important rendezvous for Nigerian immigrants, perhaps the most important next to the Nigerian church.

Although home cooking is the norm among Nigerian families, Nigerian-owned restaurants are also available to serve home dishes for those who would like to treat themselves, once in a while, to dining outside the home. Nigerian staple dishes such as main courses of jollof rice and *dodo* (fried plantain); and *iyan* (pounded yam) with *egusi* (melon) or goat meat stew, are popular in these restaurants. Indeed, the Nigerian Diaspora in today's America has easy access to Nigerian cuisine more than ever before.

Communal Identity and Socialization

Nigerians in the America Diaspora have never built their own distinct neighbourhoods like some other recent immigrant groups such as the Kurds. Despite the fact that Nigerian immigrants live in different communities, they still strive to maintain group identity and cultivate semblance of neighbourhood life. This is particularly true of the first generation of Nigerian immigrants and less true of their children, Nigerian Americans. Social events provide the best avenue for socialization by Nigerian immigrants.

Like those at home, Nigerians abroad in America delight in merriment when time permits and never fail to convert any opportunities such as weddings, child birth, and birthdays to elaborate and often expensive parties. These occasions for partying, especially weddings and birthdays, always attract large gathering of Nigerians who feast and dance to Nigerian music, sometimes supplied by life bands or disk jockeys. These events often witness the display of the rich Nigerian colourful fabrics as men and women adorn themselves in traditional attire. The typical Nigerian wedding or birthday party is not complete without the cultural tradition of "money spray" unique to Nigerians. As the celebrants dance, guests "spray" them by placing dollar notes on their foreheads. This is essentially a gesture of giving to the celebrants.

Special historical occasions also call for parties, festivities, and other social events which bring Nigerians together to socialize. Many Nigerian social and cultural organizations organize series of events on or around October 1, to celebrate Nigeria's independence and showcase its culture. A good recent example is the 2010 Nigeria Independence Day Family Fun Fair (NIDFFF), an event which featured a number of fun activities including a fashion parade and dance to celebrate Nigeria's 50th Independence anniversary.[258] Some Nigerian organizations also often commemorate July 4, America's independence anniversary with social and cultural activities.

Organizations and Associations

An important avenue through which Nigerian immigrants have sought to build an identity in America and forge stronger, more empowered communities is the formation of non-profit, largely apolitical organizations and associations. There are broadly two types of these organizations and associations in terms of the constituencies they serve and their missions. First are those that are pan-Nigerian in constitution, meaning that their mission is to protect the well-being of all Nigerians in America and advance their social, cultural, economic, and professional interests. Thus, membership of these organizations is non-partisan, and is open to every Nigerian, irrespective of ethnicity, creed, or state of origin.

There are several pan-Nigerian organizations, with bases in every major American city. While many of them do not have influence beyond the city or state of their location, a few can claim membership, or have affiliate organizations, in many of the fifty states. One of the largest pan-Nigerian organizations is the Washington, D.C., based Nigerians in Diaspora Organization-Americas (NIDO), which claims to be an "umbrella organization for all Nigerian professional groups in the Americas."[259] Conceived "to develop effective modes—through programs, policies, and advocacy for Nigerians abroad to harness their talents, expertise, and resources for Nigeria's development and nation building,"[260] it was established in October 2001 and now has chapters in many states. In the pursuit of its vision it has collaborated with other Nigerian organizations, ethnic and professional, and with interests based in Nigeria itself.[261]

Some pan-Nigerian organizations are more narrowly focused than the above in terms of their constituency. Examples are professional associations which appeal to only Nigerians in respective professions – these include groups for doctors, lawyers, nurses, academics, pharmacists, and others. There are hundreds of these pan-Nigerian professional associations, which include the Association of Nigerian Physicians in America (ANPA) for doctors, the Nigerian Lawyers Association (NLA) for lawyers, the Nigerian Nurses Association (NNA) for nurses, the Nigerian-American Public Professionals Association (NAPPA) for employees in ranking federal, state, county, and city government positions, and the Nigerian Information Technology Professionals in America (NITPA) for Nigerian IT professionals and others with interest in the profession.

Apart from professional associations, there are several other narrowly-focused socio-cultural pan-Nigerian organizations. Some are gender specific, like the Nigerian Women Association (NWA) with affiliate member organizations in many states including South Carolina, Virginia, Texas, and the District of Columbia. Alumni associations provide another example of organizations in this genre. Many Nigerian educational institutions including some secondary schools and a number of universities have branches of alumni associations in the United States. One example is Great Ife Alumni Association, USA, the United States chapter of the Obafemi Awolowo University Alumni Association. There are also Nigerian students' associations in scores of American colleges and universities.

The second major type of Nigerian organizations in America is socio-cultural associations whose membership is restricted to specific ethno-linguistic groups, thus they are clearly partisan. Some of these ethnic-based associations are open to all members of the groups, and their mandate is mainly to service the interests of the specific groups. Major examples of these associations are the Egbé Omo Yoruba: National Association of Yoruba Descendants in North America, a pan-Yoruba organization; the World Igbo Congress, open to all people of Igbo origin; and Zumunta Association, an exclusive organization for Northern Nigerians.[262] These organizations, as shown in the tables below in the case of the Egbé Omo Yoruba and the World Igbo Congress, are constituted by affiliate and associate member associations from all over the country.

Table 4: Egbé Omo Yoruba: Affiliate Chapters

Chapter	Location/Area
Concerned Yoruba Committee	Houston, TX
Egbé Isokan Yoruba	Washington, D.C.
Egbé Omo Yoruba of Greater Chicago	Chicago, IL
Egbé Omo Yoruba ti Baltimore	Baltimore, MD
Egbé Omo Yoruba of Baton Rouge	Baton Rouge, LA
Egbé Omo Yoruba of Boston	Boston, MA
Egbé Omo Yoruba, Delaware Valley	Philadelphia, PA
Egbé Omo Yoruba	Miami, FL
Egbé Omo Yoruba	MS
Egbé Omo Yoruba Staten island	New York, NY
Egbé Omo Yoruba, Greater New York	Elmont, NY
Egbé Omo oduduwa of Greater St. Louis	St Louis, MO
Egbé Omo Yoruba, Tennessee	Nashville, TN
Egbé Omo Yoruba, Greater Atlanta	Atlanta, GA
Oduduwa descendants of Tampa Bay	Tampa Bay, FL
Oduduwa Heritage Organization of Oakland	Oakland, CA
Yoruba Descendants Union, Jacksonville	Jacksonville, FL

Source, http://Yorùbánation.org/Chapters.html

Table 5: World Igbo Congress: Affiliate Chapters

Chapter	Location/Area
Igbo Union, Atlanta	Atlanta, GA
Igbo People's Congress	Austin, TX
Umunna Association	Chicago, IL
Igbo Organization of New England	Boston, MA
Igbo Community Association of Nigeria	Dallas/Fort Worth, TX
Igbo Organization of Greater Miami Valley	Dayton, OH

Igbo Cultural Association of Michigan	Detroit, MI
Igbo People's Congress, Houston	Houston, TX
Igbo People's Congress, Kansas City	Kansas City, KS
Igbo Cultural Association of Southern California	Los Angeles, CA
Igbo Association of Southern Florida	Miami, FL
Igbo Union, Nashville	Nashville, TN
Igbo USA, New Jersey	NJ
Igbo Bu Igbo of New Jersey	NJ
Nzuko Ndi Igbo, South Jersey	NJ
Ndi Igbo Development Foundation	New Orleans, LA
Igbo Organization of New York	NY
Nwannedinamba	Washington, DC
Igbo People's Forum	Philadelphia, PA
Igbo Association of Tampa Bay	Tampa Bay, FL
Umunne Cultural Association of Minnesota	Saint Paul, MN
The Nne Ji Ndi Igbo of Greater Cincinnati	Cincinnati, OH

Source: http://wicfoundationinc.org/index.php?pr=Affiliates_and_Associates

There are other types of socio-cultural ethnic associations. There are those whose membership is limited to sub-groups of larger ethnic entities. Practically all the Nigerian sub-ethnic groups represented in the United States have this type of associations. For example, the Ekiti, a sub-group of the Yoruba have an umbrella Ekiti associations known as Ekiti Associations in North America (EKAINA), with chapters which include Ekiti Progressive Union (Dallas, TX), Ekitikete Association (Chicago, IL), Ekiti Progressive Union, (Los Angeles, CA), Ekitiparapo Association (New York, N.Y), and Ekiti Association, (Houston, TX).

Some sub-group associations are even more narrowly defined in the sense that their membership is restricted to citizens of cities and towns in Nigeria. Many major Nigerian cities with sizeable number of indigenes in the United States have this type of associations. These associations, often referred to as Home Town Associations (HTA), have been prominent in Nigeria since the colonial period, and are thus, essentially, a carry-over to America. They are more popular in American cities where there is large concentration of Nigerians. Though, numerous, a typical example is the Eko Club in Atlanta, GA; an association for immigrants from Lagos, and American citizens of Lagos descent (Lagosian Americans).

In some instances, citizens of some states in Nigeria have created organizations to represent their interest in the United States while also pursuing the development of their home states in Nigeria. Associations of this type include Abia State National Association of North America, USA (ASNANA), and Kwara State Association of Nigeria, North America (KSANG).

Undoubtedly, the numerous Nigerian organizations in America, whether national, ethnic, sub-ethnic, hometown, or professional, have had a significant impact on the Nigerian Diaspora in America. Their core mission can broadly be summarized as the pursuit of the well-being, development, and progress of Nigerian immigrants and American citizens of Nigerian origin in all areas of human endeavour. This fundamental purpose of these organizations is succinctly expressed in the mission statement of the Nigerian Progressive Organization, based in Chicago, IL:

> To promote the welfare of all members of the Organization, improve the member's standard of living, and render moral support as needed. To promote bona-fide and unequivocally authentic Nigerian image through education and cultural programs directed towards the general public, by way of conference, workshops, lecture series, and other projects as may be decided upon by the general membership. To make giant strides towards the economic and social enhancement of the entire membership of the organization.[263]

Apart from the core mission of serving the interests of the Nigerian community, some of the organizations have also aimed at promoting a positive image for Nigeria in the United States. The Western mass media have traditionally and unfairly focused more on negative news from Africa than on the positive. Stories of criminal activities such as drug trafficking, credit card fraud, and advance-fee scam (popularly known as 419) by a few unscrupulous Nigerians have often made headlines in American news media, giving, not only the nation a bad name, but the Nigerian immigrant community as well. To counteract this negative image, Nigerian organizations regularly sponsor public awareness programs and cultural and social events to properly inform and educate the American public about Nigeria. Some have found it necessary to correct, through press releases and other avenues, misleading or inaccurate news perception of Nigeria. For example, in the wake of the December 25, 2009 alleged attempt of terrorist bombing of an American airline by the Nigerian, Umar Farouk Abdul Mutallab, the Egbé Omo Yoruba condemning the bungled plot, but mindful of the stereotypical inkling it might generate for Nigerians, issued the following statement:

> As Nigerian-Americans of Yoruba descent, or Yoruba residing in North America, we urge all fellow Americans to resist negative stereotyping of all Nigerians, because of the attempted callous act of ONE misguided and brainwashed individual.[264]

Other Nigerian organizations, as part of their mission, aim at assisting in the task of national development at home by instituting developmental educational and economic programs, either at communal, state, or national levels. NIDO America is closely identified with this goal as expressed in its statement of purpose and vision:

> The core vision of NIDO, deeply rooted in the organization's firm belief that Diaspora Nigerians can make significant contributions to Nigeria, is to develop effective modes—through programs, policies, and advocacy—for Nigerians abroad to harness their talents, expertise, and resources for Nigeria's development and nation building. NIDO believes that this overriding framework and philosophy resonates with every Nigerian man, woman, and organization abroad and sets the foundation for a profound opportunity to unite, collaborate, and effect needed change in our Homeland and beyond.[265]

Some of the Nigerian organizations have been able to work in partnership with local and national American organizations, especially those identified with African American interests. Through this modality, they have been able to build linkage with the larger American society.

While the hundreds of Nigerian organizations in the United States have served as an important tool for the advancement of the interests of their various constituencies, they are not without challenges. For some of the smaller ones, finance is a major issue. Some have become moribund because of this or face a precarious existence. Another major problem that often plagues Nigerian organizations, most especially the bigger ones with national outlook, is ethnic politics particularly at the leadership level.

"There's No Place Like Home" – Diaspora Relations with Nigeria

The duration of stay in America has not diminished the attachment Nigerian immigrants have for their home country. To many, even those who have become American citizens, Nigeria remains truly home, and the United States, home away from home.

Although sojourning in the Diaspora, Nigerians in the United States keep abreast of happenings at home at every level, from family issues to national politics. Most Nigerian immigrants have dual financial responsibility. They are not expected to cater to themselves alone, but also to look after the welfare of relatives left behind in Nigeria, whether immediate family members or distant relations. The obligation to support needy family members financially has become even more imperative since the Nigerian economy began to falter in the last two decades of the twentieth century, leading to inability of many households to make ends meet. A host of Nigerian households today depend, to a considerable extent, on regular money remittances from Nigerians abroad, particularly from the United States. Indeed, it has been said that after earnings from oil exports, remittances from Nigerians abroad to their families in Nigeria constitute the second major source of revenue for the country. These remittances in value have been suggested to be in excess of US$1.3 billion.[266] This is a clear indication of close connection to home by Diaspora Nigerians.

Nigerian immigrants in the United States have also maintained a bridge to their homeland through the organizations and associations they established for themselves in America. As stated earlier, many of these associations, apart from serving their members, also devote some of their resources to benefit the home community in Nigeria. Some work closely with interested American organizations especially private ones in the pursuit of this venture. Through these organizations for instance, some Nigerian institutions have received supplies of textbooks and computer equipment.

They may remain engaged in the politics of their home countries. Politicians from Ghana and other sub-Saharan countries also turn to Africans in the United States for financial support.

Mass communication revolution has greatly enhanced the ability of Nigerian immigrants to keep close ties with home. Easy access to home news of every kind – politics, economy, sports, culture – is assured by the print and electronic media as well as social media. Virtually all the major Nigerian newspapers have online editions, and thus are readily available to readers in the Diaspora. In some parts of the United States such as in the northeast, the international broadcast of the Nigerian Television Authority (NTA) are available. Numerous discussion forums and blogs exist which connect Nigerians on the two sides of the Atlantic. Social interactions media such as Facebook have also proven important vehicle of connection.

The Question of Assimilation in America

Children of Nigerian immigrants, as to be expected, are generally American in practically every sense. Many speak only English – few speak the Nigerian languages of their parents. Their accent is American, as opposed to their parents "thick" Nigerian accent. In terms of social interactions, they are often more exposed to their American counterparts. A growing trend in recent years is inter-marriage between these Nigerian Americans and native-born Americans, both white and black.

Unlike their children, Nigerian immigrants hold tenaciously to their culture. Their indigenous languages are important to them and are spoken at every available opportunity, at home, and especially at social gatherings. Certain aspects of Nigerian culture that Nigerian immigrants in America are not likely to give up any soon are Nigerian cuisine, fashion, and music. Most

Nigerian immigrant households prepare Nigerian dishes rather than American ones. The "accepted" or "respected" mode of dress on formal occasions like weddings is Nigerian attire. Nigerians are more likely to build a library of Nigerian, rather than American music CD or DVD movies. The fast growing popularity of Nollywood movies in America is noteworthy.

For many African immigrants, adapting to life in America has not been exactly easy. Often they have to contend with the prejudice of Americans who know next to nothing about Africa, and bias against them on account of their foreign origin, accent, and cultural outlook. It is common for highly qualified Nigerian immigrants to face the frustration of having to retrain in America before being eligible for employment that corresponds to their level of education. Thus, many professionals such as doctors, nurses, and lawyers, trained in Nigeria are forced to work for a long period of time in a capacity far below the qualifications obtained from home.

Nigerian immigrants, however, do not segregate themselves into an isolated group removed from mainstream America. In their home communities, work places, and through their social and cultural organizations and associations, they interact with the larger American society, and, indeed, acquire some elements of American culture. For example, the baby shower is now a common practice in the Nigerian community for pregnant women.

Conclusion

The Nigerian Diaspora in the United States still constitutes a very small segment of the American population, yet it has contributed significantly in every area of national development—academia, business, technology, sports, government, and the military. Nigerian immigrants continue to make their mark in every field as one recent case has shown that of the appointment of Dr. Olufunmilayo Falusi Olopade to a key administrative position in President Obama's White House. Dr. Olopade, who is the Walter L. Palmer Distinguished Service Professor of Medicine & Human Genetics, Associate Dean for Global Health, and Director of the Center for Clinical Cancer Genetics at the University of Chicago, was appointed a member of National Cancer Advisory Board.[268]

End Notes

245. "1871 & 1879 Liberian Students," A Digital Collection Celebrating the Foundation of the Historically Black Colleges and Universities, HBCU Library Alliance, retrieved 3/07/11 from http://contentdm.auctr.edu/cdm4/document.php?CISOROOT=/lupa&CISOPTR=528&REC=2

246. Aaron Terrazas, "African Immigrants in the United States," *Migration Information Source*, Feb. 2009, retrieved 03/7/11 from http://www.migrationinformation.org/USfocus/display.cfm?id=719#19.

247. On this subject, see Marcellina Ulunm Offoha, *Educated Nigerian Settlers in the United States: The Phenomenon of Brain Drain*, (Philadelphia: Temple University, 1989).

248. Institute of International Education (IIE), "Open Doors Fact Sheet: Nigeria, 2010, retrieved 03/11/2011 at http://www.iie.org/en/Research-and-Publications/Open-Doors

249. *ibid*.

250. Adapted from Leslie Casmir, "Bachelor's and Beyond: In America, Nigerians' Education Pursuit is Above Rest," *Houston Chronicle*, May 20, 2008.

251. "How Adeboye Designed Posters to Plant RCCG Parish," RCCG North America Website, retrieved on 03/15/11 from http://www.rccgna.org/mcm/rc/tgen.aspx?articleid=28&zoneid=5.

252. Figure is cited in "Pastor James Oladipo Fadele, Chairman of The Redeemed Christian Church of God, North America," *Mama Express Online,* retrieved on 03/15/11, from http://www.mannaexpressonline.com/pastors/pastor-james-oladipo-fadele-chairman-of-the-redeemed-christian-church-of-god-north-america.

253. An example is RCCG, Victory Temple, Bowie, Maryland, which claims 2,000 members. See its website at http://www.rccgvictorytemple.org/481164.ihtml.

254. See NCNMO's website, retrieved on 03/15/11, from http://www.nmnationalcouncil.org/.

255. For more details on NCNMO member chapters, see its website at http://www.nmnationalcouncil.org/index.php/member-chapters.

256. For more information on this community, see its website at [http://www.oyotunjiafricanvillage.org/?id=1] See Mikele Smith Omari,

"Completing the Circle: Notes on *African Art*, Society, and Religion in Oyotunji, South Carolina," *African Arts*, 24 (3), 1991, 66-75, 96; and Carl M. Hunt, *Oyotunji Village: The Yoruba Movement in America*, (Washington, D.C.,: University Press of America, 1979); and Adebayo Oyebade, "Yoruba Culture in Contemporary America," in Toyin Falola and Adebayo Oyebade, (eds.), *Yoruba Fiction, Orature, and Culture: Oyekan Owomoyela and African Literature & the Yoruba Experience*, (Trenton, N.J.: Africa World Press, 2010), 321-340.

[257.] The subject of Yoruba traditional religious practices is discussed further in Oyebade, "Yoruba Culture in Contemporary America."

[258.] See "Nigeria Independence Day Family Fun Fair in New Jersey, 2010," retrieved on 03/29/11 from *African Events* website, http://www.africanevents.com/NigerianIndieDayFairNJ2010.htm

[259.] NIDO website, retrieved on 03/18/11 from http://nidoamerica.org/

[260.] *Ibid.*

[261.] See ibid for more details on NIDO.

[262.] For the goals, missions, and activities of these organizations, see their websites viz: Egbe Omo Yoruba at [http://Yorùbánation.org/Default.htm]; World Igbo Congress at [http://wicfoundationinc.org/index.php?pr=Affiliates_and_Associates]; and Zumunta Association at[http://www.zumunta.org/]. Egbe Omo Yoruba is further discussed in Oyebade, "Yoruba Culture in Contemporary America."

[263.] Retrieved 03/29/11 from http://www.motherlandnigeria.com/organizations.html#NPO.

[264.] Egbé omo Yoruba, "Yoruba in North America Denounce Attempted Act of Terrorism," press release, December 27, 2009, retrieved on 03/24/11, from http://yorubanation.org/pressrelease/yoruba_denouce_attempted_ta.pdf.

[265.] NIDO America, "Our Purpose and Vision," retrieved on 03/24/11, from http://www.nidoamericas.org/about_ourvision.php.

[266.] Gumisai Mutume, "Workers' Remittances: A Boon to Development, Money Sent Home by African Migrants Rivals Development Aid, *Africa Renewal*,19 (3), Oct. 2005, 10. For more scholarly analysis of this subject, see Ayokunle Olumuyiwa Omobowale, Mofeyisara Oluwatoyin Omobowale and Olawale Olufolahan Ajani, "Emigration and the Social Value of Remittances in Nigeria," in Emmanuel Yewah and Dimeji Togunde, (eds.), *Across the Atlantic: African Immigrants in the United States Diaspora*, (Champaign, Ill.: Common Ground Pub., 2010), chap. 7; and Manuel Orozco & Bryanna Millis, "Remittances,

Competition, and Fair Financial Access Opportunities in Nigeria," United States Agency for International Development (USAID) Publication, Oct. 2007, retrieved 03/29/11, from http://www.thedialogue.org/PublicationFiles/NigeriaAMAP%20FSKG%20-%20Nigeria%20Remittances-%20FINAL.pdf

267. Mohammed Aman, "Blacks, Whites, and a Cultural Divide: Revelations of my American Journey," in Festus E. Obiakor and Patrick A. Grant (eds.), *Foreign-Born African Americans: Silenced Voices in the Discourse on Race*, (New York: Nova Science Publishers, Inc, 2002), xi-xix. See also Paul E. Udofia, *Nigerians in the United States: Potentialities and Crises*, (Boston, MA: William Monroe Trotter Institute, 1996).

268. Office of the Press Secretary, "President Obama Announces More Key Administration Posts," White House release, Washington, Feb. 24, 2011.

Chapter Ten

The Nigeria-United States Bi-National Commission: Scope, Achievements, Limitations and Suggestions for Review

Suleiman BABA ALI

A new stage in Nigeria-United States relations was attained on April 6, 2010, when the two countries signed the framework that established the Bi-National Commission. This whole initiative has its origin during the discussions held when the United States Secretary of State, Hilary Clinton visited Nigeria in August 2009. Subsequently, the Bi-National Commission Framework has become the structure that guides Nigeria-United States relations. Against this background, it is important to take a look at the initiative. The specific objective of this chapter is to examine the circumstances that necessitated the signing of the agreement, the scope, the achievements it has made so far, the limitations and areas that should be considered in any impending review.

Justification for Establishment

Before going into the details of the contents of the commission, there is first a need to put the circumstances that led to its establishment into perspective. In a way, the Nigeria-US Bi-National Commission is an acknowledgment of the depth of a relationship, the recognition of mutual importance and the expectations of a desired future. In terms of the depth of a relationship, it needs to be borne in mind that before the signing of the commission, the two countries had enjoyed fifty years of cordial relationship that cuts across virtually all aspects of diplomatic relations. In fact, looking at the relationship, the Nigerian envoy to the United States, Professor Adebowale Adefuye, noted:

Indeed, the history of Nigeria's 50 years of statehood will be incomplete without a mention of the proactive role of the United States in supporting us in our quest for sustainable political stability and economic development. The United States' interest in our economic and political well-being has been one of the critical factors for the progress recorded in our efforts to consolidate our democracy and deliver its dividends to the people of the country.[269]

In terms of the recognition of mutual importance, both countries have come to recognise the redoubtable role the other has been playing in international relations. While the role of the United States in global politics is unassailable, Nigeria's importance as an African power was widely recognised, especially through its massive population, its contribution to global peacekeeping and the role the country has played in providing leadership for countries in the West African sub-region. Furthermore, Nigeria is the largest recipient of direct investment by the American private sector in sub-Saharan Africa. Against this background, both countries felt that it was necessary to put the relationship under a framework that is concrete and measurable. In fact, the United States only establishes such commissions with valued and strategic partners. With its significant oil wealth and the extent of its trading links with the United States, it can be said that Nigeria had attained the status of a strategic partner even long before the inauguration of the Commission. Shortly before the signing, a commentator noted:

Nigeria supplies the U.S. with crude oil while the U.S. has supported Nigeria in public health and infrastructural development; capacity building in the oil sector; support to strengthening democratic institutions, among others. The ties which bind between Nigeria and the United States of America run deep. In 2009, Nigeria was the third topmost supplier of crude oil to the United States, even as its 'sweet Bonny crude' is of the highest quality in the world. Nigeria is the United State's largest trading partner in sub-Saharan Africa and the US is also the largest foreign investor in the country. Additionally, the US is home to a growing number of Nigerians in the Diaspora, with the most educated group of immigrants in the United States being Nigerians.[270]

In terms of future expectations, both countries felt at the time of signing the agreement that the Commission Framework would further strengthen their relationship towards the direction that would be more mutually beneficial. Indeed, both sides noted during the signing ceremony that they still had a lot to learn from each other.

But there are other things that make the establishment of this Commission important. The first is that it was the initial one of the three bi-national commissions with key African states envisioned by the Obama administration, the other two being with South Africa and Angola. The second thing was the timing of the agreement, coming as it did during the period of political uncertainties surrounding the extended illness-related absence of the late President Umaru Yar' Adua. Indeed, Secretary of State Clinton alluded to this when she noted during the signing of the Commission Framework that "the past year has been a trying one for the Nigerian people". The third issues that is worth noting about the timing of the establishment of the Commission was that it was just shortly after Nigeria had been removed from the list of countries under watch for possible terrorist activities. The formal signing of the Commission took place on April 6 2010, with the U.S. Secretary of State Hillary Clinton signing for the United States and the Secretary to the Government of the Federation, Yayale Ahmed, representing the Nigerian Government.

The expectations of both countries in signing the agreement are also worth noting. For the United States, it was expected that Nigeria would use the opportunity of the Bi-National Commission to consolidate the gains of its democracy. According to Secretary Clinton, it was expected that Nigeria "like many countries, [would] look to the future, and how to create conditions that will protect the gains that independence brought, guard against ongoing and serious threats to its progress".[271] On its part, Nigeria recognized that it also has a lot to gain from the Commission, which Mr. Yayale Ahmed saw as an opportunity of enhancing Nigeria's "chance of being a great nation". It is in the light of these expectations that this chapter now looks at the scope and contents of the Bi-National Commission.[272]

The Nigeria-United States Bi-National Commission: Scope and Content

The Nigeria-United States Binational Commission is woven around four key areas:

- Good Governance, Transparency and Integrity
- Energy and Investment
- The Niger Delta and Regional Security Cooperation
- Food Security and Agriculture

Even though there are other broad areas that it hopes to cover, the list above captures the areas considered as being vital to Nigeria's interest and also which the United States felt that it could make contributions. Immediately after the establishment of the Commission, the Federal Government inaugurated four working groups to handle the process from the Nigerian end. Because of the wide areas covered by the Commission, members of the working groups are drawn from a broad range of Ministries and government parastatals including the Independent National Electoral Commission (INEC,) Economic and Financial Crime Commission (EFCC), Independent Corrupt Practice Commission (ICPC), Nigerian Bar Association (NBA), Nigerian Union of Journalist (NUJ), Civil Liberty Organisation (CLO) Nigerian National Petroleum Commission (NNPC) and Ministries of Petroleum, Agriculture and Water Resources, Defence, Niger Delta, Finance, Power and Energy as well as the Office of the Secretary to the Federal Government and the National Security Adviser.

Good Governance, Transparency and Integrity

Both sides recognize the importance of good governance and transparency, especially what it can contribute to Nigeria's democracy and its prosperity. The Commission decided from the outset that it would focus on electoral reform and election preparations in order to achieve free, fair, and peaceful elections in Nigeria in 2011 and beyond. The hope of the Commission at its establishment was to strengthen Nigeria's democratic institutions and civil society, along with working with Nigerians themselves to fight corruption. The timing of the establishment of the Commission, just as Nigeria was preparing for a general election, was also an issue that further reinforced the importance of this component. As it is widely known, most of the elections hitherto conducted in Nigeria were controversial, with some widely known to have been massively rigged. Other key governance issues that have underlined the justification of this subject include the persistent issue of corruption and abuse of political opportunities. In summary, the Good Governance, Transparency, and Integrity Working Group was designed to address issues like electoral reform and improved administration as they are needed to help Nigeria achieve free, fair and peaceful elections in 2011. The group was also to address corruption by seeking to build Nigeria's institutional capacity and prosecutorial efforts.

Niger Delta and Regional Security Cooperation

The Niger Delta has been a major issue in Nigeria. This is not only because the region produces the bulk of the oil that gives Nigeria more than 90% of its revenue but also because militants from this region have frustrated the exploitation of oil in many parts of the region. The environmental situation too has also been at the forefront of global attention, especially through the activities of the writer, the late Ken Saro Wiwa. It is also possible that the inclusion of this aspect also serves American interest as Nigeria is a key supplier of oil to the United States and the activities of militants in the Niger Delta have affected the interest of key American oil companies, namely Exxon-Mobil and Chevron. Among others, the inclusion of regional security cooperation may also have come because of the increasing importance of the Gulf of Guinea as a source of energy supply for the United States and most of the western world. In short, the Niger Delta and Regional Security Cooperation Working Group support Nigeria's efforts to provide immediate and tangible development and economic opportunity to the people of the Niger Delta.

Energy Reform and Investment

Energy reform also came into the equation because of Nigeria's persistent desire to address its numerous energy-related problems. Despite its enormous gas, electricity remains too scarce and profits have not always been invested in ways that benefit all Nigerians, particularly the poorest. Many of the efforts made to address the problem by previous administration had only attracted very minimal success and bilateral agreements signed with many countries are only beginning to bring traces of positive result. It was thus the intention of the Commission to ensure that assistance is given to Nigeria to ensure that it meets its energy requirements. Power sector reform has been a complex issue in most countries. This is particularly true in Nigeria, which is transforming from a country with just 20 percent of its population with access to electricity, to one committed to providing power for economic growth. Thus, generalizing broadly, the Energy and Investment Working Group was tasked with improving transparency, administration, and performance of the power generation and hydrocarbon sectors.

Food Security and Agricultural Development

Despite its rich land, Nigeria has not been able to make the best in feeding its population, such that the country still spends a huge amount of money importing food. This thus makes food security an issue in the country and it is against this background that the Bi-National Commission designated a working group to address this challenge. In short, the Food Security and Agriculture Working Group was expected to work to increase reliable access to food in Nigeria and the region through improvements in agriculture and trade policy

But despite the promise raised by the initiative, there were some Nigerians who felt the need for caution right from the moment the Framework was signed. They were concerned that the whole exercise could be another form of neo-colonialism that should be resisted at all cost. Against the background of the AFRICOM initiative that was rejected by the Yar' Adua administration, some people in Nigeria suspected that the Bi-Nantional initiative was an attempt by the American government to come into Nigeria through the back door. But even while urging caution about the intention of the Americans, a Nigerian national newspaper in its editorial column also gave reasons as to why the initiative should be supported. *The Punch* Newspaper noted:

The Bi-lateral Commission must however be given every support to work. In the vicious grip of a parasitic political class, utterly contemptuous of those values, traditions and institutions critical to good governance, economic well-being and political stability, Nigeria is in desperate need of external assistance. And America is in a good position to instil some sanity in Nigeria's public domain because, depraved as Nigeria's ruling elite are, they are mindful of how the world power seeks to relate with those in public office. The country and its traditional allies could track and expose their loot and block them from migrating abroad to enjoy same.[273]

The newspaper would have expressed the minds of many Nigerians when it proffered the following advice to the Commission:

Let the Bi-National Commission stand as a demonstration of sincere commitment to the promotion of democratic values, good governance and sustainable economic development around the world. For the moral authority that America under President Barack Obama seeks to command as it confronts political and economic challenges of the time, let it prove through the Nigerian situation that it could advance such advantages at the expense of other nations.[274]

In the next section we look at the achievements that have been recorded by the American-Nigerian Bi-National Commission.

Activities undertaken and achievements recorded

A number of the activities that have been undertaken since the establishment of the Commission and the working groups have been along the lines of the main themes. The working group on "Good Governance, Transparency and Integrity" met in Abuja, in May 2010; the "Energy and Investment" working group met in Washington, D.C., in June and again in January, 2011; the "Niger Delta and Regional Security Cooperation" group met in September 2010 and the working group on "Food Security and Agriculture" met in February 2011.

Good Governance, Transparency and Integrity

As noted above, the first Working Group of the Commission took place in May 2010, just a month after the establishment of the Commission. Expectedly, it focused on Good Governance, Transparency and Integrity and it took place in Abuja. The United States was represented by the Under Secretary for Democracy and Global Affairs, Maria Otero,[275] while the Nigerian former Minister of Foreign Affairs, Odein Ajumogobia represented Nigeria. The meeting focused on a number of very critical topics, including the promotion of democratic institutions and processes, and fighting corruption.

This forum provided an opportunity for members of the Nigerian delegation made up of federal legislators, state governors, private sector, civil society and other stake holders to share insights into best practices for Good Governance and credible elections in support of democratic principles. The U.S delegation also met with Nigerian President, Goodluck Jonathan during which he reiterated his commitment to ensuring credible elections in Nigeria.

It would appear that this Working Group has recorded considerable successes. As part of this, the American government has offered assistance to the Nigerian police force and the military and peacekeeping troops. However, what seems to be the most important achievement of this sector was the assistance that was given to INEC in the conduct of the 2011 elections in Nigeria. Among the financial assistance given to INEC by the American government was a grant of US$30 million to assist in the provision of technological infrastructure towards the 2011 general elections. There can also be no doubt that the assistance given by the United States was an indication of their endorsement of Attahiru Jega as the INEC Chairman. Indeed, it was widely believed that the American government had insisted on the replacement of Professor Maurice Iwu as the head of the electoral body.[276]

Energy and Investment

The second Working Group focussed on Energy and Investment and it took place in Washington, DC in June 2010. It was co-chaired by the Permanent Secretary of the Federal Ministry of

Petroleum Resources of Nigeria and the U.S. Department of State Coordinator for International Energy Affairs. Those who came as part of Nigerian delegates included officials from the Ministry of Petroleum Resources, Ministry of Foreign Affairs, Federal Ministry of Commerce and Industry, Federal Ministry of Power, Nigerian National Petroleum Corporation, Power Holding Company of Nigeria, Nigerian Investment Promotion Commission, Economic and Financial Crimes Commission, and Nigerian Electricity Regulatory Commission. On its part, the U.S. delegation included officials from the Department of State, Department of Energy, Department of Commerce, Treasury Department, U.S. Agency for International Development, Federal Energy Regulatory Commission, Office of the U.S. Trade Representative, the Overseas Private Investment Corporation, Federal Energy Regulatory Commission, and the U.S. Trade and Development Agency.

The meeting of the Working Group was an opportunity for senior officials of the American government from the Department of Energy and other agencies in charge of the electricity sector regulation, as well as natural resources management services, to exchange views with their counterparts from Nigeria on a subject that has been of significant importance for Nigeria. From the outset, it was envisaged that the U.S. energy sector would assist in transforming Nigeria's energy sector from being state-regulated to market-driven. This would help establish a pricing system that would encourage more private investment and growth of the sector. It was expected that at the end of the exercise, Nigerians would have been exposed to the whole issue of renewable energy and energy efficiency in the country. Even before the official meeting of the Working Group, members of the American team had started suggesting that Nigeria should focus attention on solar and biomass that could be incorporated into homes for domestic use as well as agricultural waste management. Also the American team had realised from the beginning that they would have to work closely with the Nigerian Extractive Industries Transparency Initiative (NEITI), on how the audits on the oil and gas industry could change governance structures in the industry, particularly in terms of legislation and regulation.

During the June 2010 meeting, the United States Government promised to support Nigeria's desire to reform its hydrocarbon sector. The meeting recognized that there is still work to be done on the transition of major reforms and the need for transparency and further consultation with stakeholders to ensure that reforms are successful. The Government of the Federal Republic of Nigeria assured the United States Government that the reforms will be implemented consistent with World Trade Organization regulations.

Both countries recognized the importance of advancing renewable energy opportunities in Nigeria. To this end, both governments renewed their commitments to advance renewable energy in Nigeria and the U.S. Trade and Development Agency provided a grant to the Nigerian Electricity Regulatory Commission to fund technical assistance on the proposed Renewable Energy Independent Power Producer Framework in Nigeria. The Government of the Federal Republic of Nigeria has pledged to provide support to facilitate the successful completion of the framework. The Government of the Federal Republic of Nigeria also welcomed a future visit to Nigeria by the Department of Energy's Under Secretary Dr. Kristina Johnston to further explore renewable energy and energy efficiency opportunities.

The meeting was also an opportunity for the United States to call on Nigeria to optimize the opportunities provided by the African Growth Opportunities Act and the Trade and Investment Framework Agreement to encourage the country's non-oil exports into the U.S. market. Both countries discussed the possibility of negotiating a Bilateral Investment Treaty for the promotion and protection of investment in their respective countries.

Niger Delta and Regional Security

The third full working group meeting of the commission took place in September 2010 in Washington, DC and it focused on Niger Delta and Nigeria's role in regional security. This was attended by five of the oil producing regions of Nigeria, including Governors Rotimi Amaechi of Rivers, Timpreye Silva of Bayelsa, Emmanuel Uduaghan of Delta, Godswill Akpabio of Akwa Ibom and Liyel Imoke of Cross Rivers State. The first day of the meeting focused on economic and infrastructural development of the Niger Delta, while the second day was on the role of Nigeria in bilateral co-operations in the region. Also as part of the efforts to develop the Niger Delta, Governors of Niger Delta states have been working closely with the Binantional Commission. The governors first attended the meetings of the Commission held in 2010 in the United States.

Two Niger Delta states (Rivers and Delta) are working with a United States Government to understudy the American transportation infrastructure. An agreement was signed with the Pennsylvania State Government in the U.S. to commence an infrastructure exchange partnership that will see the American model being transferred to both states. Under the agreement, the Pennsylvania Department of Transportation would work with the two states to implement the partnership exchange program. Another highlight of the meeting was the arrangement made for the five governors who attended the meeting to participate in a program put together by Reta Jo Lewis, the State Department's Special Representative for Intergovernmental Global Affairs, which enabled the governors to meet and discuss areas of mutual interest with US state-level officials.

Somewhat related, but not completely connected with the Bi-National Commission was the US Coast Guard Warship, *USCGC CHASE* that the United States donated to Nigeria in 2011. This ship will assist Nigeria in monitoring security in the Gulf of Guinea and according to the Nigerian Ambassador to the US, Ade Adefuye, it will "act as a deterrent for would be-dictators and those who will not allow democracy to thrive."

Agriculture and Food Security

This was the last of the working groups to make its inaugural meeting and it took place in February 2011, in Abuja, with the Permanent Secretary, Federal Ministry of Agriculture and Rural Development, Mrs Fatima B.A. Bamidele and USAID Deputy Assistant Administrator for Food Security, Greg Gottlieb co-chairing the meeting. The Nigerian delegation included officials from the Ministry of Foreign Affairs, Ministry of Agriculture and Rural Development, Ministry of Water Resources, Federal

Ministry of Commerce and Industry, Central Bank of Nigeria, and National Investment Promotion Council. The U.S. delegation included officials from the State Department, the U.S. Agency for International Development, the Department of Agriculture, and the Department of Commerce. Representatives from both the Nigerian and U.S. private sectors also participated in the discussions.

This Working Group has taken as part of its mandate, to ensure that Nigeria gets into the level where it can "feed" itself and impact on the West African sub-region through investment in Agriculture and trade policies. The United States believe that Nigeria has the potential to do this if there is "coordinative policy responses at the federal, state and local levels, thus enabling Nigeria to resume its status as a net exporter of Agricultural commodities." Specifically, the US officials identified the role that rural women can play in improving the Nigerian agricultural sector and how improvement in this sector can dramatically improve health, education and wealth of Nigerian women. The Working Group also looked into issues like the transportation needs of small farmers, policies to address credit and input, how to attract investment to agricultural business activities and the promotion of business opportunities for women and youths. The Communiqué issued after the meeting pointed out that:

> The governments of the Federal Republic of Nigeria and the United States of America acknowledge the shared objective of strengthening the agriculture sector in the region, and that improvements in policy and its implementation can promote overall economic growth and increase the income of farmers and others in the agriculture value chain.
>
> The U.S. government will support Nigeria's Comprehensive Africa Agricultural Development Program (CAADP) Commitment and align its agriculture programs with the National Agriculture Investment Plan (NAIP) within the CAADP framework. The Nigerian government committed to achieve at least 6 per cent annual agricultural growth by allocating not less than 10 per cent of the national budget to agriculture sector, such as increasing farmer access to markets with roads and improving access to agriculture inputs, processing, and post harvest storage facilities.

The U.S. government will provide policy support for the Nigerian government to review agricultural policies that inhibit investment in the agricultural sector, and promote agribusiness loans and other mechanisms to create better jobs and build productivity in the sector. The U.S. government will provide additional policy support for Nigeria's draft biotechnology law currently under consideration by the National Assembly.

Both governments will work together to facilitate regional agricultural trade by improving the flow of road traffic along the two major trade corridors, improving the efficiency of port operations, strengthening customs operations and regulations, and reducing protective barriers and logistical hurdles pertaining to agriculture and trade. The U.S. government will assist the Nigerian government as it works to improve harmonization of regional trade policies.

Both governments will seek to connect private companies from their respective countries to encourage investment in Nigerian agriculture. Both governments intend to follow-up on these commitments and seek further collaboration to address the challenges and opportunities presented by the Agriculture and Food Security Working Group.

In short within a year of its establishment, all the elements of the Bi-National Commission had been successfully launched. In this section, there is a discussion of the Working Group activities and their achievements.

Limitations

While there can be no doubt that the Bi-Nantional Commission covers a number of subjects, there are also some issues that could have been done differently. First, some of the working groups that were brought together could have been separated and put under separate working groups because of their importance and less than ideal fit under the present arrangement. For example, the idea of putting together the Niger Delta with regional security seems to be cumbersome and it gives the appearance of lumping together two important issues that ought to form separate working components. The topics that fall under the Niger Delta heading are mainly domestic issues that relate to the internal management of affairs, while those of regional security are largely external. It may have been easier if these issues had come under separate working groups. The same applies to energy and investment. These are also two important issues that should be separated and given special attention.

Second, there are some issues that completely escaped the attention of the Commission but which are quite vital to both the United States and Nigeria. Perhaps the first noticeable omission in the content of the Commission is the subject of religious riots in Nigeria. This is a major issue in the country and there are even those who argue that the problem was even more profound than the Niger Delta issue, which may only have achieved the level of importance it has because of the centrality of oil to the Nigerian situation – not because it is as profound a security problem as the incessant religious riots in the country. Since the 1980s, no decade has passed without Nigeria experiencing religious riots that have brought the country to the focus of international attention. Indeed, at the time the Bi-National Commission came into effect, some states in the country had become stigmatized as centers of religious conflicts. These included states like Kano, Katsina, Kaduna and Plateau. On the whole, thousands of people have died as a result of these conflicts and the consequences of conflict had resulted in the Federal Government imposing a State of Emergency in one of the affected states. Given this background, the subject ought to have been included in the Bi-National Commission. What has further made the subject more profound is the fact that religious conflicts in the country has percolated into many other issues including ethnicity, party politics and other considerations.

Closely related to the issue of religious rioting is the growing problem of religious radicalization – another subject missing from the contents of the Commission. This is somewhat surprising, especially when one considers the background of the attempted suicide bombing that came shortly before the signing of the Bi-National Commission. Since the signing, the problem has become more profound, with the activities of the militant sect *Jama'atu Ahlis Sunna Lidda'awati wal-Jihad*, (which in Arabic means "People Committed to the Propagation of the Prophet's Teachings and Jihad") – widely known as Boko Haram. Indeed,

Nigeria's experience with religious fanatics began in the 1980s, when the Maitatsine religious group ignited conflicts in sections of the northern part of the country. Against the background of the incessant religious radicalization, inclusion of a clause on the subject into the Bi-National Commission would have been appropriate.

Third, the Commission seems to have only given superficial consideration to the huge problem of youth vulnerability and exclusion. Indeed, it may be said that the issue was lightly touched on under the subject of good-governance and the situation in the Niger Delta. Nigeria has a huge youth challenge and young people in the country have been involved in virtually all political and security challenges facing Nigerian society, including religious radicalisation, religious violence, and political riots.

Nigeria-US Bi-National Commission: Suggestions for Review

As the Bi-National Commission is up for review shortly, there are some areas that may need to be considered in the review process. First, there may be the need for some of the working groups that have multiple focuses to be separated. As noted above, the Niger Delta and the Regional security component and the Energy and Investment component may need to be broken down into separate groups. If this is not possible, it may then be necessary to ensure that the existing components are made to reflect the diverse segments without too much emphasis on any particular segment. Secondly, there is the need to expand the scope of the work of the Commission to include the whole subject of religious radicalisation and violence. Perhaps more than the situation in the Niger Delta, this problem seems to be the most profound security challenge facing Nigeria presently.

Conclusion

The Nigeria-US Bi-Nantional Commission is undoubtedly one of the most important developments in the history of Nigerian-US relations. Although it has only been operational for just a little over three years, the Nigeria-US Bi-Nantional Commission can be considered a huge success, especially as it has assisted in putting the relationship between the two countries in a clear framework. While activities between the two countries are not restricted only to the specified areas, issues of specific concerns have been identified and captured within a structure that gives room for regular and periodic review. What, however, seems to be responsible for the success that has been achieved by the Commission is the calibre of people that have managed it. It is to the credit of the officials of the embassies of both countries that they have been able to coordinate the various meetings involved in this complex subject. The success of this Commission has inspired imitation - both Nigeria and Germany established a Bi-National Commission, in July 2011.

End Notes

[269.] *The Will*, 29 March 2010.

[270.] Solomon Chung, "When Powerful Weak Giants Meets", Weekly Trust, 9 April, 2010.

[271.] Signing of the Binational Commission, see, http://www.state.gov/r/pa/prs/ps/2010/04/139562.htm.

[272.] *Ibid*.

[273.] *The Punch* (Lagos) 15 April, 2010.

[274.] *Ibid*

[275.] Other members of the US team included Deputy Assistant Secretary of State for African Affairs, William Fitzgerald and Deputy Assistant Secretary of State for Democracy, Human Rights and Labor, Dr Daniel Baer.

[276.] Indeed, the US Assistant Secretary of State for African Affairs Johnnie Carson had said that Maurice Iwu was incapable of organising a credible election and should be changed.

Chapter Eleven

Trends in Goodluck Jonathan's Foreign Policy

Funmi OLONISAKIN and Penda DIALLO

It is, of course, too early to undertake a comprehensive analysis of President Goodluck Jonathan's foreign policy. The proverbial statement that "the Jury is still out" may not even be applicable, as Jonathan is just two years into a full term in office as the President of the Federal Republic of Nigeria. While it is too early to tell the full story, it is nevertheless possible to discern the direction the President hopes to set. Given that he assumed office after the death of the late President Umaru Yar' Adua and administered the country for about a year before the formal commencement of his own term in office following the April 2011 elections, analysts have had the opportunity of seeing him at the helm long enough to develop an initial impression.

The objective of this chapter is slightly different from the others in this book, as it goes a bit beyond Nigeria's relations with the United States to examine more broadly the patterns that are so far discernable in Goodluck Jonathan's foreign policy. But with the slight shift in scope, it also needs to be pointed out that this chapter will still focus more attention on the relationship Nigeria, under President Jonathan, has developed with the United States. As would be expected, this chapter begins by looking at the circumstances under which he assumed power and the implications of this for Nigeria's foreign policy formulation and implementation under his administration.

Constraints of Timing and Circumstance

The circumstances of President Jonathan's assumption of office were, as noted earlier, unusual and unprecedented in the history of Nigeria.[277] This brought about considerable constraints that need to be considered in understanding his foreign policy agenda. First, at the time he assumed office as Acting President, he was effectively in a caretaker role and expected to pursue the foreign policy agenda of his predecessor. The general uncertainties at the time concerning the late President Umaru Yar' Adua's health also meant that the Acting President had to tread cautiously in order not to present the impression of overzealousness. This limited the extent to which the Acting President could take some decisions in the foreign policy arena.

But there was also domestic pressure that diverted attention from foreign policy activities. From the moment he assumed office as Acting President, Goodluck Jonathan was confronted with serious religious and communal violence across the country, especially between Muslim and Christian groups in Jos and its environs which left hundreds of people dead. This was apart from the general instability that was still prevailing, albeit in a reduced form, in the Niger Delta.

But while there were constraints along these lines, another restriction was introduced by the timing of President Jonathan's assumption of office. While the fate of the late President Yar' Adua was still unknown, the country faced one of the most profound foreign policy challenges since independence with the arrest of a young Nigerian in the United States for attempting to bomb an American commercial airline flight. As pressure on Nigeria mounted, international news agencies drew attention to the fact that these developments were taking place at a time when the fate of the Nigerian President was unknown. The subsequent inclusion of Nigeria on the global Terror Watch List presented Acting President Jonathan with his first major foreign policy challenge.

Consequently, given the background and timing of these events, the administration of President Jonathan was constrained by challenges requiring immediate attention. Once his tenure in office was more definite, the new President began the process of consolidating his position and making his imprint on the foreign policy field.

The Consolidation Phase

Not long after Jonathan assumed office, the Minister of Foreign Affairs, Ojo Madueke, was removed in a cabinet reshuffle. There was a lull for some time and during this period, the Permanent Secretary of the Ministry of Foreign Affairs, Ambassador Martin Uhomoibhi, took charge before Odein Ajumogobia, who was the former Minister of State of Petroleum Affairs, became the new Minister of Foreign Affairs. This was perhaps, the first indication that the new President was about to make a major departure from the past.

Right from the time he assumed office as President, a number of key considerations have been noticeable from some of Jonathan's activities. Indeed, five key issues are discernable:

a. Desire to improve the international image of Nigeria which had been further affected by the arrest of the Nigerian who attempted to bomb an American airline;
b. Determination to ensure that Nigeria remained active in the West African sub-region and in Africa as a whole, especially against the background of instability that was still brewing in some parts of the continent;
c. Intention to guarantee that external relations aligned with Nigeria's domestic needs, particularly in those areas where the country was trying to ensure its natural resources assist in its developmental processes;
d. Efforts to consolidate growing relations with emerging countries like Brazil, Russia, India and China; and
e. Struggle to maintain close relations with traditional global powers like the United States, Great Britain and France.

The next sections will look into each of these issues and the steps the Jonathan administration has taken to pursue them.

Improving the external image of Nigeria

Although the urge to improve the international image of Nigeria far preceded the assumption of office of President Jonathan, a number of factors further impressed the need for this on his administration. The number of Nigerians in foreign jails, for example, has given the impression that many nationals of the country are engaged in criminal and illegal activities across the world.[279] There had even been a case in the past where a senior official of the Ministry of External Affairs was murdered to avenge the fraudulent activities of Nigerians.[280] Aware of these perceptions and events, the need to improve the external image of Nigeria was paramount on the mind of the Jonathan administration. What, however, made the situation all the more profound was the arrest of Farooq Mutallab, the young Nigerian apprehended while trying to blow up an American airline flying from Europe to Detroit. This gave Nigeria very negative publicity and the image of a country engaged in terrorism was added to the negative impression many already had of a Nigeria supposedly full of criminals.

The first step the Goodluck Jonathan administration took was to ensure that the negative impression of a terrorist nation was removed and that Mutallab's act was seen as an individual action carried out by a young, impressionable and confused youth who had been indoctrinated outside Nigeria.[281] The President pursued this goal by carefully choosing Professor Ade Adefuye as ambassador to Washington. With considerable vigor and aplomb, efforts were made to ensure that Nigeria's name was removed from the Terror Watch List. There were also other activities undertaken to ensure that the image of Nigeria was improved. Although the effort to disabuse the minds of other countries that Nigeria was not a terrorist nation was largely targeted towards key Western countries, especially the United States, all other embassies and High Commissions across the world were encouraged to embark on a Charm Offensive in order to ensure that Nigeria won back the respectability that it so earnestly desired.

Also in the effort to ensure an improvement of Nigeria's image abroad, the Jonathan administration has tried to engage the Diaspora community in a continued dialogue. Indeed, the administration seems to have appreciated the fact that the best way to improve the image of the country is through its nationals living abroad. Embassies and High Commissioners have thus been encouraged to engage the Diaspora community and to participate in their activities. What seems to have made this relatively easy was that President Jonathan assumed office at just about the time that Nigeria was preparing for another election and most of the Diaspora populations were coming together to discuss their expectations for the election. It was thus possible for the various diplomatic missions to interact with the multiple Nigerian-based organizations coming together in various countries. The administration has also promised to establish a Diaspora Commission that will harmonize the contributions of Nigerians living abroad and ensure proper documentation of their input in the affairs of the nation as key stakeholders.

Another important foreign policy initiative targeted at improving the image of Nigeria is the efforts that have been made to evacuate Nigerians from violence erupting in other countries. Since President Jonathan assumed office, he has had to take decisive steps in evacuating Nigerians from countries at the threshold of anarchy. After the revolution in Egypt, the President ordered the evacuation of Nigerians from the country and when Libya too went up in flames, an evacuation of Nigerians in the country was ordered. With this, the embarrassment of Nigerians being stranded or being killed, which would have further brought the country into disrepute, was avoided.

But perhaps the most important way through which the Goodluck Jonathan administration has tried to redeem Nigeria's image was through the conduct of a credible election. Before assuming office, Nigeria had, over the years, had different election experiences, but virtually all of these had been unpleasant. Where elections had not been massively rigged or fraught with violence, they had been annulled. This had cast aspersions on Nigerian democracy and had brought the country to shame. On his assumption of office, President Goodluck Jonathan assured that his administration would give Nigeria a credible election. To ensure this, the Independent National Electoral Commission (INEC) was reconstituted and Professor Attahiru Jega was made its head. This election won international endorsement and the image of Nigeria rose considerably in the international community, especially in Africa where the country also has a strong desire to influence developments.

Active Involvement in Regional and Continental Affairs
One of the earliest pronouncements of the Jonathan administration

was a promise to continue making Africa the centre of Nigerian foreign policy. While on a visit to the United States, he told his audience at the Council for Foreign Relations that Africa would continue to attract his administration's attention. Specifically, three regional/continental issues have dominated the attention of the administration. These are: ensuring peace and stability; consolidating democracy; and developing regional/continental cooperation. The country that best exemplifies President Jonathan's commitment to all these principles is Cote d'Ivoire. Here the former President, Laurent Gbagbo refused to surrender power to Al Hassan Quattara after he had lost an election that was monitored and endorsed by the international community. This created confusion and within a very short time, complete anarchy had engulfed Cote d'Ivoire. This turned out to be particularly difficult for ECOWAS because it had to act against one of its own members. For a regional organization that had gruesome experiences like those in Liberia and Sierra Leone in its recent memory, events following Gbagbo's refusal to give up power caused considerable disquiet and the violence that occurred further aggravated apprehension.

Nigeria under President Jonathan took interest in the developments in Cote d'Ivoire. Apart from its dominant position in the region, the urge to intervene became all the more important for the Nigerian leader because he was Chairperson of ECOWAS during this time. The first step taken by President Jonathan was to recognize the election that Gbagbo refused to accept and to call on the President to hand over power. President Jonathan specifically warned the former President of Cote d'Ivoire that he would be forced out by legitimate intervention if he continued to refuse to hand over power to Quattara who was internationally recognized as having won the election. In the end Gbagbo was removed by forces led by France. This was a situation where President Jonathan had worked with President Obama of the United States to ensure a successful resolution of the problem.

In a way, Nigeria found itself in a somewhat unwinnable situation in its handling of the situation in Cote d'Ivoire, with many people claiming that Nigeria could have acted more decisively, rather than allowing France to come in and take the glory. Many observers felt that Nigeria ought to have taken a more decisive step and sent in troops to remove Gbagbo from power. Reality, however, dictated otherwise. As the ECOWAS chairperson, the Nigerian leader had to take into consideration the general opinion of other ECOWAS leaders and could not have acted unilaterally. But this apart, the President also had to take into consideration the domestic implications of another sub-regional military engagement after several years of military commitment to Liberia and Sierra Leone. It would seem that Jonathan felt that subtle pressure, while military option remained on the table, that could force Gbagbo into conformity was a far better option than outright military engagement whose duration would be indeterminable and whose consequences was clearly unpredictable.

But President Jonathan's diplomacy in Cote d'Ivoire has attracted its own set of admirers, not least among these, the Special Representative of the UN Secretary-General in Cote d'Ivoire, Young-jin Choi, who pointed out that Nigeria's early intervention, though unpopular in some quarters, in the Ivorian crisis had provided a guide for the international community. He pointed out:

> President Goodluck Jonathan who served as the Chairman of ECOWAS during the Ivorian crisis made a critical contribution by telling the truth. By guiding the ECOWAS with a clear vision and decisive action ... the Ivorian people and the international community ... are very thankful for what he did.[282]

In January 2011, President Jonathan attended the mini-summit of the AU Peace and Security Council (PSC) on the situation in Cote d'Ivoire, and this was followed by the 29th meeting of the NEPAD Heads of State and Government Consultative Committee. Being the ECOWAS Chairman, President Jonathan also co-chaired the mini-summit of the AU Peace and Security Council (PSC) on Cote d'Ivoire along with Dr Jean Ping, the AU Commission Chairperson and Mr. Ban Ki-moon, the Secretary-General of the UN.

Another country that has attracted the attention of the Jonathan administration is Sudan. Jonathan considered this problem so important that he raised it during his second meeting with President Obama (discussed later in this chapter). The Jonathan administration has always expressed concern about the situation in Sudan, especially because of the multi-dimensional nature of the crisis and the Nigerian leader specifically set time aside during the June 2011 AU Summit in Malabo, Equatorial Guinea, to discuss the situation with the President of the Sudan, Omar Bashir.

When the democratic upsurge emerged in the Arab world, the Jonathan administration appeared to find itself somewhat torn between two tendencies. While it recognized the importance of democracy and the need for autocratic leaders who had ruled their countries without election to go, the administration was also against all forms of external meddling in the problem. Consequently, there was no serious involvement in the situations in Algeria and Egypt, beyond the evacuation of Nigerians from the places where they were exposed to danger. In short, Nigeria saw the developments in the two countries as internal affairs in which it could not interfere.

The situation in Libya was, however, somewhat different and President Jonathan has reacted to it differently. While the legitimate right of Libyans to desire a change in their government was recognized, the involvement of NATO forces was something that the Nigerian President considered unacceptable. This sentiment was expressed to a delegation from Libya which visited Nigeria in June 2011. During the visit, President Jonathan asked the leaders of the delegation to convey his greetings and condolences to President Gadhafi on the death of his son, Saif Al-Arab. He further assured the delegation that he is keen to preserve the sovereignty, independence and unity of Libya and his rejection of any foreign intervention. President Jonathan also informed the delegation that Nigeria will exert every effort to end the NATO intervention in Libya.[283] Nigeria has however not fully explained its vote in support of the UN Security Council resolutions, in particular resolution 1973 (2011) which approved the imposition of a No-Fly-Zone and gave the green light for NATO military action in Libya.

Aligning External Relations to Domestic Needs

A major strategy of the Jonathan administration has been the desire to ensure that foreign policy goals are made to align with domestic needs. This had started since the Obasanjo administration and continued through the Yar' Adua era. At the centre of this principle is the philosophy that may be termed as "oil for development". The practice, which sees Nigeria give oil in exchange for infrastructural development, has brought Nigeria very close to countries like China, Brazil, India and Russia. The details of all these will be discussed later in this chapter.

Goodluck Jonathan's Nigeria and the Emerging Powers

It also needs to be pointed out that the close relations that Goodluck Jonathan has been able to develop with emerging countries like China, Brazil, India and Russia also have their antecedents in the administrations of Obasanjo and Yar' Adua. Indeed, put together, President Obasanjo visited these countries nine times while the late President Yar' Adua visited twice.[284] Indeed, in the last decade, emerging powers like China, India and Brazil have been key actors in Nigeria's foreign policy. This is not only because of the increasing economic powers of these countries but also because of the extent to which they too are willing to engage Nigeria with its vast economic and human resources.

In the relationship with Brazil, President Goodluck Jonathan has extended a hand of friendship and in January 2011, the Vice President, Namadi Sambo, further reinforce this determination during his visit to Brazil. The specific objective of this was to continue the discussion that had earlier been started by the late President Yar' Adua on the Zungeru hydropower plant and financing the Mambilla hydropower project under a joint partnership. Under the discussion, Brazil would develop Nigeria's power industry and in return, Nigeria would grant Brazil access to its oil and gas industry. This was particularly important to Nigeria, especially as the government had earlier failed in its promise to double electricity output to 6,000 megawatts by December 2009.[285] The Mambilla project would be bankrolled by the Brazilian government "from the scratch on a turnkey basis."

Nigeria and Brazil are also working together in the area of drugs and narcotics control. Both countries have realized that citizens from their respective countries and others from outside the two countries have been using both Nigeria and Brazil as routes for drugs. In fact, by April 2010, the Nigerian National Drug Law Enforcement Agency (NDLEA) had placed the Nigerian-Brazil route on red alert to cancel moves by drug trafficking syndicates.

Military links have also been developed as Nigeria has decided to upgrade its military links with Brazil and has appointed its first Defence Attaché to Brazil. The Defence Section of the Nigerian Embassy in Brazil was also commissioned by the Nigerian Vice President during his visit to Brazil in December 2010. This thus gives the impression that Nigeria wants to further extend military links with Brazil, especially against the background of the idea of the South Atlantic Zone of Peace that both countries remain committed to.

Apart from Brazil, the Jonathan administration has also been close to China and had also done oil for development exchange with the country. For example, in February 2011, the Nigerian government handed over the Olorunsogo Power station in Ogun state to a consortium led by Sepco iii Electric Power Construction Corporation of China and an indigenous company, Pacific Energy.

India too has been of specific interest to the Jonathan administration and here again the antecedent was laid by the preceding administration. With the signing of the "Abuja Declaration" between the two countries in 2007, both countries have been regularly meeting to consolidate their relations. In an interview in March 2011,[286] the Nigerian Foreign Minister, Mr. Odein Ajumogobia confirmed that the volume of trade between Nigeria and India was in the excess of US$10 billion. Nigeria desires to expand this portfolio and it was the determination to do this that made the Minister to go to India in March 2011. The visit to India in March 2011 was also to hold the 5th session of the Joint Commission with India. The Joint Commission constitutes a legal framework of the collaboration between Nigeria and India. A whole gamut of activities fit under its umbrella. The purpose of the March 2011 visit was to talk about the bilateral air service agreement which is also part of the issues under Joint Commission.[287] Under the Goodluck Jonathan administration, there has been further collaboration in the banking sector with emerging powers, notably India and China. In some cases, this has been linked to other business engagements. For example, in June 2011, an Indian company, Bharti Airtel partnered with ECOBANK in launching mobile banking. Earlier, in March 2011, China became more involved in the Nigerian Banking sector when the China EximBank granted a US$30 million trade finance facility to Access Bank Plc. The facility covers Letters of Credit and Export Credit guarantees.

The Goodluck Jonathan administration has also tried to address the alleged issue of fake drugs coming from some of the emerging powers. For example, in March 2011, the former Nigerian Foreign Affairs Minister, Mr Odein Ajumogobia and his Indian Counterpart, Somanahalli Mallaiah Krishna, signed a Memorandum of Understanding that stipulated that any Indian caught importing fake drugs to Nigeria would be jailed for life and also have their property confiscated. Also under the MOU, India agrees to pay for the prosecution of anyone suspected of counterfeiting drugs. The Indian government agreed to collaborate with NAFDAC in capacity building, training programmes and provision of funding for training of medical engineers.[289]

Goodluck Jonathan's Nigeria and the "Traditional" Powers

While the relationship with the emerging powers continues to deepen, the Jonathan administration has also continued to be close with the traditional western powers. In a way, this was a pattern of foreign policy imposed on the administration because of the historical linkage that has existed between Nigeria and these countries, especially the United Kingdom. Prime Minister David Cameron visited Nigeria on July 19, 2011 for discussion with President Jonathan during which the British Prime Minister expressed support for Nigeria "to forge ... a significant new partnership on counter-terrorism". However, one of the highlights of the visit was the joint Newspaper article written by both leaders, an abridge version of which is presented below:

> We are two leaders, from different countries and different political traditions. But we each passionately believe in the

power of trade and enterprise to change people's lives. As we are seeing now on every continent, what will lift tens of millions out of poverty in the long run is the dynamic engine of economic growth. And that means African countries buying from and selling to each other, doing business with one another and the world.

So we need to take on the obstacles to trade and growth. Despite recent strong economic growth in Africa, today just twelve percent of African trade is with other African nations. For much of the continent it is easier to trade with Europe or America than it is to trade with a neighbor. Infrastructure can be poor and overstretched, red tape endemic, and trade taxes stifling.

We are determined to seize on this success. Nigeria will work with its partners in Western Africa to liberalize trade with the ultimate ambition of Africa-wide free trade. From London, Britain will invest more than £160 million between now and 2015 in freeing up trade, including halving delays at ten key border crossings. We need greater commitment throughout the continent to regional transport corridors.

But what will transform Africa's potential in the end is truly pan-continental trade, underpinned by concrete and substantial agreements. With many African countries on the point of making the transition from dependence to sustained growth, regional trade is the golden key. Along with the efforts already made in Southern and Eastern Africa, ECOWAS, on this, the twentieth anniversary of the Abuja Treaty, is also determined to develop its own free trade area, bringing Africa a step closer to the dream of an African Economic Community from shore to shore. With a strong and unified voice in global trade, Africa can deliver a better deal for its citizens, and be a significant driver of growth for the world in the era ahead.

We need political leadership from all of Africa's leaders to achieve this. As Africa's leaders show the vision and will to get this done, so real leadership is required from the rest of the world too. Trade rules must be open and fair to all. That is why we will together be pressing the need for duty and quota free market access for the poorest countries, for sustained commitment to a global trade deal.

Never before has there been a time quite like this. We are used to thinking that the problems of our world will be always with us. But the economic revolution underway has brought within reach the steps to eradicate poverty in Africa. It is now possible to imagine an Africa no longer dependent on aid, and a real source of growth for the whole world. And the road to get there lies through freeing up the wealth creating power of enterprise and trade.

This challenge falls to our generation of leaders. For too long 55 nations' borders have been allowed to hold Africa's people back. We believe it is time to make African free trade the common purpose of the continent and the wider world. To set Africa on a path to prosperity and stability would be a wonderful legacy from our generation to the next.

President Goodluck Jonathan had found particular friendship with the French President, Nicolas Sarkozy. The friendship was further strengthened by the close relationship the two had been able to forge over Cote d'Ivoire. The Nigerian leader was invited to the 25th Africa-France Summit in Nice in May 2010 and the two leaders also met, on the sidelines of the inauguration of Ivorian President Alassane Ouattara, in Cote d'Ivoire. President Sarkozy also commended President Jonathan for the role he played as Chairman of the Economic Community of West African Countries (ECOWAS) to help restore the democratically elected government of Ouattara. France pledged its support for Nigeria's aspirations in the international arena, including her quest for a permanent seat on the UN Security Council. As of April 2011, the bilateral trade between Nigeria and France had reached 5.5 billion Euros.[290]

Another country with which President Jonathan also has remarkably warm relations is Canada. The country invited Nigeria to G20 summit scheduled in June 2010 in Ontario, which was the first time that the country was invited since it began in 2008. Canada, which held the 2010 G8 Presidency, also invited President Jonathan to participate in sideline events and to hold bilateral meetings with leaders of key G8 nations during the G8 summit in June 2010 at the Deerhurst Resort in Huntsville, Canada, despite the fact that the country was not invited for the previous meetings.

The Jonathan administration has also developed a good relationship with Britain. Indeed, Britain was among the first set of countries to indicate support for the Nigerian President when the late President Yar' Adua came back to Nigeria from Saudi Arabia following his medical treatment in that country in 2010. As a mark of admiration for the British Secretary of State for International Development, Andrew Mitchel, visited Nigeria in what was the first visit by a Cabinet Minister to Nigeria in five years. The visit was also an opportunity for the two countries to discuss further cooperation in the economic sector and in other areas like the pursuit of Millennium Development Goals, (MDG) and Security Sector Reform.

Another country that is coming to the forefront of attention for the Jonathan administration is Germany. German Chancellor, Angela Merkel, visited Nigeria in July 2011. The highlight of the visit was the decision of the two countries to establish a Bi-National Commission to oversee the expansion of economic cooperation between both countries. According to the Nigerian President, the commission would be headed by the ministers of Foreign Affairs of both countries and had ministers responsible for finance, trade, commerce and economic relations as members. The technical details of this Commission would be worked out when the new Nigerian Foreign Affairs Minister, Ambassador Olugbenga Ashiru led a Nigerian delegation to Germany, ahead of a visit by President Jonathan to Germany the following year.[291] Also during the visit of the German delegates, both countries agreed to collaborate in clinching United Nations Security Council seats.[292] But apart from bilateral relationships with individual countries, the Jonathan administration has also used the United Nations as an avenue to propagate its foreign policy agenda. With all the current international attention, the indications are that Nigeria is once again back in business and President Jonathan stands to benefit from the new international spotlight.

Goodluck Jonathan and United Nations International Organizations

An area where the Jonathan administration is also making its mark is in Nigeria's relationship with the United Nations. This again predated the administration as the foundation had been laid by the Obasanjo and Yar' Adua administrations. Apart from joining the organization in the pursuit of global peace, President Jonathan has taken active part in ensuring Nigeria's involvement in key debates at the United Nations. It is also to his fortune that during his term, Nigeria was elected twice to a non-permanent seat on the United Nations Security Council.

During his visit to the United Nations in June 2011, President Jonathan raised issue on the scourge of the HIV/AIDS and insisted that: "30 years since the beginning of the AIDS pandemic, the time is ripe for a final solution." Specifically, he called on the Security Council to set clear and decisive goals in order that efforts to maintain peace could add to the fight against HIV/AIDS and identified the problems associated with the disease as "pivotal to the development and security of Africa, in particular and the world in general". He, however, identified a national dimension to his call for global efforts to address the problem of AIDS. He noted that as the largest contributor to peacekeeping in Africa and the fourth largest in the world, Nigeria has a major stake, not only in ensuring that, "our armed forces are protected against HIV and AIDS, but also given adequate treatment".

President Goodluck Jonathan also pledged Nigeria's commitment to ensuring that HIV/AIDS prevention, treatment and care are integrated into the country's armed forces' health services. He also confirmed that the ECOWAS sub-regional transport corridor project, involving Benin, Togo, Ghana and Cote d'Ivoire, was designed to halt and reverse the spread of HIV/AIDS among various populations. There was also an assurance by the President that Nigeria would increase its level of engagement with the security services in those countries to reduce the impact of the disease in the region. But the relationship with the United Nations has also further reinforced the rapport Nigeria is developing with the United States, the country hosting the headquarters of the international organization.

Goodluck Jonathan's Administration and the United States

Between the time he assumed office as the Acting President of Nigeria in 2010 and mid 2011, President Goodluck Jonathan has visited the United States twice during which he was received by President Barack Obama. The first was in April 2010 and it was his first official visit outside Nigeria. This was a four-day working visit during which the President attended the Nuclear Security Summit and met President Obama. The timing of the visit was also important, as it was just a few months after the attempt by a Nigerian youth to bomb an American airline. This was thus an opportunity to further enhance the positive image of Nigeria. As the Nigerian Ambassador to the United States pointed out, the visit gave a tremendous boost to the country's image abroad, making Nigerians in Diaspora hold their heads high once again in national pride.

President Goodluck Jonathan's first visit to the United States saw a lot of successes. First, it was an opportunity for the American government and people and also Nigerians in the United States to meet the person who was about to fully attain the leadership position of Africa's most populous nation. Against the background of the charm offensive that was needed to redeem the image of the country after Muttalab's abortive bombing attempt, the President tried to make a positive impression on the American audience. Despite the fact that the visit was not a state-visit – which one would have expected to be associated with pomp and pageantry – it still attracted a lot of interest. While in the US, the Acting President visited the Council on Foreign Relations, the Corporate Council for Africa, and the World Bank He also met with the US Vice President and officials from the Pentagon and State Department. In addition, he is said to have met with members of the European Union, the United Nations and many powerful and influential individuals during the visit.

The second visit was made in June 2011 and this was on the invitation of the American President. The timing was particularly important as the Nigerian President had just won an election that was widely acclaimed as free, fair and credible. The objective of the second visit was to enable the two leaders to discuss regional and global developments and enhancing strong bilateral partnership between the two countries.

The trade relations between Nigeria and the United states continue to be impressive, as shown in the table below. The table shows the US trade in Goods between February 2010 when President Jonathan assumed office and the end of May 2011.

U.S. Trade in goods with Nigeria February 2010 and May 2011

Month	Exports	Imports	Balance
February 2010	310.1	2,058.7	-1,748.7
March 2010	494.5	2,728.9	-2,234.3
April 2010	323.5	2,560.4	-2,236.9
May 2010	381.8	2,512.6	-2,130.8
June 2010	301.1	2,653.8	-2,352.7
July 2010	296.8	2,700.4	-2,403.6
August 2010	287.9	2,951.1	-2,663.3
September 2010	349.9	2,808.6	-2,458.7
October 2010	349.5	2,209.3	-1,859.8
November 2010	380.2	2,116.4	-1,736.2
December 2010	376.6	2,902.4	-2,525.8
January 2011	268.6	3,144.7	-2,876.1
February 2011	331.4	2,859.3	-2,527.9
March 2011	489.0	2,972.1	-2,483.1
April 2011	397.1	2,944.2	-2,547.1
May 2011	504.3	2,801.6	-2,297.3

There has also been considerable financial assistance from the United States to Nigeria since President Jonathan assumed office. In the power sector, for example, Nigeria signed an agreement with the United States to improve power generation through the use of renewable energy. The US Trade and Development Agency (USTDA) is to provide US$323,000 technical assistance to assist the Nigeria Electricity Regulatory Commission (NERC) to develop a renewable energy framework for Independent Power Producers (IPPs). This was sequence to the discussion of the Working Group on Energy and Investment of the US-Nigeria Bi-National Commission (BNC). Besides this, the United States also assisted the Independent National Electoral Commission (INEC) with funds for the April 2011 general elections. This included a grant of US$30 million to build up its technological infrastructure towards the 2011 general elections. Also, the American government co-funded the 2010 Nigeria Education Data Survey and Digest of Education Statistics (NEDS) in Abuja.[293]

Conclusion

While it may be a bit early to give any final verdict on President Goodluck Jonathan's foreign policy, it seems clear that some patterns are getting increasingly discernable. First, it seems that the government wants to pursue the policy of aligning foreign policy to domestic developmental needs. This can be seen in the various links the government has been establishing with emerging powers like Brazil India and China. Among others, the increasing links with these countries is targeted towards addressing Nigeria's energy problem. Indeed, the government want to align foreign policy to the realization of the country's Vision 2020, which aspires that by the year 2020 "Nigeria will be one of the 20 largest economies in the world, able to consolidate its leadership role in Africa and establish itself as a significant player in the global economic and political arena." Second, President Jonathan has shown interest in maintaining Nigeria's traditional interest in the West African sub-region. This is most evident in its position in Cote d'Ivoire and in the leadership it provided while serving as the ECOWAS Chairperson. This is also a policy based on precedent, as Nigeria has always played a dominant role in the affairs of the West African sub-region. Third, the Jonathan administration has tried to maintain cordial relationship with the dominant global powers, especially the United States, Great Britain and France. Indeed, President Jonathan is one of the few leaders that have visited the United States twice within 18 months and on both occasions held meetings with the American President. Relationship with other key countries like France and Great Britain continues to be cordial. On the whole, it would appear that the foreign policy of the Jonathan administration has so far been positive. With the President now in a full term in office, it is likely that some of these policies will be fully developed. Also, with the appointment of a career diplomat, Ambassador Olugbenga Ashiru, as the Minister for Foreign Affairs – the third time in the history of the Ministry[294] – it is expected that the foreign policy agenda of the administration will be well anchored and made to be more in synergy with domestic concerns.

End Notes

277. There had been two cases somewhat similar but also uniquely different: the process of Obasanjo assumption of office after Murtala Mohammed's death and that of Abubakar Abdulsalam after the demise of Sanni Abacha.. But these were not under constitutional processes as the constitution had then been suspended. There were thus no process that could have brought out the opposition and objection people may have had about the succession processes. Apart from this, the circumstances of the deaths in both cases were sudden, unlike the case with Goodluck Jonathan that first acted for some time as the President before formal acceptance of office as President.

278. Although the Amnesty Exercise had considerably reduced the incidence of violence in the Niger Delta, there were still remnants of violence as at the time Goodluck Jonathan assumed office.

279. For example, as at May 2010, it was estimated that there are up to 20,000 Nigerians languishing in various British. See, Dimeji Kayode-Adedeji, "20,000 Nigerians in UK Prisons", www.234next.com/

280. In February 2003, Mr. Michael Lekara Wayid, Nigeria's consul in the Czech Republic, was shot dead by a Czech national at the Nigerian Embassy in Prague. The Czech had been a victim of a Nigerian-organized advanced fee fraud, popularly known in Nigeria as "419" after the Criminal Code.

281. Mutallab had been schooled in England (University College London) and had been in contact with Yemen prior to his attempt.

282. *Punch* (Lagos) 7 June 2011.

283. He made this position when the Libyan Foreign Minister Abdullahi Oubaidi met him in his office in Abuja.

284. The itemised visits are Obasanjo Brazil 2, Russia, 1; India, 4 (one of which was a private visit) and China, 2. On his part, Yar'Adua only visited Brazil and India on one occasions each.

285. It was calculated that the Mambilla project in the country's north-eastern state of Taraba will generate 2,600 megawatts when completed.

286. Interview with Odein Ajumogobia *ThisDay* (Lagos) March 22 2011

287. *Ibid.*

288. *ThisDay*, (Lagos) March 22 2011.

289. *This Day* (Lagos) March 30 2011.

290. See *The Punch* (Lagos) 25 April 201.

291. See, "Nigeria-Germany bi-national commission under way, *Nigeria Tribune* (Ibadan) 15 July 2011.

292. Ayodele Adesanmi, "UN Security Council Seat: Nigeria/Germany to Cooperate" *Nigerian Tribune* (Ibadan), 15 July 2011.

293. William Ekanem U.S-Nigeria Relations: A 12 months Assessment, *Business World* March 31 2011.

294. The first career diplomat to be the Minister for Foreign Affairs is Ambassador Ignatius Olisemeka, who was the Minister in the Abacha administration, while the second was Ambassador Olu Adeniji under President Olusegun Obasanjo.

Chapter Twelve

Looking at the Public Perception of Nigerians in the United States from within: President Goodluck Jonathan and the Making of a New Image

Laolu AKANDE

A new phase in US-Nigeria relations began on 29 March, 2010 when President Barack Obama welcomed Ambassador Adebowale Adefuye to the White House. Shortly after Adefuye's arrival, the US entered into a strategic Bi-National Commission with Nigeria, signed 6 April 2010 at the State Department (discussed at length in Chapter Ten above). Before the end of that month, then Acting President Goodluck Jonathan was received by President Obama in Washington DC. During this meeting according to Jonathan himself, Obama spoke highly of US-based Nigerians.[295] While this positive momentum may not immediately reveal deeper perception challenges the Nigerian nation has been contending with in the United States, nonetheless, they create an opportunity for a new beginning and a chance to reorder things.

The recurring challenges of Nigeria's public perception issues in the United States have not always been located only within government-to-government relations. There have been times that frictions at that level have generated immense perception worries, but where the real problem lies is in the nature of the American media reporting on Nigeria.

A country's foreign policy generally addresses the issue of how nations can maintain their good names abroad. It is for that reason that the objective of this chapter is to review the evolution of Nigeria's public image in the US in recent years, consider the attempts made since the beginning of the Jonathan presidency to address the situation, and offering insight from within, as a US-based journalist. No nation can be contented nor should be when its image abroad is generally questionable. This is especially so when the more favorable developments and the inspiring news items about such a nation and its people are regularly being overwhelmed by a consistent brush of negativity.

Prevalent Public Perception

Perception is often what constitutes reality in the consciousness of an individual or the public. And in the life of a nation what constitutes the national self-concept that feeds perception, is not merely the domestic condition, history and culture of the people, but also the attitudes and reactions of other nations, especially those nations considered not only as global leaders but seen as friendly. The United States is not only a global leader in the community of nations, but Nigerians and the Nigerian government more often than not perceive Americans in friendly terms.

However, perceptions may easily become one sided for three reasons. First, perception involves a process of selection of certain information out of a larger pool. Regardless of whether selection is made by an individual or the media, a great deal of information is simply knocked out in what is not always a value-free elimination. Secondly, in the manner in which public perception is organized, information that is not deemed easily understandable perhaps due to huge cultural differences and nuances is either misunderstood or simply set aside. Thirdly, the way public perceptions are interpreted depend on previously determined mind sets, which again leaves enough room for the potential of bias and even at times ethnocentrism.

These factors underscore the understanding and significance of whatever is widely held as the dominant perception of Nigeria in a country such as the United States. Unfortunately however, at least since the mid to late 90s when military dictatorship took Nigeria to the pariah status in the community of nations, Nigeria and Nigerians have not enjoyed a sustained positive image in the United States. Apart from the human rights violations and the abridgement of democratic rights which the military perpetrated,

Nigeria's image problem in the US can also be traced to several other factors including the widespread Internet expansion of 419 at home and abroad, financial and drug-related crimes, especially by some Nigerians in the United States, domestic corruption at home, and governance challenges.

The American print and broadcast media has imprinted a Nigerian label on 419 over the years, simply calling it "Nigerian 419 scams." The preponderance of such reports in the US has overwhelmed the many and otherwise significant recognitions and impacts that quite a good number of Nigerians in the US have recorded.[296] And since by nature, news is more appealing when it is negative, Nigeria has been at the short-end of the stick in terms of media coverage that is more damning than complimentary. Equally, media scholars have always highlighted the fact that a media organization or outlet is set-up with a specific goal or sets of goals in mind based on the Agenda-setting theory of the press. Therefore the reportage of Nigeria by the western and American media is often seen as reflecting the agenda-setting roles of such media and less reflective of the completely accurate, fair and balanced view of the Nigerian condition in the US.

While the general factors militating against the image of the country abroad persist and have become like music in the ears of the average American journalist, new sources of discontent against Nigeria and Nigerians are also often highlighted. For instance, earlier this year a Nigerian-American in the state of Texas was involved in a fire incident which saw her day care business burnt, killing American children. Jolted and perhaps in panic, or out of fear the Nigerian involved travelled to Nigeria. The American media[297] quickly deemed the disappearance an escape, calling her a fugitive, thus causing further depreciation to the country's image. The fact that Nigerian authorities were actively involved in securing her return and that she voluntarily stepped forward once she realized the interpretation of her movements, did not get enough play in the media. Instead, the US media played up the slant that she was "caught" and extradited back to the US.

On virtually every major TV network including CNN, there has been one major negative report on Nigeria. Well-known talk show hosts like Oprah Winfrey have also not been left out depicting what, at times, are accurate reports about fraud perpetrated in the US and also at times about the condition of poverty in Nigeria. Thus, often dramatic American TV news reports on Nigeria are clear sources of the development of a negative public information level against Nigeria among the average American TV audience. Either deliberately or otherwise, the American media has actively propagated and maintained a perception about Nigeria which has had tremendous impact not only on the image of the country and its citizens in the US but elsewhere in the world. Yet what is undeniable is that while this view is not entirely baseless, it has not been an accurate depiction of the totality of the Nigerian national ethos. Indeed while the Nigerian government and people must take responsibility for their own inadvertent contributions to feeding what has truly become a negative western media bias against Nigeria, the western media cannot in fairness acquit itself of reproducing sometimes distorted and slanted perception about the country and its people here in the US or in Nigeria.

A few years ago, the protests from Nigeria on the characterizations and generalizations following these reports increased with formal official reactions from the Nigerian government. For instance in December 2006, ABC (perhaps America's second largest TV network) did an unflattering report on 419 email scammers in Lagos which elicited sharp responses from Nigeria. Later on 15 April 2010, the BBC did a rather slanted documentary on Lagos with the misleading title 'Welcome to Lagos.' This documentary, which highlighted the intensity of poverty in Lagos slums, sparked some protests both from Nigerians abroad and even government officials at home. It was not the accuracy of the reporting or lack of it, but how it characterized and stigmatized the entire commercial capital of the country at a time decent efforts were at play to win greater foreign investment. Indeed there are those in Lagos who felt the report undermined the efforts of Governor Babatunde Fashola, who is well-known for actually attempting to clean up the city.[298]

The Significance of Image in International Relations

International relations theory suggests that there are perceived strategic relationships that "can be conceived of as a function of perceived relative power, perceived culture, and the perceived threat or perceived opportunity that a subject believes another actor represents."[299]

According to the Columbia University professor, Mahmood Mamdami in his book Saviors and Survivors the western media do not take Africa that seriously. He argued:

> When corporate media does focus on Africa, it seeks the dramatic which is why media silence on Africa is often punctuated by high drama and why the reportage on African wars is more superficial than in-depth ...those who rely on the media for their knowledge of Africa come to think of Africans as peculiarly given to fighting over no discernable issue...

The other option is to portray Africa in the exotic fashion! But generally and by extension, it is the same way the American media presents its coverage on Nigeria. So, even when the reporting may be factual, it still lacks a true understanding or a fair representation of the totality of the issues involved. There is indeed no incentive on the part of the western media generally to treat a country like Nigeria better. If Nigeria is therefore to be taken seriously there has to be a conscious and consistent effort at projecting a more accurate, fairly balanced image that represents the intrinsic values, hope and aspirations of the nation and its resilient peoples. The task is however often herculean because the western media can become hegemonic agents, reproducing the prevalent perception. And with the "conniving" attitudes and pranks of some Nigerians who get involved in varying crimes in the United States, creative and sustainable strategies are imperative to address this lopsided perception. Such strategies ought not to rely heavily on the "goodwill" of the same western-oriented media.

In house Ambassadorial crisis and a Diplomatic Lacuna

While Nigeria and other African or developing nations may not expect a fairer treatment from the western media, the internal contradictions of the Nigerian system itself sometimes generates enough steam for the continuation of what was already a confounding situation. In 2009, an unprecedented altercation broke out and got wide reportage in the Nigerian news circuit globally between the then Foreign Affairs Minister, Chief Ojo Maduekwe and the immediate past Nigerian Ambassador to the United States Chief Oluwole Rotimi, a retired senior military officer. Based on media reports, what seemed to be an uneasy working relationship between them soon burst into the open. The Ambassador allegedly refused to yield his diplomatic ticket to the minister to attend the much-talked about inauguration of Barack Obama as the first African-American President of the United States on January 20, 2009.

The US government had insisted that its invitation to the event would be directed only to the resident diplomats and envoys, meaning that all other foreign dignitaries interested in attending the historic event would have to do so through their embassies in Washington, DC. Maduekwe later arrived in the US with a fairly large government delegation but without an invitation. Then Ambassador Rotimi on the other hand refused to yield his invitation, but personally attended the inauguration to the consternation of the minister. One month later, after unhelpful media leaks of distasteful exchanges of correspondence between the two top officials, Rotimi was recalled.

ThisDay newspaper which had a reporter in Washington DC at that time, Feb. 14, 2009 reported the recall thus:

> President Umaru Yar'Adua has approved the immediate recall of Nigeria's Ambassador to the United States, retired Brigadier-General Oluwole Rotimi, for 'gross insubordination'...sources at the Nigerian embassy in Washington DC said the decision to recall Rotimi followed his running disagreement with the Foreign Affairs Minister, Ojo Maduekwe, over issues bordering on activities of the mission, policy, protocol and hierarchy.

Here was just an all-out depreciation of the Nigerian image in the US. On several Internet web sites, some monitored by US government officials and reporters, unprintable comments were posted exposing the exchange of unflattering and disdainful remarks between Maduekwe and Rotimi. Others also toed either lines with vicious observations that extended uncomfortably beyond the immediate confines of the dispute. It was an unnecessary yet self-hurting experience for Nigeria and Nigerians, especially in the US.

In all, Rotimi spent about a year as Ambassador. He arrived March 31, 2008, and presented his credentials on 8 April 2008 to the then US President George W. Bush. His recall however meant Nigeria would not enjoy the services of a substantive envoy in the US. The recall is by itself not a welcome image in matters of diplomacy and could have only added fuel to the disparaging of the country's public perception in the US. But more significantly, and for the purposes of this essay, it was during the absence of a substantive Nigerian Ambassador in the US that the 2009 Christmas day attempted bombing of a US jetliner by Umar Farouk Abdulmutallab took place.

As the news broke in the US and spread fast on a global scale with the labelling of "a Nigerian terrorist," there was no response or reaction on any of the American media for days from the Nigerian embassy to attenuate the insinuations against Nigeria because of Abdulmutallab's wicked and irresponsible behavior. There was no Ambassador to defend Nigeria's image even at the US government level and it was no surprise that in short order Nigeria's name was added to the terror-watch list as a country of interest. An avoidable and lamentable diplomatic gap had ensued between Nigeria and the United States. Even though there was another senior diplomat who acted as Ambassador, the diplomatic culture of Washington DC paid substantially less attention to an acting ambassador than it would have to a substantive Ambassador who the US President had personally received.

The Abudulmutallab Conflagration and the Hanging Threat of a Terrorist Label

Before the December 25, 2009 failed attempt to blow-up a US jetliner heading to Detroit, Nigeria was not in danger of receiving a US government terrorist label. However, in its own response to the rude shock of another terror-attempt on its soil, the US government felt it had to take some immediate drastic action which included adding Nigeria to the list of *countries of interest* regarding terrorism.[301] The US Transportation Security Administration (TSA), an agency under the Homeland Security Department took the decision within days after the 2009 Christmas Day terror attempt and even though the decision earned the rebuke of some US Senators, the addition of Nigeria's name was an additional worry and assault on the image of the country and its many US-based citizens.

By the following week, on 3rd January 2010 the CNN reported the TSA decision that added Nigeria's name to the watch-list thus:

> The TSA said in a statement announcing the new measures that 'effective aviation security must begin beyond our borders.' A senior government official, not authorized to speak on the record, provided CNN with the full list compiled by the Department of Homeland Security and the State Department of 14 countries that fall under the TSA's 'countries of interest' label -- which will automatically trigger the enhanced screening. The State Department lists four countries as those that sponsor terror: Cuba, Sudan, Syria and Iran. The other 10 countries of interest are Afghanistan, Algeria, Iraq, Lebanon, Libya, Nigeria, Pakistan, Saudi Arabia, Somalia and Yemen, the government official said.

The news was a case of putting salt on a wound! Apart from Nigeria's name being soiled by such a damaging list, Nigerian passengers heading to the US from any part of the world would also undergo what the TSA called enhanced security screening at the departing airport. According to the TSA:

> ...passengers flying into the United States from certain countries will be subject to enhanced screening techniques, such as body scans and pat-downs, including the requirement that "all passengers on U.S.-bound international flights will be subject to random screening.

To be sure, no one in Nigeria or among US-based Nigerians gave any kind of succor to Abdulmutallab or his attempted terror plot – he was roundly condemned and rightly so. There was unanimity in the Nigerian response, but what irked many Nigerians within and outside the government including those based in the US was the addition of Nigeria's name to that ignoble list just for the 'sins' of one man. Indeed Nigerians in a certain groundswell of public opinion after the 2009 Christmas Day episode roundly dismissed Umar Farouk Abdulmutallab as a troubled child, raised rarely in Nigeria and short of the "good life" nature of the average Nigerian, who would not normally seek after suicide. Why the actions of such a one would then become the yardstick to determine Nigeria's fate in the official estimation of US security minders became an issue of instant frustration.

As a foreign correspondent, I got the chance to express this frustration. I questioned the US government's decision to treat the whole Nigerian nation with such a disgraceful tag. At a press briefing on 22 January 2010, by an American government official, Mr. Mike Hammer, I asked the following question via a video-conference link:

Q: Why Nigeria's name was added to the list of countries of interest because of the "sins" of one man, whose father had taken the unusual step of forewarning the US authorities? When the shoe-bomber, Richard Reid, from Britain was caught in similar circumstances, the name of Britain was not added to the list?

In response to my question Mr. Hammer said:

Thank you very much for your question; I am glad you asked it. I'll make three points:
- One, after the December 25th incident, it was clear that we needed to take measures that protect aviation. Protecting aviation serves the entire world as we have citizens, of course, from the entire world that are flying back and forth whether it is to the United States or elsewhere.
- The listing, in no way, is meant to be discriminatory against any individual or nationality. What is important here to realize is that we need to take some measures, but already, Secretary Napolitano of the Department of Homeland Security had said that she would personally review each of

the countries listed. And this is an evolving process.
- So, I understand the issues that you raised, the issues that Senator Leahy had raised; we are very well keen about the concerns. But it's a balance here in that we need to take the necessary steps to protect aviation and as well as taking into consideration what other measures, in co-operation, of course, with a number of countries around the world. And that is what, in fact, we are doing at the moment.[302]

Later in my news report[303] I noted that:

> The decision of the executive arm of the US government to add Nigeria's name to the security and terror list of countries of interest has been coming under attacks generally from the US and on Wednesday directly from the US Senate.

While Mr. Hammer's response served to calm restive nerves at least for a while, and also brought with it an expectation of a review in Nigeria's favor, a significant damage to the country's image was already done. More so, his response left many things unsaid. For instance the US official was hard-pressed to justify the label on Nigeria perhaps because hitting Nigeria in such a way was not considered too risky. Nigeria's image had become that tenuous!

It is reasonable to assume that the prevalent negative public perception of Nigeria in the US might have made it fairly easier for the US government agency, TSA, to lump the nation among some well-known and self-professing terror havens like Libya, Afghanistan, Iraq, Lebanon, Pakistan, Saudi Arabia, Somalia and Yemen. A commentator in a leading Nigerian newspaper *Punch*[304] summarized the impact of the Abdulmutallab saga saying:

> ...what Umar Farouk Abdulmutallab did was to add salt into our injury, because, already, our image as a nation has been damaged globally in negative ways before his criminal and murderous attempt to bomb a passenger aircraft that was preparing to land in Detroit, Michigan, United States of America.

In that respect the commentator urged that as a nation Nigeria needed to "take the issues of rebranding seriously, before we become outcasts in the eye of the world." He was referring to the project of the federal government launched by then Information Minister Dora Akunyili to rebrand Nigeria as a means of addressing the problematic international image that has recurrently become the lot of the country.

Significantly, that terrorist designation by the TSA is one of the unusual occasions and topics where both the Nigerian government and its people strike the same chord, another proof that the label represented what was clearly seen by all as a national stigma. While commenting on that designation of Nigeria as a country of interest on the US terror watch list, Akunyili herself declared that:

> ...it is unfair to include Nigeria on the U.S list for tighter screening because Nigerians do not have terrorist tendencies.... It is unfair to discriminate against over 150 million people because of the behavior of one person.[305]

USAfricaonline reported further that before the designation it was difficult enough for the reputation of Nigerians "seen (by some) as a base for scam and con men/women and will get worse with the latest addition of the global scar of terrorism."

That said it all.

Absence of a Substantive Ambassador in Washington DC and the Crisis of an Indisposed President

On the day the news broke that a Nigerian was held responsible for the attempt to blow up a US jetliner, Abuja had no substantive envoy in Washington DC. To make matters worse, even in Abuja, the nation's capital, no one could conclusively explain the whereabouts of the then President Umaru Yar'Adua. By December 25, 2009, the ailing president had already been away for nearly a month in a Saudi Hospital. President Yar' Adua left Nigeria November 23, 2009 on what was said to be a medical vacation. Later it was disclosed that the president was suffering from pericarditis, an inflammation of the membrane surrounding the heart, which can restrict its normal beating. As days turned to weeks with no official reported updates, rumors swirled in the country and abroad about how long it might take for President Yar'Adua to return, and if he were still be alive.

In the US, President Obama and a few other top officials in the American administration had taken responsibility for addressing the American people personally. From Aso Rock in Abuja, however, there was no equal presidential response or seriousness in response to what was clearly a national and international crisis.

The then Vice President Goodluck Jonathan was engulfed in a succession crisis as the incredible perception grew in the country that the indisposed President Yar'Adua had not relinquished power to him, effectively stalling government business. Jonathan's silence therefore may be seen as his own way of staying put and not willing to be seen as angling for power, the very power, which a group then known as a "cabal" made up of a few presidential aides and relatives, wanted to hijack from him. The constitution was clear on the procedure for transfer of power, but the management of its implementation by this "cabal" imposed a different but telling reality and image. The cabal's goal seemed to be the prevention of the then Vice President from carrying out the powers and role of the president. This therefore made matters worse for the image of the nation at such a moment when a presidential voice and face were particularly imperative.

Instead what was heard from Abuja, the federal capital, was a press statement signed by the then Information & Communications Minister, Prof Akunyili, the following day, a 'third-best' option, even if the delay is overlooked. It should have been the President speaking at such critical moments, on the same day, or failing that with his indisposition, his Vice President. According to the statement:

> The Federal Government of Nigeria received with dismay the news of an attempted terrorist attack on a U.S. airline. We state very clearly that as a nation, we abhor all forms of terrorism....the Vice President of the Federal Republic of Nigeria, Dr. Goodluck Ebele Jonathan, has directed Nigerian security agencies to commence full investigation of the incident. While steps are

being taken to verify the identity of the alleged suspect and his motives, our security agencies will cooperate fully with the American authorities in the on-going investigations. Nigerian government will be providing updates as more information becomes available.

But in Washington, DC, where the whole episode was happening there was not even an attempt to respond immediately. Some US-based Nigerians have recounted[306] how the CNN and other US media were desperate to speak to an official of the Nigerian Embassy in Washington DC. All through the initial days of the news of Abdulmutallab's arrest there was complete silence from the Embassy, short of a reported faceless appearance of an unnamed Nigerian diplomat once on CNN. A formal appearance by a Nigerian Ambassador or even a Special Envoy specifically on the matter would have highlighted Nigeria's seriousness and positioned its image for some instant mitigation in the western media which made a big deal of the Nigerian identity. Perhaps it would also have arguably prevented the unilateral addition of Nigeria's name to the US terror watch list.

Enter President Goodluck Jonathan, and the Way Forward

One of the positive impacts of the eventual transfer of power to then Acting President, Dr. Goodluck Jonathan was a lift-up for Nigeria's image abroad, especially in the United States. As if to underscore its own strategic interests in the resolution of the political impasse that followed Yar'Adua's prolonged absence from office, on 8 February 2010, the United States Government sent the US Assistant Secretary of State for Africa Ambassador Johnnie Carson to meet the then Vice President, in Abuja, just a day ahead of his designation as Acting President by the Nigerian National Assembly.

Many in the international community including the United States had always favored the assumption of presidential powers by the then Vice President, Dr. Jonathan, in the absence of the president. According to a statement by the US Government:

Nigeria's constitution is strong and clear in its provisions, so now it is the responsibility of the government and the Nigerian people to demonstrate their shared commitment to democratic governance respect for human rights, and the rule of law.

(Nigeria) an important regional leader on the continent and a valuable member of the international community, it is critical that Nigeria set a strong example through its firm and continued adherence to these principles.[307]

Previewing the Jonathan-Carson meeting, a Nigerian Newspaper *Daily Trust* on that day[308] reported that "Carson's visit comes at the time of political tension over the absence of President Umaru Yar'Adua who has been in Saudi Arabia since November 23 receiving treatment for a heart condition." The paper also significantly observed that the "relationship between Nigeria and the United States was strained after Nigeria was placed on a terror watch list following an alleged failed bombing of a US plane by a Nigerian, Umar Farouk Abdulmutallab, on Christmas Day," 2009. It was an accurate depiction as the strain was fast becoming a diplomatic communication breakdown. But the meeting and the designation of Dr. Jonathan as Acting President proved transformative at least in terms of the direction of US-Nigeria bilateral relationship at that time.

By the next month, March 2010, a substantive Nigerian Ambassador was received by President Obama at the White House, an event that did not take place for a year after the federal government had recalled the former Ambassador Oluwole Rotimi. Speaking at the White House on March 19, President Barack Obama while receiving Adefuye's Letters of Credence applauded Nigeria for taking steps to restore confidence in the nation's political system while adhering to democratic principles, in clear reference to the eventual transfer of power to the Vice President. According to Sahara Reporters: [309]

> Mr. Obama said the United States was encouraged by Acting President Jonathan's public promises to strengthen democratic reforms, improve the economic environment, and address the on-going violence and impunity seen in the Niger Delta and

Jos. Obama in his own words noted that 'We look forward to supporting these efforts to improve the lives of all Nigeria's citizens.'

The new envoy himself a professor of History and tested hand in the art of diplomacy, rose to the occasion. In his speech at the ceremony, Ambassador Adebowale Adefuye spoke in the spirit of a new beginning, and underlined many of the issues, which retained a tremendous impact on Nigeria's Image in the US. Adefuye restated very early in his speech that America:

> is one of our closest allies and a country which has identified with us at all times.
>
> Indeed, the history of Nigeria's 50 years of Statehood will be incomplete without a mention of the proactive role of the United States in supporting us in our quest for sustainable political stability and economic development. The United States' interest in our economic and political well-being has been one of the critical factors for the progress recorded in our effort to consolidate our democracy and deliver its dividends to the people of the country. These underscore the uniqueness of the relationship between the United States and Nigeria.

Ambassador Adefuye quickly pointed out most significantly that Nigerians based in the US, just like Americans based in Nigeria, are playing positive roles in their communities here, a direct approach towards underlining how much the 'new administration' in Washington, DC and Abuja will consider the issue of the country's image here in the US. It may have worked as Acting President Jonathan later disclosed that US President Obama spoke glowingly of Nigerians in the US at their first meeting in April 2010.

Also quite early in the speech, Ambassador Adefuye put the December 25, 2009 terror attack right in front of the US President for review. It was a right move as it addressed the single most important issue in the relationship of both countries and also the core driver of Nigeria's image in the US at the time:

Your Excellency, President Obama, the incident of the December 25, when a Nigerian was caught on a Detroit-bound plane with a bomb is condemnable and has been severally condemned by Nigeria. This event, serious as it is, is a one-off incident and ought not to have warranted the classification of Nigeria as a country of interest in the fight against terrorism. I have been asked by His Excellency Goodluck Jonathan to again convey Nigeria's shock at this and urge you to revisit this issue as soon as possible."

In a matter of weeks afterwards, US President Obama personally invited then Acting President Jonathan to the US. Although the visit, held between 11 - 14 April, 2010, was not the typical presidential state visit, it still sent the signal that the relationship between Nigeria and the US was now on an upswing. During that visit then Acting President Jonathan, apart from participating in President Obama's Nuclear Security Summit in Washington DC, also met Vice President Joe Biden, President of the World Bank Bob Zoellick and other influential American and international groups and individuals. The Acting President had the occasion to redefine the Nigerian image to the listening ears of many friends of Nigeria who were simply waiting for such an opportunity.

As I reported in *The Guardian* on Sunday April 18, 2010, that visit may have in fact made the nation proud again in America:

> Acting President Goodluck Jonathan's recent visit to the United States may have offered Nigeria a new lease of life in the US and on the wider global scene, going by comments in Washington DC about the four-day visit from Sunday to Wednesday, last week.
>
> Jonathan, who simply became the toast of the US capital city on arrival, last Sunday 'met all who mattered' in Washington DC and was actively sought after by several US groups and international agencies. In all the meetings, opened to public, there were not enough rooms for Nigerians and Americans, diplomats, businessmen, top officials and others who wanted engagement with the Nigerian leader.
>
> At one of the several meetings to which the Acting president was invited on Wednesday, hosted by the Corporate Council

for Africa, CCA, a Caucasian American attendee, stood up and openly declared that the Acting President Jonathan has within a few days in the US "repaired the reputation of Nigeria" by his visit and the level and warmth of welcome that he enjoyed. A ready applause from the luncheon room greeted the observation.

From the point of view of the US government the report also noted a favorable comment by a US government official just a day after Jonathan left the US capital thus:

> ... the deputy assistant Secretary of State for Africa, William Fitzgerald, said publicly on Thursday, in Washington DC, that "Nigeria is important to stability and progress worldwide, as well as in Africa," emphasizing the closeness of U.S.-Nigeria ties.
>
> Nigeria is very important," Fitzgerald, stressed, adding that, "on the continent, it is the most populous nation, the largest contributor of peacekeepers, the largest producer of oil, and the largest recipient of direct investment by the American private sector.
>
> Whether providing critical leadership in ECOWAS (Economic Community of West African States), engagement in West Africa, or, from the perspective of its current seat on the U.N. Security Council, Nigeria plays a role far beyond its own borders.[310]

No one was now left in doubt that both Nigeria and the US at the bilateral level were now on the same wave length again. That by itself offers a great opportunity also for the rebuilding of a stronger and positive image and public perception for Nigeria and its people in the eye of the American public.

At the end of the week that President Jonathan visited Washington, DC/Maryland region, after he was already back in Nigeria, his name had become a pop quiz question on a popular Baltimore FM radio station 88.1. The question was "whose country's president's name starts with the word Goodluck?" A new tone had been set in US-Nigeria relationship, and the Nigerian image in the United States was on the rise again!

With this new tone, several positive developments were recorded in short order that shored up Nigeria's image tremendously in the US:

- A few days after Ambassador Adefuye presented his Letters of Credence to President Obama, the US government announced new airport security measures, which meant Nigerians were no longer singled out for enhanced airport screening.
- On April 2 then US Assistant Secretary of State for Public Affairs P.J. Crowley announced in Washington, DC while addressing reporters that the particular emphasis given to 14 countries including Nigeria after December 25, 2009, was neither sustainable nor efficient. "Since that time, we've been engaged in intensive dialogue with those countries," he said.
- Within a week of that announcement, a visit to Nigeria was set up by the US Secretary of Homeland Security, Janet Napolitano, under whose department, the TSA had, in January, made the determination to include Nigeria and Nigerians under the enhanced airport screening after the Abdulmutallab incident.
- About the same time the State Department announced that the US government was also now ready to grant a long-held request of Nigeria for the resumption of a US-Nigerian Bi-national Commission, which had been in place between the two countries during the Clinton administration but was suspended afterwards by President George W. Bush. It is believed that Nigeria is the first country in Africa under the Obama administration to enjoy such an agreement. It was signed just a week ahead of the Jonathan visit.

A sudden revival had taken place in US-Nigeria relations and the Nigerian international image will be the better for it!

Conclusion

The Jonathan presidency inherited a troubled international perception, particularly in the United States. Its intervention so far has been largely positive, particularly because of the dramatic circumstances that birthed the presidency after a time of diplomatic lull and the absence of both a president in Abuja and a substantive Ambassador in Washington, DC.

The new Ambassador, Adefuye, has clearly captured both the imagination of the American government and those of many US-based Nigerians in ways that were not previously known. An experienced diplomat, Adefuye has managed and continues to positively engage both the US government and Nigerian-Americans articulate a vibrant vision about Nigeria's potential and painted a robust image for Nigeria. For instance, the Ambassador has chaired a major Awards Dinner to celebrate high-flying Nigerians in North America and continues to hold town hall style meetings with Nigerians across the US.

President Goodluck Jonathan figured out early enough that one major determinant of Nigeria's image on the global scene was the issue of electoral credibility. And in the US, the promise of a free and fair election was an opportunity to remold the image of the country in America. As it turned out, the comparative success of the April 2011 election prompted another American visit for President Jonathan and this time, a reception at the White House in June 2011-a further boast under the belt of the Jonathan presidency.

Yet challenges remain, especially on how to promote and maintain a more positive image for Nigeria. Nigeria's foreign policy-makers should diligently explore new and creative ideas on how to promote the good name of the country abroad. Here in the US, there are several high flying Nigerians, credible organizations, including Nigerian-owned media, who should become active agents with the Government in promoting and protecting the good name of the nation in the US.

At home, the management of public information should become more active such that the President and other top Nigerian officials become more accessible to the local and international media in a manner that captures the news and media cycle more in a proactive rather than reactive way.

Conclusion
Surveying the Past and Seeing the Future

Shola OMOREGIE and Abiodun ALAO

As shown in the preceding chapters, Nigeria's relations with the United States are varied and diverse, cutting across economics, military, trade, culture, education and a string of formal and informal contacts among the citizens of both countries. Indeed, what we have been able to do in this book is just to scratch the tip of a proverbial iceberg. What started on a small scale at the time of Nigeria's independence in 1960 had by 2010 become undoubtedly the most complex and most extensive diplomatic relations between the United States and any African country. In a way, the extensive, even if occasionally difficult relationship between the United States and Nigeria should be expected, as both countries have a lot of things in common. This, in fact, prompted one of the foremost African academics, Professor Ali Mazrui, to observe that Nigeria is the closest approximation to the United States in Africa. Both are structured as democratic Federal republics. Both have amended their constitutions to redress grievances of previously marginalized groups and both have undergone painful civil wars and post-war reconstruction. Both have had military leaders who have or are playing roles in politics and both have found themselves having to play important roles in shaping the affairs of their immediate surroundings. In short, looking back carefully into their pasts, both countries share similarities over a broad spectrum of their history, even if both had adopted different methods in meeting the consequences and challenges of their past.

Several key issues have emerged in the US-Nigerian

relationship in the last fifty years and the preceding chapters have shown how that relationship has passed through shifts and twists. In a rather curious way, each decade of the relationship seems to have had peculiar features associated with them: the first witnessed the establishment of the relationship and the experience of the Nigerian civil war, while the second was preoccupied with disagreements and/or agreements over southern Africa. The third decade, on its part, focused on the redefinition of the relationship after the end of apartheid. The challenge of the fourth decade was how to manage the relationship with military dictatorship and the trampling of democracy while the fifth decade centered on the relationship with a new democratic Nigeria.

Broadly, the basis of the relationship between Nigeria and the United States would seem to be built on two major premises. These are the desire to ensure cordial relations that will be mutually beneficial to both countries, while the second is to ensure global peace. Indeed, all the various ramifications of the relationship would seem to be rooted to these two considerations. As shown in the preceding chapters, attitudes and the positions of the two countries have shifted and changed over the decades, but both have tried to ensure that situations are managed to prevent a major breakdown in the relationship. In this concluding chapter we attempt two things: first is to review the past fifty years of United States – Nigerian relations; while the second is to identify and discuss the key issues that are likely to dominate relations in the future.

Reviewing the Past

In the course of the first fifty years of Nigerian independence, the issue of Southern Africa seemed to be the most dominant. The US/Nigerian relationship moved through several phases on this topic: that of mutual critics, allies or opponents. It is important to note that there has never been a phase of indifference. With the liberation and/or independence of all the countries in the region, during which Nigeria was in the vanguard of the anti-apartheid campaign that ended white minority rule, a key issue that had been a contentious recurring feature in the relationship between the two countries was removed and both countries have had to face issues that are more pertinent to their mutual affairs.

But what seems to be the most important singular event in the fifty years was the December 2009 attempt by Umar Farouk Abdul Mutallab, a Nigerian national, to bomb an American airline, an unfortunate development that put the strong relationship between the two countries to test. Far from ending the relationship, this unfortunate event was followed by both countries busy exploiting different ways of working together to combat the issue of terrorism.

As one looks back over the whole of the relationship between the governments of both countries, the most cordial phases of the relationship between Nigeria and the United States were those when President Kennedy was in the White House and Tafawa Balewa was the Nigerian Prime Minister and again during the administrations of Presidents Jimmy Carter and Olusegun Obasanjo in America and Nigeria, respectively. Undoubtedly, the most difficult phases were those when the Clinton administration had to contend with President Babangida's nullification of the June 1993 election and later with President Sani Abacha's flagrant violation of human rights. With President Obama in the White House, the future holds enormous promise for a solid and fruitful relationship.

What seems to be the most important issue for the United States today is the consolidation of democracy in Nigeria after decades of military dictatorship. This also falls in line with Nigeria's interest, as the country struggles to consolidate its nascent democracy. The concurrence of position on this seems to bring the governments and peoples of both countries together. Even in Nigeria, where radicals always view relationship with the United States with suspicion, there seems to be some form of acceptance of America's interest and commitment in the consolidation of democracy in Nigeria. This is better demonstrated in the support by the United States for the building of democratic structures within the government and in the civil society in Nigeria. The United States also played a significant role in the transition to civilian rule through relentless and intense pressure on the regimes of Presidents Babangida and Abacha to end military rule. Further, following the end of military dictatorship, significant assistance has also come from the United States in the effort to nudge the Nigeria military to recognize and subordinate itself to democratic control. Military to military contacts are also maintained, with military training in the United States for members of the Nigerian Armed Forces.

A review of the economic relations between the two countries has shown that both consider this cooperation extremely important. Even when there were serious diplomatic disagreements in the past, as were the cases during the nullification of the June 1993 elections and the hanging of Ken Saro-Wiwa and other activists, trade continued with very minimal reduction. As shown in this book, economic relations between both countries have focused largely on oil and it seems almost certain that this is likely to remain for quite some time to come, especially as the United States continue to show greater interest in oil from the Gulf of Guinea. There have also been important agreements that are likely to consolidate economic links between both countries. However, there are still key areas of concern in the economic sphere. For a very long time, many Nigerians believed that trade between Nigeria and the United States was one-sided and that Nigeria needed significant investments and technological transfers that this US-centric trade did not offer. There have also been concerns that American oil-multinational corporations had worked hand-in-glove with successive military dictators that had victimized the population and encouraged corruption. However, while governments of both countries sometimes try to conceal their differences, criticisms have always come from the public, especially the media and the intellectuals in both countries. To the chagrin of some Nigerians, the criticism coming from some quarters in the United States tend to be one sided and at times blown out of proportion. Former United States Ambassador to Nigeria, John Campbell, in his latest book portrays Nigeria as "dancing on the brink," an exaggeration that overlooks the strength of Nigeria in pulling through, even in the most difficult circumstances, the civil war and the military regimes of Generals Babangida and Abacha.

The activities of Nigerians in the United States and American citizens in Nigeria have been major issues between the two countries. Indeed, Nigerian citizens, including distinguished professionals in many fields in the United States are the country's most important exports and there can be no doubts that these Nigerians are making giant strides in the United States, even if there are also those whose activities are on the negative side. However, the activities of Nigerians in the United States raise a number of issues as to long-term implications of credible workforce that should assist in the development of Nigeria. Those who are engaged in criminal activities have also been at the centre of attention, especially as it has resulted in a situation where Nigeria has had a negative press in the United States. Both sides have, however tried to play this down. As a former American Ambassador to Nigeria pointed out "for every incidence of crime and fraud, there are ten remembered experiences of friendship … of working towards shared values of higher productivity and growth. Even when they do not make the newspaper, these experiences shape attitudes and actions".

American involvement in socio-economic and health-related issues in Nigeria has also been a major factor during the last fifty years. While this was not a major issue initially, the 1990s and 2000s witnessed the deep involvement of the American Government, agencies and individuals in addressing of diseases like HIV/AIDS, malaria, diarrhea and a host of others. Specifically, the contribution of individuals like former Presidents Jimmy Carter, Bill Clinton and George W. Bush as well as Microsoft founder Bill Gates are noteworthy. Also to be noted here are the activities of the various American foundations involved in the promotion of education in Nigeria, especially foundations like Ford, Carnegie, Rockefeller and a host of others.

There is the need to ask the fundamental question as to how both countries see their relationship over the last fifty years. The governments of both sides understand that there have been hiccups in the relationship, hence the title of this book "Twists and Turns", but at the same time, both appreciate that, to a very large extent, the relationship has been mutually beneficial. The opinions of the peoples, especially on the Nigerian side, are, however, more complex. To most Nigerians, the relationship is not based on equality and the desire of the United States has always been seen to dominate Nigeria. The interest of the United States in Nigeria, as far as most Nigerians are concerned, is basically over Nigeria's oil and that all the advertised interests on democracy and human rights in Nigeria were mere subterfuges to further milk the resources of their country. This is a position the United States has persistently denied, but it is also one that still has believers in the light of the nature of the strategic value of Africa as a whole to the United States. This perception, whether true or not, needs to be addressed. The support and assistance provided by the United States towards the current electoral process is a step in the right direct, although it carries with it, the risk that the United States Government is favoring President Goodluck Jonathan. The same attitude was displayed by a certain region (the North) during the Obasanjo administration when this part of the country reacted negatively to the improved relations during that period as support for Obasanjo and his third term agenda.[311] While there are those in Nigeria who look at the US questioningly, there are also some in the United States government who calculate that Africa is of low strategic value.

In concluding the discussion on the review of the past, there is therefore the need to appreciate the fact that both countries, in their relationship, have always come from different angles, even if there are similarities in their broad positions. First, it has to be noted that the United States is a global power, with interests spread all over the world, of which Nigeria and indeed, Africa, is just a negligible part. Nigeria, on its part, is a developing society whose main interest and goals is largely continental, even if it equally desires global stability as demonstrated in its participation in the United Nations global peacekeeping operations. The differences in the spheres of their focus has inevitably resulted in situations where both sides have often accused the other of either going too far or not going far enough. Apart from the issue of Southern Africa mentioned earlier, another area where Nigeria expected the United States to have shown greater consideration was in the area of global trade, which many in Africa believed for a very long time to be against African interest. The cooperation between the two countries in international peacekeeping operations as demonstrated during the Obasanjo administration in bringing peace to Liberia and close collaboration in Somalia, is a clear proof that both can work together in the interest of Africa rather than on solely national interests.

Looking into the Future

It would appear that in the coming years, the relationship between Nigeria and the United States will center, among others on six major things: consular issues, especially on the politics of Visa issuance; consolidation of democracy in Nigeria; the problem of religious radicalization; the issue of drug/narcotics and Advanced Fee Fraud; management of regional stability; and imbalance in trade relations.

Visa Issuance

There have been persistent concerns by Nigerians that it was always difficult to obtain a visa to visit the United States. The American authorities have, however, said that the difficulties in obtaining visas for Nigerians have been rooted to two areas: documentation fraud and narcotics. The American Embassy in Nigeria argues that enormous counterfeiting of documents such as birth certificates, marriage certificates, school records, etc. often slows the process of visa applications. But the United States government has also said that the problem of visa issuance in the past should not be heaped on the door-step of Americans alone. For example, at a stage, the American government said that it was as difficult for Nigerians to get visas to visit the United States as it was for Americans who want to come to Nigeria. In a speech at the Nigerian Institute of International Affairs in April 1987, the American Ambassador to Nigeria, Princeton Lyman, pointed out that two American journalists representing two of the most prestigious newspapers in the United States waited for 6 months to get visas to Nigeria. At a time when Nigeria was clamoring for American investment, American businessmen could not get entry visas to the country. Such consular problems were not peculiar to only the United States. This was a systemic and general difficulty which President Obasanjo tackled aggressively when he assumed office in 1999. It was an issue to which he attached the greatest importance and priority, to the extent of taking severe disciplinary action against erring staff at the Nigerian Embassy in the United States.

Although the problem still exists on both sides, things seem to have improved considerably. Various systems have been introduced to ensure that visa application processes are speeded up and rejection rate reduced once application requirements are complied with. The introduction of the American lottery has also increased the chances of Nigerians having access through the normal channels to the United States. It is most likely that the years ahead will continue to witness issues and complaints on the issue of visa issuance and both the American consulate in Nigeria and the Nigerian embassy and consulates in the United States seem to appreciate this situation and are trying to cope with the challenges.

Consolidation of Democracy in Nigeria

Efforts to consolidate Nigeria's democracy are almost certainly going to be at the center of United States-Nigerian relations for the foreseeable future. From all indications, the United States is impressed with developments in Nigeria along this direction. While there had been concerns about the conduct of elections in Nigeria, there also seems to be greater hope with the new leadership of the Independent National Electoral Commission (INEC) and with the efforts it has made to improve elections in Nigeria. It seems certain that greater encouragements will be given to the Commission in the years ahead. It is also envisaged that American assistance will come to the building of institutions that can further strengthen democracy.

Religious Radicalization

Since the ill-fated attempt by a Nigerian to bomb an American plane in December 2009 and the subsequent inclusion of Nigeria in the Terror Watch List, the US has shown deep interest in developments in Nigeria on the crucial subject of Islamic radicalization and how this can affect the United States and Nigeria's relations. Although Nigeria's name was subsequently removed, domestic issues in the country, particularly in northern Nigeria continue to give the United States considerable concern. While the Nigerian Government has taken serious steps to bring this problem under control, such as the recent adoption of an anti-terrorism bill by the Nigerian National Assembly, it is critically important for both countries to strengthen their collaboration in bringing this menace under control.

The issue of Drug/Narcotics and Advance Fee Fraud
This is a subject that has been at the forefront of relations between the two countries for quite some time. For example, in 1986, INTERPOL statistics indicated the arrest of 1003 Nigerians for drug trafficking in 1986. Although the figures have gone down quite significantly, this still remains a problem and also one that is most likely to engage attention of both sides for quite some time to come. But while the issue of drugs and narcotics seem to be going down, allegations linking Nigerians to different forms of advance fee fraud still seem to be high. While it is suspected that many other nationals who are not Nigerians are posing to be nationals of the country in their criminal activities along these lines, there is no doubt, judging from the number of arrests made by the authorities of both countries, that some Nigerians have been (and are still) deeply involved in crimes of this nature. It seems certain that efforts to ensure that the impact of the activities of those criminal elements engaged in these activities are reduced. This will be crucial to Nigeria-United States relations in the years to come.

Management of Regional Security
The United States has always considered Nigeria vital to regional security in West Africa and the country has undertaken this creditably well in Liberia and Sierra Leone. This is likely to continue for quite some time to come, especially with the developments in Cote d'Ivoire where the position of Nigeria, as Chairman of ECOWAS, on this issue has been praised by the United States and vindicated by the support of the international community for the early decision of ECOWAS to endorse Mr. Alassane Ouattara as President-elect. With the United States reluctant to get involved in local conflicts, the country is likely going to rely on regional powers to address local skirmishes and, in the case of West Africa, Nigeria fits the bill.

What, however, is likely to increase the importance of Nigeria's regional position in US - Nigerian relations is the Gulf of Guinea initiative. As shown earlier in this book, this is a region of extreme importance to the United States which recognizes the crucial importance of Nigeria in the Gulf of Guinea equation. Although America's interest in the AFRICOM initiative has reduced, especially as the initiative has not received support from crucial countries like Nigeria and South Africa, however, the endorsement the initiative has received from Liberia is most likely to be a factor in the calculation of both Nigeria and the United States to hold on to their respective positions. On the whole, it is most likely that the situation in West Africa and the entire Gulf of Guinea will remain a key issue of interest in the Nigeria-United States relations for quite some time to come.

On the whole, it is difficult to write a history of a relationship that has every prospect of perpetual survival, and all that this book has done is to take a look at key aspects of Nigerian – American relations. Of course, we concede that there are aspects of the relationship that are not covered in this book, but we hope that the key issues identified are enough to capture the twists and turns in the first fifty years and to generate interest in the future relationship of the two countries.

End Notes

295. I was present when then Acting President Jonathan met with a group of US-based Nigerians at the Nigerian Embassy on April 14, 2010, where he said this while addressing the Nigerians.

296. For instance last October 2010, when a group of Nigerians and Empowered Newswire honored "Top 50 Nigerians" in North America, to mark Nigeria's 50th Independence Anniversary in collaboration with the Nigerian Embassy, such rarely make news in the US media. This is despite of the fact that these Nigerians in the US and Canada have distinguished themselves and excelled in their American and Canadian communities.

297. See Lindsey Wise and Terri Langford in article titled *Day care Owner now a Fugitive,* Houston Chronicle, February 28, 2001. Although she traveled to Nigeria even before she was charged, the newspaper still called her a fugitive.

298. Gbenro Adeoye, *Lagos is not a Slum City,* 234next.com, April 28 reports that some among the leadership of the Nigeria Bar Association in Lagos State "condemned the documentary and stated that it undermined the efforts of Governor Babatunde Fashola."

299. Herrmann, Richard K.; Voss, James F.; Schooler, Tonya Y. E.; Ciarrochi, Joseph, *Images in International Relations,* published by the *International Studies Quarterly* Vol. 41, No. 3 (Sept., 1997).

300. Constance Ikokwu, now a deputy editor at *ThisDay* newspaper was then the Washington Bureau Chief for the Nigerian daily newspaper *ThisDay.*

301. That list had existed before besides the list of countries deemed to be state sponsors of terrorism. Both lists maintained by the US State Department. But Nigeria was never considered in those categories. A *New York Times* news report on January 3, 2010 by Eric Lipton noted that "the addition of Nigeria, Pakistan and Saudi Arabia to the "country of interest" list marks the first time that citizens of those countries will be subject to automatic additional screening for flights to the United States."

302. See US State Department web site for verbatim –Q&A format-report of 22 January 2010 Foreign Press Briefing given by Mike Hammer, who was then Spokesperson of the US government National Security Council. Hammer, a very knowledgeable US public official is now the

Assistant Secretary of State for Public Affairs at the State Department.

[303.] After the briefing with Hammer, I wrote a front page report: *White House Offers to Review Countries on Watch List* in *The Guardian* on Sunday, January 24, 2010. That report highlighted the illogicality of the decision to add Nigeria's name to the list.

[304.] Gordon Chika Nnorom, Letter to the Editor, *Punch* Jan 1, 2010.

[305.] USAfrica Online, one of the earliest Nigerian- owned internet news sites based in the US, reported on 4th January 2010.

[306.] Some of them who had working knowledge spoke to me as a reporter on conditions of anonymity about how embassy officials were unprepared to make a facialapperance even when networks like CNN was seeking some Nigerian government perspectives through the Embassy.

[307.] http://nigeria.usembassy.gov/pr_05062010b.html

[308.] 8 February edition of the paper.

[309.] A leading Nigerian news website known for its anti-establishment style.

[310.] Jim Fisher, Staff Writer at the US State Department Public Affairs Section in America.gov, a US government web site on April 15, 2010.

[311.] *Nigeria: Dancing on the Brink* by John Cambell).

List of Contributors

Temilade ABIMBOLA is an Associate Professor at the Warwick Business School. Her doctorate was obtained from Aston University in England and her articles have appeared in key academic journals like *Journal of Product and Brand Management, International Marketing Review, and Journal of Brand Management*.

Funso ADESOLA is a Ph. D. holder and Senior Lecturer in the Department of International Relations, Obafemi Awolowo University, Ile-Ife, Osun State. Nigeria. He was an Exchange Scholar in the Study of United States Institute on US Foreign Policy, sponsored by the Bureau of Educational and Cultural Affairs, United States Department of State, Washington DC; and hosted by University of Florida, Gainesville. USA. He is the author of *International Relations: An Introductory Text, National Security in Nigeria's Relations with its Neighbours* and published widely in reputable local and international journals. His research interests are on security studies, geopolitics and international relations of Africa.

Joseph AIHIE teaches International Relations at Okada University Igbinedon, where he was the formal Head of Department. He holds a Bachelors in History and Political Science and Masters in Political Science from the University of Ibadan. His Doctorate in Political Science was obtained from the Igbinedion University, Okada. He has published articles in a number of local and international journals.

Laolu AKANDE is a US-based Nigerian journalist and the longest serving African correspondent at the United Nations, which he has covered continuously for over a decade. He has also reported about the US and North America for leading Nigerian newspapers including *The Guardian*, which he represents as Bureau Chief in North America. In his coverage of the US, he has interviewed President George W. Bush in the White House,

Secretary of State Colin Powell, United Nations Secretaries-General Kofi Annan and Ban Ki-Moon and several other global newsmakers. He is also the publisher of Empowered Newswire, a US-based independent news agency reporting for *The Punch* and other leading Nigerian newspapers and web sites. Akande has served as an adjunct professor in US schools including State University of New York, SUNY and Suffolk County Community College, where he is currently teaching Human Communication courses. He is married to Olawunmi and they are both blessed with two teenage children.

Ronke AKO-NAI is a Lecturer in the Department of International Relations, Obafemi Awolowo University, Ile-Ife, Nigeria. She obtained her B.A. in History from the University of Ibadan and a Masters' and Doctorate in International Relations from the Obafemi Awolowo University. She was a Grantee of the Council for the Development of Social Science Research in Africa {CODESRIA} Dakar, Senegal. She specializes in developmental studies and human rights and has published widely in reputable local and international journals.

Abiodun ALAO is a Senior Research Fellow at the King's College London. He was educated at the Universities of Ibadan, Ife and London where he holds a Bachelors in History, Masters in International Relations and Doctorate in War Studies respectively. His published books on African Security include: *The Tragedy of Endowment: Natural Resources and Conflict in Africa*, Rochester: University of Rochester Press, (2007); *The Mau-Mau Warrior*, (OSPREY Warrior Series), Oxford: Osprey Publishing, 2005; *The Role of African Regional and Sub-regional Organisations in Conflict Prevention and Resolution*, Geneva: UNHCR Working Paper Series, No. 23, (2000), *Security Reform in Democratic Nigeria*, London: CDS Conflict Security and Development Working Paper Series, No. 2. 2000; *Peacekeepers, Politicians and Warlords: The Liberian Peace Process*, Tokyo and New York: United Nations University Press. (Co-Authored with John Mackinlay and Funmi Olonisakin) 1999; *Africa after the Cold War: The Changing Perspective on Security*, Trenton, New Jersey: African World Press, 1998. (Co-Edited with Adebayo Oyebade); *The Burden of Collective*

LIST OF CONTRIBUTORS

Goodwill: The International Involvement in the Liberian Civil War, Aldershot: Ashgate Publishers. 1996; *Brothers at War: Dissidence and Rebellion in Southern Africa*, London: British Academic Press. 1994; *African Conflicts: The Future without the Cold War*, London: Brassey Publishers, 1993.

Suleiman Baba ALI is a Public Relations consultant based in Abuja, Nigeria. He was educated at the Ahmadu Bello University and the University of Lagos.

Kehinde BOLAJI is on the staff of the Economic Community of West African States (ECOWAS). He holds a Bachelor and Masters degrees from the University and he is currently completing his doctorate in Political Science in the same University.

Penda DIALLO is a doctoral student at the University of Edinburgh, Scotland. Her Masters Degree in International Relations was obtained at St Andrews University.

Kunle OJELEYE was educated at the Obafemi Awolowo University, Ile Ife, where he read International Relations for his Bachelors and at the King's College, University of London where he had a Masters in Law and Diplomacy and a Doctorate in War Studies. He is the author of *The Politics of Post-war Demobilisation and Reintegration in Nigeria*. Farnham: Ashgate, 2010. He is a Visiting Lecturer at the Osun State University, Oshogbo Nigeria.

Funmi OLONISAKIN is the Director of Conflict Security and Development Group at King's College London. She holds a Bachelors degree from University of Ife in Political Science and her Masters and Doctorate in War Studies from King's College London. Prior to this, she worked at the United Nations Office of the Special Representative of the Secretary-General for Children and Armed Conflict (OSRSG/ CAAC), as Adviser on Africa. She has held research and visiting positions at the University of Lagos (Nigeria) and the Institute of Strategic Studies, University of Pretoria (South Africa). She has written extensively on African Security issues. Her books on the subject include: *Peacekeeping* in Sierra Leone: The Story of UNAMSIL, Boulder Co: Lynne Reinner Publishers, 2007; *Global Development and Human Security* (co-authored with Robert Picciotto and Michael Clarke with Foreword by Sir Lawrence Freedman), Transaction Publishers, 2007; *The Challenges of Security Sector Governance in West Africa*, (co-edited with Bryden and Ndiaye), Lit Verlag, 2007; *Security Sector Governance in Africa: A Handbook*, (co-authored with Nicole Ball, Kayode Fayemi and Rocklyn Williams), Lagos: Centre for Democracy and Development, 2004; *Reinventing Peacekeeping in Africa: Conceptual and Legal Issues in the ECOMOG Operations*, (The Hague: Kluwer Law International), 2000; *Peacekeepers, Politicians and Warlords: The Liberian Peace Process* (Co-authored with Mackinlay and Alao) Tokyo: United Nations University Press, 1999.

Shola J. OMOREGIE is the former Representative of the United Nations Secretary-General in Guinea-Bissau and Head of the United Nations Peace-building Support Office in Guinea-Bissau (UNOGBIS) from 2006 - 2008. He is founder and President of Africa Peace Support, LLC, an international consulting firm. He retired from the United Nations in December 2008, having had a dedicated and distinguished service at the United Nations Secretariat spanning over three decades — 1978 - 2008. From 1978 – 1983, he served in Botswana as the first Resident Representative of the United Nations Commissioner for Namibia. He subsequently served in various capacities at the United Nations, including as Representative of the United Nations Commissioner for Namibia in Angola (1988-1990); Secretary of the UN Special Committee on Peacekeeping Operations (1992-1994); and Chief of Branch of the UN Security Council Charter Research Branch. He was educated at the University of Lagos, Lagos, Nigeria, where he earned a B.SC (Honors) in psychology. He is the author of a new book, *Witness to Transformation – My Years at the United Nations* and publisher of Africa Peace and Security Monitor, a quarterly political and security analytical newsletter.

Adebayo OYEBADE is Professor of history at Tennessee State University, Nashville. He holds a Ph.D. in history from Temple

LIST OF CONTRIBUTORS

University, Philadelphia. He is the editor of a two-volume book on Nigeria, *The Transformation of Nigeria: Essays in Honor of Toyin Falola* (2002), and *The Foundations of Nigeria: Essays in honor of Toyin Falola* (2003). His other books include: *Africa after the Cold War: The Changing Perspectives on Security* (1998) Co-edited with Abiodun Alao. *Culture and Custom of Angola; Yoruba Fiction, Orature, and Culture: Oyekan Owomoyela and African Literature & the Yoruba Experience,* (Trenton, N.J.: Africa World Press, 2010) (Co-edited with Toyin Falola).

INDEX

9/11, 147, 170, 186, 214, 215

Abacha, Sani, 91, 275
Abiola, Kudirat, 95
Abiola, Moshood, 89
Abubakar, Abdulsalami, 97
Abubakar, Atiku, 161
Abuja, 88, 138, 145, 148, 157, 159, 160, 163, 166, 175, 185, 223, 224, 227, 242, 244, 249, 251, 263-265, 267, 270, 287
Aburi Agreement, 56-59
Adams, Justice Arlin, 87
Adamu, Alhaji Hassan,97
Adefuye, Adebowale, 167, 217, 253, 267
Advance-fee scam (popularly known as 419), 208
Afghanistan, 123, 142, 172, 260, 262
Africa House, 23
African Unity (AU), ix, x,
African-American Labor Center, 90
AFRICOM, 128, 133-135, 150, 162, 222, 282
Agbami project, 184
Agriculture, 45, 46, 227
Aguiyi-Ironsi, Johnson, 80, 98, 99
Ahmadu Bello University, 30, 52
Ahmed, Yayale, 219
Aiyetoro Comprehensive High School, 48

Ajumogobia, Odein, 224, 235, 242, 243
Akinyemi, Bolaji, 10, 126
Akpabio, Godswill, 226
Akunyili, Dora, 263
Algeria, 18, 172, 260
Al-Qaeda, 111, 170, 172
Amnesty International, 90
Anglo-Nigerian Defence Pact, 36, 129
Angola, 85, 102, 103, 107-111, 113, 117-119, 131, 140, 219, 288, 289
Ankrah, Joseph, 57
Annan, Kofi, 163, 286
Apartheid, 120, 274
Appolo, Major, 58
Apter, David, 33
Arthur D. Little consulting, 49
Artic National Wild Life Refuge, 140
Ashiru, Olugbenga, xii, 246, 250
Association for Better Nigeria, (ABN), ix, 88, 89,
Awlaki, Anwar al, 172
Awolowo, Obafemi, 49, 61, 205
Azikiwe, Nnamdi, 19, 21, 22, 24

Babangida, Ibrahim, 87
Balewa, Abubakar Tafawa, 6, 32, 54
Balogun, Tafa, 160, 161
Bamidele, Fatima B., 227
Bashir, Omar, 240

Benin, 131, 247
Bethune, Mary McLeod, 23
Biafra Lobby, 42
Biafra, 62, 63, 65, 66, 71, 73, 75, 76, 78
Biden, Joe, 167, 268
Buhari, Muhammadu, 85-87, 98, 118, 120, 129
Bush, George W., 133, 152, 155, 156, 175, 259, 270, 277, 285
Bush, George, 121
Business Council for International Understanding, 93
Business Week, 93

Calabar, 12, 20, 23, 50, 135, 149
Cameron, David, 243
Campbell, John, 174
Capitalism, 33, 36, 44, 170
Carnegie Endowment for International Peace, 5, 93
Carrington, Walter, 94, 96
Carson, Johnnie, 167, 232, 265
Carter, Jimmy, 7, 92, 111, 142, 156, 159, 175, 275, 277
Centre for Democracy and Development, 92, 288
Centre for Democratic Studies, 89
Certificate of Origin, 111
Cheney, Dick, 140, 141, 183
Chevron, US Oil Company, 5, 167, 184, 188, 190, 221
Christ Apostolic Church, 201
Christianity, 200
Churchill, Winston, 23
Clinton, Bill, 2, 4, 7, 97, 151, 152, 154, 155, 156, 277
Clinton, Hillary, 217
Cohen, William S., 137

Cold War, 6, 24, 25, 27, 37, 53, 62, 81, 98, 99, 106, 107, 110, 118, 128, 143, 286, 287, 289
Colonialism, 22, 25,
Columbia University, 19, 20, 21, 257
Commonwealth of Nations, 129
Communism in Nigeria, 34
Communism, 34, 108, 170
Comprehensive Secondary Schools, 48
Congo, 34, 38, 43, 60, 62, 131
Congress of Nigerians Abroad, 95
Congress, US, 61, 72, 73, 90, 121, 124, 153
Congressional Black Caucus, 167
Consumer Access to a Responsible Accounting of Trade Act (CARAT), 111
Cote d'Ivoire, 131, 157, 163, 238, 239, 243, 245, 247, 250, 281
Court of Appeal Edict, 58
Crime, 163
Crowley, P. J., 270
Cuba, 12, 172, 260
Czechoslovakia, 62

Deeper Life Ministry, 201
Delany, Martin Robinson, 13-16
Democracy, 4, 6, 7, 25, 27, 34, 37, 40, 41, 79-81, 83, 85-99, 115, 131, 133, 146, 148, 151-155, 159, 162, 163, 165, 173, 174, 176, 180, 187, 192, 218-220, 224, 227, 232, 237, 238, 240, 267, 274, 275, 278-278-280, 288
Dewey, Eugene, 83
Dikko, Umaru, 80,
Diversity Immigrant Visa

INDEX

Program, often referred to as "Green Card Lottery", 190, 197, 198
Diya, Oladipo, 97
Drugs, 94, 96, 159, 241-243, 281
Dwight David Eisenhower, 18, 26, 31, 32, 54

Eastern Nigerian Housing Corporation, 50
Eastern Region, Nigeria, 24, 41, 48, 55-59, 61, 70, 72
Easum, Donald, 109, 110,
Edop-Idoho Offshore, 184
Education - Nigerians in the US, 19, 20, 23, 40, 47, 48, 49, 138, 153, 195, 198, 199, 205, 242,
Egypt, 60, 133, 171, 237, 240
Eket, 65
Emigrationists, 13, 14,
Enugu, 10, 20, 23, 26, 46, 51, 58, 59, 75, 78
Equatorial Guinea, 240
ERHC Energy, 190
Eritrea, 131
Ethiopia, 131, 163, 197
European Union (EU), ix, 160, 248
Exxon Mobil, US Oil Company, 167, 184, 188, 190, 221

Facebook, 211
Farah, Douglas, 94
Farrakhan, Louis, 95
Fawehinmi, Gani, 88
Federal Advanced Teachers College Lagos, 47
Federal Electoral Commission, 85
Finland, 114

First National Development Plan, 47, 49
First Republic, Nigeria, 5, 24, 27, 31, 33, 37, 38, 40, 41, 45, 47, 48, 49, 51, 179
Fitzgerald, William, 232, 269,
Ford Foundation, 50
Ford, Gerald R., 108, 111, 186
Foreign Corrupt Practices Act, 191
Foreign Relations Committee (US), 95
Frontline States, 113

G8 Summit, 245
Gadhafi, Maumar, 240
Garba, Joseph, 104, 109, 125, 186
Garvey, Marcus, 22
Gates, Bill, 7, 159, 277
Gbagbo, Laurent, 238, 239
Ghana, 2, 56, 131, 165, 166, 197, 211, 247
Giwa, Dele, 88
Goodlatte, Bob, 136
Gore, Al, 152
Gottlieb, Greg, 227
Government of National Unity (GNU), 108
Gowon, Yakubu, 41, 54, 56, 59, 68, 70, 81, 83, 98, 99, 159
Great Britain, 60, 235, 250
Guinea-Bissau, 288
Gulf of Guinea, xiv, 8, 74, 128, 135, 221, 227, 276, 281, 282
Gulf Oil, 38, 142

Hall, Tony, 111
Halliburton Scandal, 5, 10, 191
Hammer, Mike, 261, 283
Harvard University, 48

Hausa people, 11, 43
Herskovits, Melville Jean, 23
Herter, Christian, 26, 53
Howard University, 19, 21,
Human Rights Watch, 90, 160

Ibadan, 28, 29, 46, 48, 49, 51, 78, 99, 125, 146, 252, 285, 286
Igbo people, 11-13, 19, 56, 206, 207
Ikimi, Tom, 93,
Ikpeme, Justice Bassey, 88
Immigration and Nationality Act (US), 89
Imoke, Liyel, 227
International Republican Institute, 160
Iran, 169, 172, 260
Iraq, 142, 172, 260, 262
Islam, 95, 169-172, 200, 202, 280
Israel, 60
Ita, Eyo, 21
Iwu, Maurice, 232

Jackson, Jesse, 90
Jega, Attahiru, 169, 174, 224, 237
Johnson, Lyndon B., 27, 37, 60
Johnson-Sirleaf, Ellen, 160
Johnston, Kristina, 226
Joint Development Zone (JDZ), ix, 190
Jonathan, Goodluck E., xii, 9, 167, 168, 174, 224, 233, 234, 236, 237, 239, 241, 242, 243, 245, 246, 247, 248, 250, 253, 264, 265, 268, 269, 271, 278
Jordan, 60
Jos, 20, 23, 234, 267
Journal of Commerce, 93

Kano, 18, 20, 48, 109, 169, 230
Kansteiner, Walter, 142, 183
Katsina, Hassan Usman, 129
Kaunda, Kenneth, 112
Kellogg Brown & Root, 191
Kennedy, Edward M., 124
Kennedy, John F., 27, 32, 37, 38, 54
Kenya, 8, 96, 114, 170, 197
Ki-Moon, Ban, 167, 239, 286
King, Coretta Scott, 93
King, Rev. Martin Luther Jr., 24, 30, 93, 106
Kingston, Jack, 136
Kissinger, Henry, 7, 42, 69, 105, 106, 109, 110, 117
Krishna, Somanahalli M., 243
Kufuor, John, 166

Lagos, 5, 12-14, 16, 18, 20, 23-26, 29, 35, 42-44, 47, 51, 54, 68, 72, 75, 76, 78, 84, 90, 95, 100, 110, 125, 126, 136, 149, 150, 164, 176, 177, 193, 201, 208, 232, 251, 252, 256, 283, 287, 288
Lagosian Americans, 13, 208
Lebanon, 172, 260, 262
Legal Education Edict, 58
Lewis, Reta J.O., 227
Liberia, 87
Libya, 237, 240
Locke, Alain, 23
Lyman, Princeton, 119, 122, 123, 126, 279

Machel, Samora, 112
MacNeil Lehrer News Hour, The, 93
Madueke, Ojo, 134, 135, 235

INDEX

Maitatsine, 231
Majority Rule, in Southern Africa, 101, 103, 105, 107, 109, 111, 113, 115, 117, 119, 121, 123, 125
Malawi, 131
Mali, 131,
Malu, Victor, 132, 133
Mandela, Nelson, 124, 175
Marwa, Mohammed, 169
Mazrui, Ali, 273
Mbadiwe, Kingsley O., 19, 20, 22-24
Mbu, Matthew, 32
McCurry, Michael, 94
Meeks, Gregory, 136
Merkel, Angela, 246
Michaelmore, Marjorie, 5, 39
Michigan State University,
Military rule, 52
Mitchel, Andrew, 48
Mobil, 38, 167, 184, 188, 190, 221
Moeller, Robert, 133
Mohammed, Murtala, 84, 85, 98, 99, 103, 108, 109, 111, 251
Moor Plantation, 46
Mountain of Fire, 201
Mozambique, 102, 103, 113, 119
Mugabe, Robert, 105, 112
Mutallab, Umar Farouk Abdul, 236
Muzorewa, Bishop Abel, 115

Namibia, 116
Napolitano, Janet, 172, 270
Nation of Islam movement, 95
National Council of Nigeria Muslim Organization in the USA, ix, 201
National Security Council's Interdepartmental-Group Study on Southern Africa, 105
Neo-colonialism, 131, 222
New York Times, The, 93
New York University, 20, 280
Niger Delta, 142, 221, 226
Nigeria Afro-Asian Solidarity Organization (NAASO), 84
Nigeria, 2-8, 10-12, 14, 16, 18-20, 22, 24, 26-30, 32, 34-38, 40-52, 54, 56, 58, 60, 62, 64, 66, 68, 70, 72-80, 82-84, 86-90, 92, 94, 96, 98-110, 112-116, 118-120, 122-130, 132, 134, 136-140, 142-144, 146, 148-154, 156-160, 162, 164-166, 168, 170, 172-174, 176-180, 182-192, 194, 196, 198-200, 202, 204, 206, 208, 210, 212, 214, 216, 218, 220, 222, 224-226, 228, 230, 232-238, 240-250, 252, 254, 256, 258, 260-262, 264, 266, 268, 270, 272, 274, 276, 278, 280-282, 284-290
Nigerian Army, 52, 132
Nigerian Central Bank, 50
Nigerian Foreign Service, 26
Nigerian National Petroleum Corporation, 184
Nigerian Progressive Organization, 208
Nigerian-Anglo Defence Pact, 34
Nigerians in Diaspora, x, 204, 248
Nigeria-United States Bi-National Commission, 217, 220
Nixon, Richard M., 42, 44, 66, 68, 69, 83, 111
Nkomo, Joshua, 112
Nollywood, 212
Nordchurch aid airlift to Biafra, 63
Norland, Donald R., 141

Northern Region, Nigeria, 16, 41, 46, 50, 169, 231, 280
Nzeribe, Arthur, 89

Obama, Barack, 2, 10, 140, 167, 172, 223, 247, 253, 258, 266
Obasanjo, Olusegun, 84, 92, 97-99, 103, 111, 153, 156, 157, 159, 175, 252, 275
Obiozor, George, 1, 45,
Ogoni, 93, 97
Oguta, 20
Ohio University, 48, 49
Oil, 38, 127, 139, 141, 142, 183-185, 187, 189-191, 203, 218, 226
Ojike, Mbonu, 19
Ojukwu, Odumegwu, 41
Okereke-Onyuike, Ndi, 164
Okonjo-Iweala, Ngozi, 159
Okotie-Eboh, Festus, 182
Olopade, Olufunmilayo Falusi, 212
Omoruyi, Omo, 89,
Onibiyo, Adelabu, 164
Onitsha, 20, 23
Organisation of African Unity (OAU), x, 6, 60, 71, 101, 104, 108, 113, 117, 160
Orisa worship, 202,
Orizu, Akweke Nwafor, 19, 20, 22-24
Osomo, Mobolaji, 161
Osuji, Fabian, 161
Otero, Maria, 224
Ouattara, Alassane, 245, 281
Owen, David, 114
Oyo Empire, 12,
Oyotunji African village, 8, 202, 213, 214

Pakistan, 172, 260, 262, 283
Palmer, Joseph II, 26, 32, 77
Paris Club, 153, 159
Payne, Donald, 90
Peace Corps, 38, 39, 52, 78
People's Democratic Party, 161-162
Philips Petroleum, 38
Pickering, Thomas, 98
Ping, Jean, 239
Point Four Program, 26
Port Harcourt, 20, 23, 48
Postcard incident, 39

Reagan, Ronald, 87, 116, 117, 156
Redeemed Christian Church of God (RCCG), X, 201, 213,
Reno, Janet, 153
Revenue Collection Edict, 58
Revolutionary United Front, 144
Rhodesia, 102
Robeson, Paul, 23
Rockefeller Foundation, 47, 126, 227
Rockefeller, Nelson, 26
Roosevelt, Eleanor, 22, 23
Roosevelt, Franklin Delano, 23
Rotimi, Oluwole, 258, 259, 266
Rusk, Dean, 81, 82

Salomon Brothers, 93
Sambo, Namadi, 241
Sao Tome and Principe, 160, 190,
Sarkozy, Nicholas, 245,
Saro-Wiwa, Ken, 276
Saudi Arabia, 166
Savimbi, Jonas, 110
Senegal, 100, 131, 163, 176, 286
Sese Seko, Mobutu, 62

INDEX

Shagari, Shehu, 85, 86, 115, 116, 118,
Sharia, 169
Sheikh El Zakzaky, 171
Shultz, George, 190
Slavery, 12-14, 28
Smith, Ian, 101, 103, 111
SNDP, 69
Sokoto, 20, 46, 146
Somalia, 7, 8, 160, 172, 197, 260, 262, 278
Soremekun, Kayode, 96, 100
South Africa, 101, 112, 116, 118, 119, 131
Southern Region, Nigeria, 117, 126
Soweto massacre, 101
Sub-Saharan Africa, 197
Sudan, 113, 157, 172, 197, 239, 240, 260
Sule, Yusuf Maitama, 120
Sunday Times, 117, 126
Syria, 60

Taylor, Charles, 158, 160, 164, 176
Terror Watch List, 8, 172, 173, 234, 236, 259, 263, 263, 266, 280
Texaco, 38
Thatcher, Margaret, 116, 120
Time Magazine, 93
Transition to democracy, Nigerian, 90
Twadell, William, 131, 149

Uduaghan, Emmanuel, 226
U.S.-Nigeria TIFA, x, 185, 188
Udoh, Peter, 83
Uganda, 131, 176
Uhomoibhi, Martin, 235
UNITA, 107, 108, 110, 111

United Nations, 246-248, 287, 288
United States, 2-4, 6, 8, 10, 12, 14, 16, 18, 20, 22, 24, 26, 28, 30, 32, 34, 36, 38, 40-42, 44, 46-48, 50, 52-78, 80, 82, 84, 86-88, 90, 92, 94, 96, 98-102, 104, 106, 108, 110-112, 114-116, 118-130, 132, 134, 136-144, 146-148, 150, 152, 154, 156-158, 160, 162, 164, 166-168, 170, 172, 174, 176, 178-180, 182, 184-192, 194-196, 198-200, 202, 204, 206, 208, 210-216, 218, 220, 222, 224, 226, 228, 230, 232, 234, 236, 238, 240, 242, 244, 246-250, 252-254, 256, 258, 260, 262, 264-266, 268, 270, 272, 274, 276-280, 282-284, 286, 288, 290
University of California, 47, 48,
University of Ife, 46, 205,
University of Nigeria, 48
University of Pittsburgh, 50
US National War College, 129
US State Department, 144, 145, 283, 284
US/Nigeria Bi-National Commission, viii, 8, 9, 143, 145, 191, 217, 219, 220, 222, 223, 227, 229-232, 246, 249, 253, 270
USAID, 5, 46-48, 92, 182, 215, 227
USSR, 34, 35, 44, 62

Vance, Cyrus, 4
Vietnam War, 42
Vorster, John, 108, 112

Wabara, Adolphus, 161
Wachukwu, Jaja, 32
Wall Street Journal, The, 93

Wallace Henry, 23
Walters, Vernon, 121
Washington, D.C., 223
Watt, Melvin, 136
Western Region, Nigeria, 46, 48, 61, 182
Westphal, Michael A., 141
White House, 51, 175, 271, 284

Yar'Adua, Shehu Musa, 92
Yar'Adua, Umaru, 134, 166, 168, 219, 233, 234, 258, 263, 266
Yates, Mary, 133, 134
Yoruba people, 5, 8, 11-13, 28, 61, 202, 206, 207, 209
Yorubaland, 13-15
Young, Andrew, 92, 114

Zaria, 20, 50
Zimbabwe, 105, 115
Zimbabwe-Rhodesia, 115
Zoellick, Robert, 167, 268

www.ingramcontent.com/pod-product-compliance
Ingram Content Group UK Ltd.
Pitfield, Milton Keynes, MK11 3LW, UK
UKHW041416180426
11947UKWH00007B/155